Daily
Encouragement
for Single Women

Daily
Encouragement
for Single Women
365 Devotional Readings

BARBOUR
PUBLISHING

INTRODUCTION

God has a special place in His heart for you, single sister! Whether you're still searching for Mr. Right or happily unattached, He has big plans for your life.

Inside *Daily Encouragement for Single Women* you'll find reminders of God's love for you, His beloved daughter, as well as help to face the challenges each day brings.

With a devotional reading for each day of the year, you will be able to focus your thoughts on God's wisdom and promises throughout the Bible to help you turn your struggles into success. You'll be encouraged and gently challenged at times to make beneficial changes to your own attitudes and actions.

Singleness has its own set of unique challenges. But with your heavenly Father by your side, you have access to all the wisdom, resources, and strength you need to accomplish everything He has called you to do. We hope these readings are an encouragement along the way!

THE PUBLISHERS

WHAT SEASON ARE YOU IN?

*There is a time for everything,
and a season for every activity under heaven.*
ECCLESIASTES 3:1 NIV

Many single women wonder if they're in a season, or if they will remain single forever. Even Christian women can get hung up on God's timing. If relationships move too slowly, we get frustrated. One of the exciting things about God being at the helm is that He knows every season of our life, even before it comes.

So, what season are you in, daughter of God? Are you in an autumn season? Life seems to be slowing down? Perhaps you're in a bleak winter, where potential relationships with the opposite sex seem impossible. Maybe you're entering a springtime season, where your hopes are lifting and new possibilities rise up at every turn. Or perhaps you're in the middle of summer, where everything is in full bloom.

Regardless of where you are, God is ready to meet you there. He alone knows when the seasons will shift—but when they do, watch out! Change is ahead. Flexibility is key as you make the transition from one season to another. Don't give up, and don't let confusion or fear kick in. Trust God. He's the creator of the seasons.

Lord, I'm not always sure what season I'm in. And things do seem to be changing. . .a lot. Just about the time I think relationships are going in one direction, they shift. Today I give You the many seasons of my life. Walk me through them. . .hand in hand.

HE ENJOYS YOU

*The LORD your God is in your midst, a mighty one who will save;
he will rejoice over you with gladness; he will quiet you by his love;
he will exult over you with loud singing.*

ZEPHANIAH 3:17 ESV

Memory is a powerful part of each one of us. Perhaps you can see your father cheering you on in a sports event or you remember your mother stroking your feverish forehead while you lay sick in bed. With those mental pictures comes a recollection of emotion—how good it felt to be cheered and encouraged—how comforting it was to be loved and attended.

Zephaniah's words remind us that God is our loving parent. Our mighty Savior offers us a personal relationship, loving and rejoicing over us, His children, glad that we live and move in Him. He is the Lord of the universe, and yet He will quiet our restless hearts and minds with His tender love. He delights in our lives and celebrates our union with Him. We can rest in His affirmation and love, no matter what circumstances surround us.

*Lord, help me remember that You are always with me
and that You delight in me. Remind me that I am
Your child and that You enjoy our relationship.*

Sweet Aroma

The heartfelt counsel of a friend is as sweet as perfume and incense.
Proverbs 27:9 NLT

When you think of the word *comfort*, what comes to mind? Maybe it's a favorite pair of jeans or a well-worn sweatshirt. It might be chocolate or homemade mac and cheese—foods that soothe in a difficult time. Or perhaps it's a luxurious bubble bath, complete with candles and relaxing music.

While all these things can bring temporary relief, God's Word tells us that finding true comfort is as simple as sharing heart-to-heart with a friend. Whether it's over coffee, dessert, or even on the phone, a cherished friend can offer the encouragement and God-directed counsel we all need from time to time.

Friendships that have Christ as their center are wonderful relationships blessed by the Father. Through the timely, godly advice these friends offer, God speaks to us, showering us with comfort that is as sweet as perfume and incense. So what are you waiting for? Make a date with a friend and share the sweet aroma of Jesus!

Jesus, Your friendship means the world to me. I value the close friendships You've blessed me with, too! Thank You for the special women in my life. Show me every day how to be a blessing to them, just as they are to me.

FULL OF GRACE

Let your conversation be always full of grace, seasoned with salt,
so that you may know how to answer everyone.
COLOSSIANS 4:6 NIV

Inflection. Tone of voice. Attitude. Maybe you remember your mom saying, "It's not what you say, but how you say it." Words not only convey a message, they also reveal the attitude of our hearts. When our conversation is full of grace, even difficult truths can be communicated effectively. But how do we season our words with grace?

Grace is undeserved favor that extends unconditional love to another. Whether you're communicating with friends, family, or coworkers, it's important to show that you value them. Put their needs above your own. Communicate truth within the context of love. Show compassion and forgiveness. Demonstrate understanding and an openness to receive their input. Respect their opinion. Rather than striving to drive home your point, try to understand theirs. Seek to build them up. Convey encouragement and hope. Be positive.

When our conversations are full of grace, people will enjoy communicating with us. They will walk away blessed by the love we have shown. Today, in your conversations, extend God's grace to those hungry to experience His love.

Dear Lord, may I view each conversation as an opportunity to
extend Your grace to others. May my words be a blessing. Amen.

A Prosperous Soul

Beloved, I wish above all things that thou mayest prosper and be in health,
even as thy soul prospereth.
3 John 1:2 KJV

Twenty-first-century women do everything conceivable to keep their bodies and their minds in good shape. They work out, watch their calories and carbs, and take excellent care of their skin and teeth. On the outside, many women appear to be in excellent health. But what about their souls? What would it profit a woman to be completely fit on the outside and have a sin-sick soul?

Maybe you're one of those women who thrive on staying in shape. Perhaps you even put your external body on the front burner of your life, paying particular attention to diet, exercise, and appearance. As you think about your overall health, consider your soul. Have you given your heart and life to the Lord Jesus Christ? If so, are you spending time with Him? Praying? Reading His Word? These things are necessary for a healthy soul.

Today's scripture is so encouraging. God wants us to prosper and He loves for us to be in good health, even as our souls prosper. If we really think about that, we have to conclude that the health of our soul is even more important than our physical health. Spend some time today giving your soul a workout.

Lord, sometimes I pay more attention to the outside than the inside. I care more about what people can see than what they can't. Today I draw near to You. Make me healthy. . .from the inside out.

LEAD, FOLLOW,
AND BLESS

*You go before me and follow me. You place your
hand of blessing on my head.*
PSALM 139:5 NLT

A kindergarten teacher explained the rules to her new students. "When we walk down the hall," she said, "I will always go first, and you must not pass me." Immediately the children asked why. She told them she would be their guide to help them know which way to go. She added that it would help her keep track of them. "I don't want to tell your parents that I lost you when they come for you!" she teased. *The teacher would go before her students.*

The admiral of a ship took a crew of navy recruits on board. He covered standard procedures of the ship. "If the ship goes down," he said, "get the life rafts and save yourselves. I will come behind you. Once I know that all of you are safe, I will follow." *The captain would follow his sailors.*

A young mother tucked her daughter into bed. The child mumbled sleepily, "Mommy, why do you put your hand on my head before you leave my bedroom?" The smiling mother answered, "I place my hand on your head as I pray for you, sweetie. I ask God's blessings on you as you sleep." *The mother placed her hand upon the head of her child.*

God is all three. *He leads you. He follows you. He places a hand of blessing upon your head.* An omnipresent Father has you in His care.

God, thank You that You lead me, have my back, and bless me daily. Amen.

Between Miracles

*Then the LORD said to Moses, "I will rain down
bread from heaven for you."*
Exodus 16:4 NIV

By the moaning and groaning, you'd never know that the
Israelites had just been miraculously freed from slavery. They
knew firsthand of Pharaoh's hard heart and had witnessed
horrifying plagues that tortured their enemies. And yet, days
later, when they were stuck in the desert, they doubted God's
faithfulness. They wondered if God had forgotten them and if
they would starve. God's answer? Another miracle. This time He
rained down bread from heaven. A tangible, daily reminder that
He would continue to provide for the Israelites, in spite of their
lack of faith.

Have you ever experienced a miracle? A job offer in just
the nick of time? An unexpected check in the mail? It's easy
to praise God in the face of answered prayer and miraculous
provision. We readily acknowledge His work and praise Him
for His faithfulness. But all too soon, we feel stuck in the desert
and wonder what on earth God is up to. Is He listening? Has He
forgotten us completely? Somewhere in our distant memory is
a miracle, but sometimes we just want to cry, "What have You
done for me lately?"

Circumstances change. God does not. The next time you're
stuck in the desert between miracles, remember the manna.

*Father, how sorry I am that I forget Your faithfulness, in spite of Your
continuing provision for me. Help me to remember and
help me to be grateful. Amen.*

THE MIND OF CHRIST

Let this mind be in you, which was also in Christ Jesus.
PHILIPPIANS 2:5 KJV

Living an independent life isn't always easy. Making decisions, both big and small, falls solely upon one person. Unanswered questions constantly bring on doubt and fear. What if I lose my job? What if my car breaks down? What if my bills are more than my paycheck? What if I get sick?

When negative thoughts bombard your mind, quickly replace them with scriptures like these:

"The things which are impossible with men are possible with God" (LUKE 18:27 KJV).

"My grace is sufficient for thee: for my strength is made perfect in weakness" (2 CORINTHIANS 12:9 KJV).

"I can do everything through him who gives me strength" (PHILIPPIANS 4:13 NIV).

"But my God shall supply all your need according to his riches in glory by Christ Jesus" (PHILIPPIANS 4:19 KJV).

A daily dose of God's Word will bring your focus back to recognizing that God is in control of every situation, no matter what circumstances or decisions come your way.

*Dear God, it's my desire to be more like You. When fear creeps in, fill my
mind with positive thoughts from Your Word and fill
my heart with Your peace. Amen.*

SELF-EXAMINATION

Let us test and examine our ways, and return to the LORD!
LAMENTATIONS 3:40 ESV

What if you could follow yourself around for the day, carefully examining all that you do? Look at your schedule—your choice of activities, the people you talk to, the things you listen to and watch, the habits being formed, the thoughts you think. Maybe your heart desires intimacy with God, but a real day in your life leaves no time for solitude. God often speaks to us in the stillness and silent spaces. How will we hear Him if we're never still?

Taking time to reflect, to think, and to examine oneself is a necessary step in moving toward intimacy with God. Before we can turn back to Him, we must repent of the things that moved us away from Him in the first place. As we set aside time for solitude and reflection, the Holy Spirit will gently show us these things if we ask. He will show us the sins we need to confess and give us the grace of repentance. Experiencing forgiveness, our fellowship with our heavenly Father is restored.

Lord, help me to still myself before You and be willing to examine my ways. Speak to me through Your Holy Spirit of what is wrong in my life. Give me the gift of repentance and allow me to enjoy the sweetness of Your forgiveness.

A Holy Longing

As the deer pants for streams of water, so my soul pants for you, O God. My soul thirsts for God, for the living God. When can I go and meet with God?

Psalm 42:1–2 NIV

When you think of the word *longing*, what images come to mind? We long for so many things, don't we? We long for someone to love us, to tell us how special we are. We long for financial peace. We long for a great job, the perfect place to live, and even the ideal friends.

God's greatest desire is that we long for Him. Today's scripture presents a pretty clear image. We should be hungering and thirsting after God. When we've been away from Him, even for a short time, our souls should pant for Him.

If we were completely honest with ourselves, we'd have to admit that our earthly longings usually supersede our longing for God. Sure, we enjoy our worship time, but we don't really come into it with the depth of longing referred to in this scripture. Ask God to give you His perspective on longing. He knows what it means to long for someone, after all. His longing for you was so great that He gave His only Son on a cross to be near you.

Father, my earthly longings usually get in the way of my spiritual ones. Draw me into Your presence, God. Reignite my longing for You.

WALKING IN
GOD-CONFIDENCE

*If my people, who are called by my name, will humble themselves and pray
and seek my face. . .then will I hear from heaven and will
forgive their sin and will heal their land.*

2 CHRONICLES 7:14 NIV

Some people consider humility a weakness. Others think humility
means never talking about yourself or always putting yourself and
your accomplishments down. Christians often confuse humility with
low self-esteem, believing we should not think of ourselves as worthy,
because Jesus Christ was the only perfect person.

But when we accept Christ as our Lord and Savior, His life
becomes ours. We are no longer slaves to sin, but we own His
righteousness. So we don't have to go around thinking that we're
scum.

Our Savior walked in total God-confidence—knowing
that His steps were planned—and He had only to listen to His
Father's heartbeat to know which way to go. He could withstand
insults, persecutions, and dimwitted disciples because He knew
who He was and where He was headed.

Today, live in total God-confidence, knowing you'll be able
to withstand the pressures life throws at you, because He is your
life.

*Father God, I praise You for Your forgiveness and healing.
Thank You that I am called by Your name.*

HIS PERFECT STRENGTH

*"My grace is sufficient for you, for my power is made perfect in weakness."
Therefore I will boast all the more gladly about my weaknesses, so that
Christ's power may rest on me.*

2 CORINTHIANS 12:9 NIV

How do you define stress? Perhaps you feel it when the car doesn't start or the toilet backs up or the line is too long at the grocery store. Or maybe your source of stress is a terrible diagnosis, a late-night phone call, a demanding boss, or a broken relationship. It's probably a combination of all of these things. You might be able to cope with one of them, but when several are bearing down at once, stress is the inevitable result.

It has been said that stress results when our perceived demands exceed our perceived resources. When the hours required to meet a deadline at work (demand) exceed the number of hours we have available (resources), we get stressed. The most important word in this definition is *perceived*. When it comes to stress, people have a tendency to do two things. One, they magnify the demand ("I will *never* be able to get this done"), and two, they fail to consider all of their resources. For the child of God, this includes His mighty strength, which remains long after ours is gone.

In an uncertain world, it is difficult to say few things for sure. But no matter what life throws our way, we can be confident of this: our demands will *never* exceed God's vast resources.

*Strong and mighty heavenly Father, thank You that in my weakness
I can always rely on Your perfect strength. Amen.*

THE SIMPLE LIFE

I want you to live as free of complications as possible. When you're unmarried, you're free to concentrate on simply pleasing the Master.
1 CORINTHIANS 7:32 MSG

Cyndi watched in amazement as her sister's life seemed to run at 105 miles per hour. Abby had gotten married two weeks after high school graduation. Now, at age twenty-three, she had three kids in tow and no time outside of parenting, housekeeping, marriage, and a part-time job. Abby seemed frazzled every waking moment.

"If I could do it over again," Abby confided in her older sister, "I'd have allowed myself to grow up—get some life experience—and figure out who I am before jumping into marriage and kids."

Do you ever see the drama surrounding some of your married friends and appreciate the simplicity of your own life? Too often we focus on what we don't have, but God wants us to look at the opportunities we have because of our singleness.

Our uncomplicated lives may allow us to offer help to others when a need arises. Maybe there's an opportunity to develop a new ministry or outreach program that God lays on our heart. When we do as Paul says in 1 Corinthians and "concentrate on simply pleasing the Master," we'll find our focus shifts from self to Jesus—an attitude adjustment that's guaranteed to bring true fulfillment.

Father, thank You for the blessing of simplicity in my life. Help me to find true contentment every day by focusing my energies on pleasing You and only You.

UNCHAINED!

For you did not receive a spirit that makes you a slave again to fear, but you received the Spirit of sonship. And by him we cry, "Abba, Father."
ROMANS 8:15 NIV

Imagine how difficult life would be inside prison walls. No sunlight. No freedom to go where you wanted when you wanted. Just a dreary, dark existence, locked away in a place you did not choose, with no way of escape.

Most of us can't even imagine such restrictions. As Christians we have complete freedom through Jesus Christ, our Lord and Savior. No limitations. No chains.

Ironically, many of us build our own walls and choose our own chains. When we give ourselves over to fear, we're deliberately entering a prison the Lord never intended for us. We don't always do it willfully. In fact, we often find ourselves behind bars after the fact, then wonder how we got there.

Do you struggle with fear? Do you feel it binding you with its invisible chains? If so, then there's good news. Through Jesus, you have received the Spirit of sonship. A son (or daughter) of the Most-High God has nothing to fear. Knowing you've been set free is enough to make you cry, "Abba, Father!" in praise. Today, acknowledge your fears to the Lord. He will loose your chains and set you free.

Lord, thank You that You are the great chain-breaker! I don't have to live in fear. I am Your child, Your daughter, and You are my Daddy-God!

LIFE'S DISTRACTIONS

When they found Him, they said to Him, "Everyone is looking for you."
But He said to them, "Let us go into the next towns, that I may preach
there also, because for this purpose I have come forth."
MARK 1:37–38 NKJV

The Sunday school director approached a young woman in the hallway. "I know you're capable of leading the high school department. You're not serving in any capacity at this time. Won't you consider the position?" The young woman felt cornered. Her gift was not teaching, and she dreaded the prospect of Sunday mornings with teenagers. Yet there was an opening, and she'd feel guilty if she didn't help out the church leader. What to do?

In Jesus' ministry, He was called upon to heal the sick and speak to the multitudes. Yet despite the clamor of the crowds, He knew His purpose. Instead of getting sidetracked and following the people's agenda, Jesus knew His priority was prayer and recognizing God's will. He never allowed people's demands to distract Him from His calling.

God designed us for a special purpose. Using our gifts is what we're called to do. When we step into a situation He didn't design for us, we're being disobedient. Filling a position just because there is an opening is never a good idea. We need to find our gifts and use them for God's glory.

Lord, point me on the path You would have me follow.
Keep me from becoming distracted. Amen.

BODY AND SPIRIT

Don't you know that you yourselves are God's temple
and that God's Spirit lives in you?
1 CORINTHIANS 3:16 NIV

Amy fell into bed with a moan. She'd been on her feet all day for her retail job, and she felt old and tired.

I need to start exercising, she thought for the hundredth time that week. Every Monday she resolved to take better care of her body, but by Tuesday she had fallen back into old bad habits. *Why do I do this?* she wondered. *Lord, help me!*

The next day, Amy called a friend to ask if she'd help keep her accountable in her exercise. "I want to change," Amy said. "But I need encouragement."

Our physical shells house the very spirit of God, and God created our bodies, so we are called to be good stewards of them. It's hard with our modern, busy lifestyle to make health a priority, but we can ask God for wisdom and discipline. After all, if He asks us to do something, He will equip us for the task.

Do you treat your body as the temple of God? What habits do you have that could change? Perhaps you could drink less soda, eat more fruits and veggies, or get more exercise. Do you smoke? Resolve to quit. Do you work at a desk all day? Get some fresh air during your lunchtime. Your body and your spirit will thank you!

Lord, give me the discipline to make wise choices about what I drink and eat. And help me to make exercise a priority.

FROM OLD TO NEW

Therefore, if anyone is in Christ, he is a new creation;
the old has gone, the new has come!
2 CORINTHIANS 5:17 NIV

Just a few weeks earlier, six inches of snow were piled atop Mrs. Baker's patio table. It looked like a huge birthday cake with white frosting.

Today, springtime has warmed away winter's chill. Mrs. Baker plants bright pink impatiens and golden orange marigolds in her flower garden. She smiles, remembering the recent snow as she walks past the wrought-iron patio table and places a potted ivy in its center. What a change a few weeks brought to that table!

Before we come to know Jesus, our hearts are as cold and dead as winter, full of sin. We may do many good deeds. But no amount of good can bring a new creation to an unsaved soul. Only the grace of God has that kind of power.

As sunny springtime melts the frigid winter days and brings forth new life, so the Son of God brings new life to sinners saved by grace.

The old has gone. The new has come. Praise the Lord that He saves sinners and brings us into new life, our sins forgiven by His grace.

God, I believe in Jesus and that He died for me. Make a new creation of me.
Forgive my sins. Save me that I might have an abundant life here on earth
and eternal life in heaven when I die. Amen.

SPEAK, LORD

The LORD came and stood there, calling as at the other times, "Samuel!
Samuel!" Then Samuel said, "Speak, for your servant is listening."
I SAMUEL 3:10 NIV

The Lord spoke—*out loud*—to the young boy Samuel.
Although this incident happened thousands of years ago,
Samuel's response teaches us important lessons today. The boy
viewed himself as God's servant and revealed a heart that was
committed to obedience. Maybe that's why the Lord chose to
speak to this youngster.

Although the Lord's call today is different than in Old
Testament times, He still speaks to hearts that yearn to listen. The
Lord speaks powerfully through His Word, the Bible. The Holy
Spirit also whispers truth to our hearts. Even other people and
His creation may reveal God's message to us.

The Lord most often communicates to servant hearts that are
ready to listen—hearts committed to obedience. Servant hearts
trust that God's ways are best even when they might be difficult.
They covet His counsel and seek His voice.

The Lord longs to communicate with us. Is your heart
receptive to His call today? Work toward being able to say
sincerely, "Speak, Lord, your servant is listening!"

Dear Lord, may I have a servant's heart that's committed to
obedience. Speak, Lord! Amen.

I Am a Friend of God

When Jesus saw their faith, he said,
"Friend, your sins are forgiven."
Luke 5:20 NIV

Friendships are critical to women, and godly friendships are the best. Can you even imagine a world without your girlfriends in it? Impossible! Who would you share your hopes and dreams with? Your goals and aspirations? Oh, what a blessing women of God are! They breathe hope and life into us when we need it most. They laugh along with us at chick flicks. They cry with us when our hearts are broken.

Isn't it amazing to realize God calls us His friend? He reaches out to us with a friendship that goes above and beyond the very best the world has to offer. Best of all, He's not the sort of friend who loses touch or forgets to call. He's always there. And while your earthly friends might do a good job of comforting you when you're down, their brand of comfort doesn't even begin to compare with the Lord's. He knows just what to say when things go wrong, and knows how to throw an amazing celebration when things go well for you.

Today, thank the Lord—not just for salvation, not just for the work He's done in your heart, not just for the people and things He's placed in your life—but for calling you His friend.

Oh, Lord, I'm so blessed to be called Your friend! You're the best one I'll ever have. Thank You for the kind of friendship that supersedes all boundaries.

HE IS YOUR CONFIDENCE

For the LORD will be your confidence, and will keep your foot from being caught.
PROVERBS 3:26 NKJV

Sometimes we wish for more confidence. A job interview or a social situation we are facing may make us nervous. A new situation we're thrown into may cause us to worry. Will we be dressed appropriately? Will we know what to say?

Those are the times to remember that the Lord is always with us. He has promised never to leave or forsake us. He tells us we are His little lambs and He is our great Shepherd. He upholds us with His righteous right hand. He leads us along still waters and restores our soul. These are just a few of the promises of God regarding the care He provides for His children.

The next time you need some confidence, instead of worrying or trying to muster it up on your own, seek God. Read 2 Corinthians 12:9 and remember that in your weakness, God shows up to be your strength. He will be your confidence.

God, be my confidence when this world brings situations in which I feel insecure or inadequate. Thank You.

OMNIPRESENT GOD

If I rise on the wings of the dawn, if I settle on the far side of the sea, even there your hand will guide me, your right hand will hold me fast.
PSALM 139:9–10 NIV

Have you ever moved when it wasn't your choice? Maybe it was a job transfer. Or maybe finances required you to downsize from a house to an apartment. It may have been an adjustment to move out on your own after living with roommates. Perhaps you were needed back in your hometown to care for a sick relative. No matter the reason, a move is always somewhat unsettling.

Do you remember as a child when your family went to your grandparents' home for Christmas? Maybe you panicked at the thought of spending the night away from home on Christmas Eve. What if Santa didn't know where you were?

Think of how unsettling it was to lose a tooth while on vacation. Did the tooth fairy make visits to hotels? How would she ever locate the correct room number in order to deposit the dollar for the tooth under your pillow? Yet Santa and the tooth fairy always showed up! Amazingly, they knew right where you were.

So does God! He is omnipresent, *always present everywhere.* Our human minds cannot conceive it, but it is true. Wherever you live or travel, whatever unfamiliar place you find yourself in, remember God is there with you to guide you and to hold you tight.

Father, thank You that You are always with me to guide and protect me. Amen.

SHINING LIGHT

"You are the light of the world. A city on a hill cannot be hidden."
MATTHEW 5:14 NIV

Jesus' disciples knew all about darkness. Centuries before electricity had been harnessed to provide light, individuals made do with fires and oil lamps. When the sun went down, darkness ruled.

So when Jesus told His followers that they are the light of the world, the image meant a great deal to them. Light that overtakes the darkness—light to illuminate the way to the Savior. What an amazing concept!

Jesus tells us twenty-first-century followers to be light, too, boldly and unashamedly flooding the darkness that surrounds us. How do we do it? First, by living the life God calls us to—not sinless, but forgiven. Second, by sprinkling our conversations with evidence of our faith. Did something good happen? Share that blessing with others and give God the credit for it. When someone asks about the peace they see in you, share the joy of Jesus.

Being a light of the world is not about being a Bible thumper or bashing others over the head with religion. It's about living out genuine faith that allows Christ's light to break through our everyday lives. With that goal in mind, shine!

Jesus, You are my true light. Even though I alone can't shine as brightly as You, I ask that You shine through me as I seek to follow after You. I know I won't be perfect, but I also know that Your grace has me covered. Amen.

People Pleaser vs. God Pleaser

We are not trying to please men but God, who tests our hearts.
1 Thessalonians 2:4 NIV

Much of what we say and do stems from our desire to be accepted by others. We strive to make a certain impression, to shed the best light possible on ourselves. Wanting to be viewed as successful, we may decide to exaggerate, embellish, or even lie. It's difficult to be true to ourselves when we care so much about the acceptance and opinions of others. Impression management is hard work, so it's good to know God has a better plan!

Rather than being driven by the opinions of others, strive to live your life for God alone and to please Him above all else. God knows our hearts. He perceives things as they truly are. We cannot fool Him. When we allow ourselves to be real before Him, it doesn't matter what others think. If the God of the universe has accepted us, then who cares about someone else's opinion?

It is impossible to please both God and man. We must make a choice. Man looks at the outward appearance, but God looks at the heart. Align your heart with His. Let go of impression management that focuses on outward appearance. Receive God's unconditional love and enjoy the freedom to be yourself before Him!

Dear Lord, may I live for You alone. Help me transition from a people pleaser to a God pleaser. Amen.

SURROUNDED BY
HIS PRESENCE

*Then the cloud covered the tabernacle of meeting, and the
glory of the LORD filled the tabernacle.*
EXODUS 40:34 NKJV

God wants us to enter worship with a heart prepared to
actually meet Him. He longs for us to come in the frame of mind
where we're not just singing about Him, we're truly worshipping
Him with every fiber of our being. He wants wholehearted
participants, not spectators.

God promises to meet with us. When we come into His
presence, if our hearts and minds are truly engaged, He often
overwhelms us with His goodness, His greatness, His Word.
Think about the last time you truly "engaged" God—met with
Him in a supernatural way. Has it been awhile?

It's the Lord's desire that we come into His presence regularly,
not in an "I have to get this over with" frame of mind, but a
"Lord, I am so blessed to get to spend time with You!" attitude.
When we meet with Him in that mindset, the shining-greatness
of the Lord will be revealed, and His glory will fill that place.

*Lord, I long to meet with You—really meet with You. I don't want to
go through the motions, heavenly Father. I want Your glory to fall, Your
shining-greatness to overwhelm me. Today I offer myself to You, not as a
spectator, but a participant in Your holy presence.*

REDEEMING LOVE

*"For a brief moment I deserted you, but with great compassion I will
gather you. In overflowing anger for a moment I hid my face from you, but
with everlasting love I will have compassion on you,"
says the LORD, your Redeemer.*
ISAIAH 54:7–8 ESV

Contrasting opposites are at work in this beautiful passage
from Isaiah: a brief desertion but a great gathering; momentary
anger but everlasting love and compassion. There is purpose in
His every word. The Lord is passionate about His chosen people.
Though they felt deserted, it was short-lived; God's intent was to
gather them back with great care. He was angry and hid His face
but could never deny His eternal love that would redeem them.

Just as God loved the Israelites and spoke to them through
Isaiah, so does He love each of us. His heart has not changed
through the ages. He still allows us times in which we feel
deserted, yet He will pursue us and draw us back to Himself. Sin
still angers Him, but He is tender and merciful toward those He
loves. His ultimate act of compassion for us was when He poured
out His wrath on Jesus at the cross, when He gave His Son to be
our Redeemer. He bought us back at the highest price when we
had no way to bring ourselves to Him.

*Father, thank You for forgiveness and restoration. In the dark times,
help me to remember Your everlasting love and grace to me.*

GIVER OF GOOD THINGS

For the LORD God is a sun and shield; the LORD will give grace and glory;
no good thing will He withhold from those who walk uprightly.
PSALM 84:11 NKJV

Worry is such a useless practice, like spinning wheels on a vehicle that takes you nowhere. And yet we women are notorious for it. The Bible advises us to let each day take care of itself. We are promised that God will provide for us.

Psalm 84:11 says that God is not a withholder of good things from His children. He knows us. He created us and put in us our own unique dreams, preferences, and hopes. When you begin to worry, read this verse. Put it on your bulletin board at work and your bathroom mirror at home. Read it aloud each time that worry begins to creep in.

Your heavenly Father is not "the big man upstairs" looking down upon you and laughing at the unfulfilled desires in your life. He wants to give you good things. Often His timing is different than ours, but His plan is always to bless and never to harm us. Look for the blessings in each day, and keep bringing your desires before the Lord in expectation.

Father, sometimes I wonder why You don't just pour down from heaven the
blessing that I cry out for. Give me patience, and help me to see the good
gifts from You in each day—even the small ones. Amen.

OVERWHELMED BY LIFE

*"The waves of death swirled about me; the torrents of destruction
overwhelmed me. . . . In my distress I called to the LORD. . . . From his
temple he heard my voice; my cry came to his ears."*

2 SAMUEL 22:5, 7 NIV

Some days the "dailyness" of life seems like a never-ending
grind. We get up, eat, work, rest—and do it again the next
day. Then when tragedy strikes, we're swept up in grief. What
once seemed doable now seems a huge challenge. Depression
sinks its claws deep into our spirit. Fatigue sets in, and we are
overwhelmed: life is hard. We may be tempted to question, "Is
this all there is?"

Here's the good news: there's more. God never meant for us
to simply exist. He created us for a specific purpose. He longs
for us to make a difference and show others His love and grace.
What's more, He never asked us to do life alone. When the waves
of death swirl around us, and the pounding rain of destruction
threatens to overwhelm us, we can cry out to our heavenly Father,
knowing that He will not let us drown. He will hear our voice,
and He will send help.

So, next time you feel that you can't put one foot in front of
the other, ask God to send you His strength and energy. He will
help you to live out your purpose in this chaotic world.

*Lord, thank You for strengthening me when the "dailyness" of life
and its various trials threatens to overwhelm me.*

CONTENT IN HIM

But godliness with contentment is great gain.
1 TIMOTHY 6:6 KJV

Even the strongest Christian can struggle with discontentment. We're conditioned by the world to want more—of everything. More money, nicer clothes, a bigger house, a better-paying job. We're rarely satisfied with what we have.

And when we're single, the "I Wish I Had This or That" list can get pretty long. If we don't get the things we long for—a spouse, children, a home, a better car, or nicer clothes—sometimes our discontentment shifts into overdrive. But what can we do about it?

Today, take stock of what God has already done for you. Take a look at the areas of your life in which you've been struggling with discontentment. Hasn't God already given you people who pour into your life? Hasn't He made sure you have a roof over your head and food to eat? Has He not provided you a way to get to and from work?

Instead of focusing on all of the things you don't have, spend some time praising Him for the things you do have. Offer the Lord any discontentment, and watch Him give you a contented heart.

Lord, I confess that I'm not always content. I find myself wishing life were different sometimes. Today I thank You for the many things You've already done in my life. Take my discontentment and replace it with genuine peace.

GRATITUDE

*Not that we are competent in ourselves to claim anything for
ourselves, but our competence comes from God.*
2 CORINTHIANS 3:5 NIV

In times of trouble or weakness, when circumstances seem
beyond our control, we pray. But when life is moving along
smoothly and we have a handle on life, it is easy to forget who
God is and who we are.

Scripture teaches us that everything comes from God, even
our achievements. Have you ever thought of your résumé as
being God's work? When someone retires, do we thank God for
their lifelong ability to work, to contribute, and to provide? Our
good health, a stable home, deep and abiding friendships. . .who
gets credit for these?

Are you known for being prompt, polite, and professional? Who
taught you those things? Who sent those teachers into your life?

Spend some time looking at the ordinary, good things in
your life today—the things you take for granted as being yours.
Pause to thank God for giving them to you. Acknowledge
the Giver behind every good thing you have received or
accomplished.

*Heavenly Father, I have been blind to the goodness that dwells in You. I
have moved through my days all too quickly and claimed as my own doing
the gifts You have bestowed. Thank You for all Your gifts to me.*

Take My Hand

*I have no regrets. I couldn't be more sure of my ground—the One I've
trusted in can take care of what he's trusted me to do.*
2 Timothy 1:11–12 MSG

Ever feel like giving up? Throwing in the towel? Some days it's
hard to find the resolve to persevere. Despite our human frailties,
our heavenly Father is there to grab our hands and pull us to our
feet. He isn't impressed with what we do in life but with how we
tackle each day. He wants us to gaze at Him and know He's there
to take care of us despite the overwhelming odds life brings.

Paul could have given in. The man was shipwrecked,
beaten, imprisoned, and persecuted, and yet he kept on giving
the Lord praise. He preached the good news of Jesus and faced
the consequences of his actions. Few of us will face the same
persecution, but we have the same Spirit within us that Paul did.
He told Timothy he had no regrets because he was sure of the
One he served.

Are you sure today of the One you serve? When coming to
grips with difficulties, do you turn to the Creator of the universe
and ask for help? You should. He's available. Just reach out and
take His hand. He'll be there.

*Lord, teach me Your love. Let me feel Your embrace.
I choose to trust in You. Amen.*

HOPE

Why are you downcast, O my soul? Why so disturbed within me? Put your
hope in God, for I will yet praise him, my Savior and my God.
PSALM 42:5–6 NIV

If you've ever been depressed, you're not alone. Depression
can be caused by circumstances, biology, environment, or a
combination of all of those things. Research indicates that as
many as 25 percent of Americans suffer from depression at some
point in their lives.

We are blessed with scriptural accounts of godly people like
David and Jeremiah who struggled with depression. These stories
let us know that it's a normal human reaction to feel overcome by
the difficulties of life.

While feeling this way is normal, it doesn't have to be the
norm. As Christians, we have hope. Hope that our circumstances
will not always be the way they are right now. Hope that no
matter how dismal the world situation seems to be, God wins in
the end. Hope that eternity is just on the other side.

Hope is like a little green shoot poking up through hard,
cracked ground. When you're depressed, do what David and
Jeremiah did—pour out your heart to God. Seek help from a
trusted friend or godly counselor.

Look for hope. It's all around you, and it's yours for the
taking.

Father, even when I am depressed, You are still God. Help me to
find a ray of hope in the midst of dark circumstances. Amen.

A New Song

He put a new song in my mouth, a hymn of praise to our God.
Psalm 40:3 niv

David was in a bad spot. He describes it in the Psalms as a "slimy pit. . .the mud and mire." Ever been there?

Often a person suffering from depression feels as if she is in a pit, unable to get out. Certainly a pit is not a place of rejoicing or singing!

Life is hard, and we are human. We make mistakes. We suffer. We fail. We lose. We crumble. Sometimes we can't even see God through the gray cloud of hopelessness.

Perhaps after losing a loved one or going through another difficult season in life, you felt as if you would never be happy again. Thankfully, one of the greatest gifts God gives His children is the gift of a "new song."

If you are in a place of sadness, trust in this. There will come a day, an hour, a moment when God will transform gloom into joy. Your feet will be planted on a mountain, where once you fought to climb out of a valley.

Be steadfast. Trust in the dark what He showed you in the light. Suffering is but for a time, and God's mercies are new every day.

Father, when You find me in the pit, put a new song of praise in my heart, that I might live again a life of abundance and joy. Amen.

FEAR-FREE

You will not fear the terror of night, nor the arrow that flies by day.
PSALM 91:5 NIV

Were you afraid of the dark when you were a little girl? It's hard to be comfortable when you can't see what's out there, right? Even as a big girl, the nighttime hours can still be a little scary. Seems like we're most vulnerable to fears and failures in the wee hours, when the darkness closes in around us.

So, how do you face the "terror of night" without fear? You have to grasp the reality that God is bigger and greater than anything that might evoke fear. He's bigger than financial struggles. He's bigger than job stress. He's even bigger than relational problems. Best of all, He can see in the dark. He knows what's out there and can deal with it. All it takes is one sentence from Him: *"Let there be light!"* and darkness dispels.

We serve an awesome and mighty God, One who longs to convince us He's mighty enough to save us, even when the darkness seeps in around us. So don't fear what you can't see. Or what you *can* see. Hand over that fear and watch God-ordained faith rise up in its place.

Father, I'm glad You can see in the dark. Sometimes I face the unseen things of my life with fear gripping my heart. I release that fear to You today. Thank You for replacing it with godly courage.

IMMOVABLE LOVE

"For the mountains may depart and the hills be removed, but my steadfast love shall not depart from you, and my covenant of peace shall not be removed," says the LORD, who has compassion on you.
ISAIAH 54:10 ESV

Mountains are steadfast and immovable. Even small parts of mountains are not easily moved. Nature's forces take centuries or tremendous energy to do so. Snow, glacial ice, mountain streams, rain, and wind move one grain of sand or pebble at a time. Volcanoes release tremendous energy to alter a mountain's shape. When man wants to build a highway through a mountain range, the power of dynamite is needed to cut tunnels through rock, and the road must twist and turn to adapt to the terrain.

God says His love is even more immovable. Mountains will move before His love will leave us. Hills will depart easier than God would remove His covenant of peace with us. In the sacrifice of Christ on the cross, He demonstrated His amazing love for us, and Jesus became our peace. Romans 5:1 (ESV) says, "Therefore, since we have been justified by faith, we have peace with God through our Lord Jesus Christ." Regardless of what we have done or will do, God's love is set upon us. By faith, we have only to believe what Jesus has done for us.

Father, thank You for Your immovable love, for the permanence of Your covenant of peace, and for my righteousness, which does not come from my good works but from Christ's sacrifice for me.

FIX YOUR EYES

*So we fix our eyes not on what is seen, but on what is unseen. For what is
seen is temporary, but what is unseen is eternal.*
2 CORINTHIANS 4:18 NIV

The majestic oak's enormous trunk was three feet in diameter.
For more than one hundred years, buds had formed each spring
and leaves had dropped each fall. But one spring, the leaves were
not as plentiful as in previous years. That summer the leaves
suddenly turned brown. Soon it was painfully obvious that the
great white oak had died.

What a visual reminder that the things of this world will
someday pass away. Although the oak had lived many years, it no
longer produced oxygen—no longer shaded the backyard. Even
trees have life spans.

There are very few things that can be counted on to last
forever. Souls are eternal; they remain even when our earthly
bodies decay. We need to see beyond the physical by focusing on
the spiritual. There is life beyond what we are experiencing in this
moment.

Spend your energy and resources on those things that will
last: your relationships with your heavenly Father and with
others. Love God. Love people. Then you won't fear being cut
down like the majestic oak. You will live into eternity in the
Lord's presence.

*Dear Lord, help me keep an eternal focus and perspective in this life.
Allow me to "see" what is unseen. Amen.*

RED HIGH HEELS

*Don't be concerned about the outward beauty of fancy hairstyles, expensive
jewelry, or beautiful clothes. You should clothe yourselves instead with the
beauty that comes from within, the unfading beauty of a gentle and quiet
spirit, which is so precious to God.*

1 PETER 3:3–4 NLT

Fashion gurus love to tell women what to wear. Many like to
recommend one pair of red shoes—preferably sassy high heels—
to spice up a lady's wardrobe. Proponents of the advice say having
one special pair of shoes to wear when feeling down or depressed
can turn a woman's whole day around, making her feel beautiful
and powerful.

While fashion trends are fun and we all want to look well-
groomed, we can't forget where true beauty and power come
from. Wasn't it Jesus who taught us not to place our treasure in
physical things like our bodies or worry about where our clothes
will come from? He promises to provide for us.

Shoes scuff, necklaces break, and fabrics fade, but true
beauty starts from within. When we allow God to dress our
spirits in robes of love, joy, peace, patience, kindness, goodness,
faithfulness, gentleness, and self-control, our inner beauty will far
outshine anything we put on our physical bodies.

*Dear Father, I want to be a woman whose inner beauty far surpasses my
outer beauty, so that when people see me they are pointed to You and rejoice
in Your creation.*

A MEMBER OF
THE FAMILY

*Consequently, you are no longer foreigners and aliens, but fellow citizens
with God's people and members of God's household.*
EPHESIANS 2:19 NIV

If you grew up in a large family, then you certainly know the pros and cons of being one of many children. But you also know just how wonderful it feels to belong—to really, truly belong to something bigger than yourself. Yes, being in a family has its ups and downs, but it sure beats going it alone.

God is the ultimate Father. And He's got a lot of kids in His family. But there's always room on His lap for another child. How wonderful to know He's made you part of His household! You're not an outcast. You're not a stranger on the street, one who doesn't belong. You not only belong—you're priceless to Him. He loves you more deeply than you can fathom! And guess what? He knows just how to make you feel like you're an only child, even with all of those other brothers and sisters around. Best of all, no sibling rivalry!

Today, praise the Lord for making you His child. Thank Him for His amazing love. Celebrate that you have a heavenly Father and a houseful of godly siblings.

*Oh, Daddy God! Today I'm reminded just how much You love me—Your
daughter. Thank You for inviting me into Your wonderful family. I praise
You for loving me as if I were an only child.*

REMEMBERING GOD'S MARVELOUS WORKS

Seek the LORD and His strength. . . . Remember His marvelous works which He has done.
1 CHRONICLES 16:11–12 NKJV

Jamie spent the last few months of a busy year taking care of her aging mother. Her dad had died several months before, leaving Jamie's mom with a mountain of paperwork, financial stress, and unfinished business.

As an only child, Jamie felt the weight of responsibility. And she resented her dad for not leaving his affairs in better order. She even resented her mom for leaning on her only daughter too much.

Those were in the crazy moments. In her saner times, Jamie remembered that God had healed her dad of cancer not once, but twice, and he had enjoyed a long life of ministry and service. She recalled that her mom had found a Christian attorney who was helping them sort through her father's estate at a fraction of his normal fee. And she reminded herself that God had kept her safe on her weekly commute and given her extra money at just the time she needed it for gas and meals.

How do you remind yourself of the marvelous works God has done in your life? When times are hard, it's wonderful to look back in a journal or Bible and see His goodness, answers to prayers, and interventions recorded. It may keep you sane, and it will help you give thanks, even when the going is tough.

Lord, help me to remember that You have done marvelous things for me.

THINK BIG

"For as the sky soars high above earth, so the way I work surpasses the way you work, and the way I think is beyond the way you think."
ISAIAH 55:9 MSG

Anne heard a missionary speak at church, and a dream to serve in China was born in her heart. After graduation from high school, she would go.

But World War I began and kept her dream on hold. She began a teaching career that spanned the years until she retired at sixty-five. On the day of her retirement, she filled out an application to serve as a missionary but was rejected because of her age. Undecided about her future, she packed her car and drove north to a small town in need of a teacher.

Anne continued to pray about her heart's desire. In the late '60s, an age discrimination bill was passed. Anne filled out the form to become a missionary and went to China. She had a big dream—one large enough for God to fill.

We should dream big and ask God for direction in life. We humans are impatient and want what we want right now. But our Father in heaven knows better. He has created a world that unfolds according to His timetable.

We must dream, think big, and wait for God to reveal the plan. He's in control.

Dear Lord, You know my heart's desire. Help me to wait upon Your answer for my life. Amen.

FINANCIAL STRAIN

"No one can serve two masters. Either he will hate the one and love the other, or he will be devoted to the one and despise the other. You cannot serve both God and Money."
MATTHEW 6:24 NIV

Do you ever get nervous when you watch the news and see reports about the stock market? Does your head spin when you see the prices rise at the gas pump? Can you feel your heart race when you look at your bills in comparison to your bank statement? Even though many of our day-to-day activities depend on money, it's important to remember that money is not a provider or sustainer. Only God can provide for you and sustain you. When we begin to focus on and worry about money, then we are telling God that we don't trust Him.

As you feel yourself start to worry about money, stop and change your focus from wealth to God. Thank Him for what He has provided for you and then humbly ask Him to give you wisdom about your financial situation. Be at peace as you remember that you can absolutely trust God to provide for you and to sustain you.

Dear God, help me not to worry but to trust that You will provide for me. Help me to be devoted to You only. Amen.

HEAD AND SHOULDERS, KNEES AND TOES

Now the body is not made up of one part but of many.
1 CORINTHIANS 12:14 NIV

JoAnn struggled to fit in with the people in her neighborhood, and even the people in her church. She wondered if she would always feel like a square peg in a round hole. Convinced she would never find her place, she retreated to the safety of her home, where books and television became her primary source of comfort. In short, she gave up on trying to find her place in the body of Christ.

Perhaps you can relate to JoAnn. Maybe, in your singleness, you're struggling to fit in. Remember, daughter of God, He has created you uniquely, with specific gifts. The body of Christ is made up of many members—all ages, colors, shapes, and sizes, with a variety of spiritual gifts.

Make a conscious decision today not to retreat. Even if you've struggled to fit in, give it another try. Pray about the specific gifts God has placed within you, then ask Him—and your church leaders—where you can best serve Him. You might be surprised at the new directions in which the Lord leads you.

Father, I don't always know where I fit. Sometimes I feel there's not a place for me, even at church. I know I'm a part of Your body, and all of the parts work together. So, stir up the gifts, Lord, then place me where I can be most effective.

REACH OUT

But people who aren't spiritual can't receive these truths from God's Spirit.
It all sounds foolish to them and they can't understand it, for only those
who are spiritual can understand what the Spirit means.

1 CORINTHIANS 2:14 NLT

Imagine yourself visiting France but unable to speak the
language. Everywhere you go, people are conversing in a tongue
that you cannot decipher. Although you're lost, asking for
directions seems useless. You drive around aimlessly, confused
by street signs that don't make sense. People honk as you enter
the exits and yell as you navigate the roundabouts. Even though
you're trying your hardest, the French judge you as an idiot.

In the same way, unbelievers may feel confused trying to
navigate the unfamiliar territory of spiritual truth. They don't
have the ability to understand it because they don't have the Holy
Spirit as a teacher to guide them. The Bible may not make sense
to them, but don't be quick to judge. Hope isn't lost!

God likely has placed unbelievers in your life that He wants
you to reach out to. Share your faith with them in words and
actions they can understand. Pray the Lord opens their hearts to
receive Jesus as Lord and Savior. Then the Holy Spirit will dwell
with them, giving them the ability to comprehend spiritual truth.
Pray that these lost "tourists" will find Jesus soon!

Dear Lord, help me not judge those who don't know You. Instead,
may I pray that You intercede to show them the way. Amen.

THE BLESSING OF FAMILY

God sets the lonely in families.
PSALM 68:6 NIV

Singleness does not have to equal loneliness, but sometimes it does. If you are lonely, God wants to set you in a family. If you live near family, consider spending more time with them. Attend more of your nephew's baseball games or your niece's recitals. Set up an evening every month to meet at a restaurant with your family. Stop by your parents' home for a visit now and then. Family support is important, especially for single women.

Sometimes God provides a family that comes in a different form, such as a small group or community group at church. It may be a women's Bible study group or a Sunday school class. As a Christian, you are part of God's family. There will always remain in this world a remnant of God's people; therefore, there will always be a family available for any believer.

God sets the lonely in families. What a beautiful blessing!

Lord, thank You for the family You have given me. Help me to surround myself with other believers in the family of God as well. Amen.

Protecting Angels

*For he will command his angels concerning you to guard
you in all your ways.*
Psalm 91:11 NIV

The SUV was completely totaled after being rear-ended
by a semitruck. After flipping end over end, the SUV landed
upright. Mangled pieces from the vehicle were scattered along the
highway.

It was hard to imagine anyone surviving such an accident,
but the five occupants—a husband and wife and their three
granddaughters—walked away from the scene with minor
injuries.

Have you ever experienced a miraculous accident like this?
It wasn't luck that kept you safe; it was the protecting hands of
God's angels watching over and keeping you safe, just as the
angels did for the family in the SUV.

Take great comfort in knowing that God loves you so much
that you are being guarded and protected by an elite group of
heavenly host.

*Dear Lord, no matter where I go, in my heart I always know that Your
angels are with me night and day, keeping me safe in every way. Amen.*

CONSISTENT RIGHTEOUSNESS, CONSTANT PEACE

"Oh that you had paid attention to my commandments! Then your peace would have been like a river, and your righteousness like the waves of the sea."
ISAIAH 48:18 ESV

P eople are drawn to bodies of water. Pick any place on earth where there is a beautiful sea, lake, or river, and there you'll find hotels, cabins, boats, marinas, docks—everything that goes with being near and enjoying the water. Many of us find we can relax easily near water. At the seashore, we are lulled by the rhythm of the waves as they unceasingly roll in. At the river's edge, we are mesmerized by the current. The river is always moving downstream, an endless supply of water passing by.

Isaiah 48 tells us that if we follow God's commandments, our peace can be as constant as a river and our righteousness as consistent as waves at the shore. On the other hand, disobedience to God's commandments results in an inconsistent lifestyle and an interrupted peace. We should examine our lives in light of God's Word, asking the Holy Spirit to reveal areas where we do not follow His commandments. When we confess our sin, He is faithful to forgive us, and we can begin again. We can ask Him to help us believe that His way is right. We can ask for the desire and resolve to follow Him.

Lord, show me the areas in my life where I am not paying attention to You. Lead me to consistent righteousness and constant peace.

SLOWLY, STEADILY,
SURELY. . .

"This vision is for a future time. It describes the end, and it will be fulfilled.
If it seems slow in coming, wait patiently, for it will surely take place.
It will not be delayed."

HABAKKUK 2:3 NLT

Ah, patience. It's the stuff frustration is made of. And yet it's a virtue the Lord expects His people to have plenty of.

In this fast-paced world, we want what we want and we want it *now*. We don't want to have to wait. And we don't have to—for most things. Microwaves speed up the cooking process. Fast-food restaurants hand us our food as we zip through the drive-thru. Internet access gives us instant access to people, places, and things all over the world. And cell phones give us the chance to connect with folks in a hurry.

Oh, if only we could learn the value of slowing down—of waiting in God's presence. Take another look at today's scripture. Sometimes the things we're waiting on come slowly. Similarly, God's plans may come slowly, but they come steadily, surely. God is going to do what He says He'll do. We don't know when, exactly, but we can be found faithful while we're waiting.

What are you waiting on today? Is your patience wearing thin? Apply the slowly, steadily, surely principle and watch God work—in His time.

Lord, I'm used to things moving really fast. And yet I find myself in a
waiting season. Give me patience, Lord, and remind me daily that Your
timetable is the only one that matters.

FORGIVE...
AND FORGIVE AGAIN

Then Peter came to him and asked, "Lord, how often should I forgive
someone who sins against me? Seven times?"
"No, not seven times," Jesus replied, "but seventy times seven!"
MATTHEW 18:21–22 NLT

Monica's grandmother had crossed the line once again.
Every family gathering, without fail, Nana would start with the
questions and hurtful remarks. Easter dinner was no exception:
"Monica, why aren't you dating anyone yet?" "Don't you hear
your biological clock ticking?" "Since you can't seem to find
someone, I think you should sign up for a dating service."

People—even loved ones—sometimes say and do hurtful
things that leave us feeling sad, bitter, or outraged. Maybe these
people will realize they've wronged us and will ask for forgiveness,
but often they—like Monica's grandmother—think they're
helping and never know the hurt they're causing us.

Instead of holding a grudge against these people, Jesus has
another answer: hand the hurt over to Him and forgive. Not just
once or twice, but again and again. . .and again. Forgiveness is a
process that is successful only with God's help. After all, He's the
perfect example of forgiveness, forgiving us again and again. . .
and again.

Jesus, You know the struggle I have in forgiving the people who hurt me.
Give me the strength I need to completely let go of the bad feelings I have
and forgive them, just as You have forgiven me.

THINK ABOUT THIS

*Whatever is true, whatever is noble, whatever is right, whatever is pure,
whatever is lovely, whatever is admirable—if anything is excellent or
praiseworthy—think about such things.*

PHILIPPIANS 4:8 NIV

Jessica's friends jokingly called her obsessive, and deep down,
Jessica knew they were right. But she couldn't help it. Once she
started worrying about something, she just couldn't stop.

Lately she had been concerned about her brother, who was
serving in the military overseas. She couldn't stop thinking about
all the things that could happen to him, and it was starting
to interfere with her life. She spent hours online every day,
reading everything she could find about the country in which
he was serving. After a few months she became withdrawn and
depressed, not wanting to leave her house or her computer for
even a few hours.

Our thought patterns can powerfully influence our emotions.
This is no surprise to students of scripture—God's Word tells us
to think about things that are positive, uplifting, praiseworthy,
and true. And for good reason. When we dwell on dismal
thoughts, we begin to believe them. When we believe them, we
start to feel defeated and depressed. Positive thoughts have the
opposite effect and can make a dramatic difference in our outlook
on life. What negative thoughts do you need to eliminate today?

*Lord, forgive me for the negative and self-defeating thoughts I've allowed
to bring me down. Help me to think about the things that honor You, and
thank You for the way this changes my attitude and my heart.*

A New Name

*"To everyone who is victorious I will give. . .a white stone,
and on the stone will be engraved a new name that no one understands
except the one who receives it."*
REVELATION 2:17 NLT

In the classic book *Hinds' Feet on High Places*, the main character, Much-Afraid, is invited by the Chief Shepherd to travel from her home in the Valley of Humiliation to the glory of the High Places. This is a difficult decision for Much-Afraid. The journey is long and her companions will be Sorrow and Suffering. And although it is indeed painful, in the end she is rewarded with a home in the High Places and a new name: Grace-and-Glory. Much-Afraid is transformed by her journey, and her new name reflects this glorious transformation.

Throughout scripture, God changes the names of His children as an outward expression of inner transformation. Sarai and Abram receive God's promise and are called Sarah and Abraham. Jacob prevails and is called Israel. Saul the persecutor becomes Paul the evangelist.

What is your name? Perhaps you are Fearful. Timid. Weak. Like Much-Afraid, we are in the midst of a long and painful journey. At times it seems that our only friends are Sorrow and Suffering. But don't lose heart! Your glorious destination and your new name are waiting for you, and you can be sure that it will be more than worth the journey.

Father, thank You for the promise of a new name in heaven's glory. Amen.

FIRSTFRUITS

*Honor the LORD with your possessions, and with the
firstfruits of all your increase.*
PROVERBS 3:9 NKJV

A young woman in a new career faced several business
decisions alone. She did her best to handle her finances but often
found things out of balance. Sometimes the paycheck didn't quite
stretch to cover the month. And she struggled with something
else, too. She found herself overwhelmed with guilt every time
she heard a sermon on tithing. How could she possibly give 10
percent of her income with money already so tight?

Giving the firstfruits of your income isn't always easy, but it's
a part of God's master plan for your success in life. It's tough to
see how giving something away can actually benefit you, isn't it?
But God promises to meet your every need if you're faithful in
this area. In fact, He actually challenges us to test Him.

So, have you tested Him with your finances? If you're
struggling financially, bring your fears to God. He will give
you the courage you need to write that first check to your local
church. And then, as His provision is proven out, your faith and
courage will grow. Loosen your grip on your pocketbook, woman
of God. You will find the Lord faithful in this area if you just
trust Him.

*Lord, I'm scared to give. There, I've said it. I'm scared to give because I'm
afraid there won't be enough left over to cover my bills. Help me loosen my
grip in this area, Father. And take away my fears. Make me a giver!*

WHAT DO YOU WORSHIP?

But worship only the LORD, who brought you out of Egypt with great
strength and a powerful arm. Bow down to him alone, and
offer sacrifices only to him.
2 KINGS 17:36 NLT

When Hildy heard her preacher say, "We all worship something," she had to agree. In high school, she worshipped the quarterback on the football team. In college, she worshipped her grades. During law school, she worshipped her professors.

These days, she worshipped her body, spending hours at the gym. And on other days, she bowed down to the idol of food, taking in way more than she needed. She figured she deserved it because she exercised so much. *At times*, Hildy admitted to herself, *I worship material things.* Being single and prosperous gave her a lot of discretionary income, and she didn't always use it well.

Forgive me, Lord, she whispered in her heart. *Forgive me for putting such silly things on the throne of my heart. Help me to put You first, and to ask for Your guidance in using my money, time, and talents for You.*

What do you worship? Food? Television? The opposite sex? Your dreams and goals? Today, determine to take those idols off the throne and put God back in His rightful place.

Lord, I'm so sorry that I worship other things instead of You. Have mercy on me and show me how I should use the resources You've graciously given me.

SIMPLY SILLY

A cheerful disposition is good for your health.
PROVERBS 17:22 MSG

Jeanne Calmont died at the age of 122, after outliving twenty-seven French presidents, and entered the *Guinness Book of World Records* as the world's oldest woman. When asked the secret of her longevity, she replied, "Laughter!"

It's a scientifically proven fact that laughter lowers blood pressure and strengthens the immune system. It helps overcome depression. In short, laughter is good medicine. A "spoonful" each day will add much to our lives.

Paul had so much joy that he sang and won his jailors to Christ. Imagine the effect we could have on our world today if our countenances reflected the joy of the Lord all of the time: at work, at home, at play. Jesus said, "I have told you this so that my joy may be in you and that your joy may be complete" (John 15:11 NIV).

Is your cup of joy full? Have you laughed today? Not a small smile, but laughter. Maybe it's time we looked for something to laugh about and tasted joy. Jesus suggested it.

Lord, help me find joy this day. Let me laugh and give praises to the King. Amen.

YOU EITHER TRUST HIM
OR YOU DON'T!

*Trust in the LORD with all thine heart; and lean not unto thine own
understanding. In all thy ways acknowledge him, and he
shall direct thy paths.*
PROVERBS 3:5–6 KJV

Trusting the Lord isn't always easy," Candace confided at her
women's Bible study after they read Proverbs 3:5–6.

"You're right—it's not always easy, but it's pretty simple. You
either trust Him or you don't," Sandy said.

Talk about an enlightening statement! It was straight to the
point. True friends often tell you the truth just as they see it.

The world is filled with personal trials, and we often struggle
with them alone. We may be worried about finances. The sudden
loss of a family member or friend may grieve or depress us.
A good friendship may be strained over misunderstanding or
outright nastiness. No matter what the situation, trials often leave
us feeling anxious and confused.

Today, if you're facing a difficult trial, try trusting the Lord
with all of your heart. Not just a little piece of your heart, but
all of it. Don't try to figure things out. God already has them
under control, and He holds all the answers to your unanswered
questions.

Remember, it's really pretty simple: you either trust Him or
you don't.

*Dear Lord, I trust You with all my heart and all my being. I acknowledge
You as Lord of my life. Thanks for making it pretty simple. Amen.*

WHAT IS WRITTEN
ON YOUR HEART?

These commandments that I give you today are to be upon your hearts. . . .
Write them on the doorframes of your houses and on your gates.
DEUTERONOMY 6:6, 9 NIV

In many Jewish homes today, there is a small container attached to the doorway. Inside the box is a tiny scroll containing the words of Deuteronomy 6:9. This is known as a mezuzah and serves as a tangible reminder of God's ancient covenant with the Israelites and His desire to have first place in their lives.

In the Old Testament, God's law was written on scrolls and passed down from generation to generation. In the New Testament, we learn that Jesus both fulfilled the old covenant and introduced a new covenant. This new covenant is written on our hearts (see Hebrews 10:16). God's Word is our scroll and it confirms the truths that He has already written on our hearts through the Holy Spirit. In spite of this, we sometimes forget.

What are some practical ways you can remind yourself, each day, of the truth of God's Word? Copy verses on index cards to carry with you, or better yet, commit them to memory. Listen to the Bible on CD or to songs composed from scripture. Whatever you do, always be looking for fresh ways to remember the truth that God has written on your heart.

Father, thank You for writing Your truth upon my heart. Help
me to look for tangible reminders of Your truth. Amen.

RUNNING ON EMPTY

I have observed something else under the sun. The fastest runner doesn't always win the race, and the strongest warrior doesn't always win the battle.
ECCLESIASTES 9:11 NLT

Jan struggled to be the best at everything she tried. She worked harder than anyone in her office, joined nearly every ministry at her church, taught wonderful Bible studies, and gave the best parties of anyone in her women's group. She cooked better, dressed better, kept a better home, and was never seen in public without her game face on.

There was only one problem. Before long, Jan was running on empty. She had little left to give. Her quest to appear perfect before a watching world crumbled around her. Not only was she not perfect, she couldn't keep up with the crazy schedule anymore.

Can you relate to this woman? Are you trying too hard? Always rushing here and there, involving yourself in a dozen things? Has keeping up appearances become an issue? Watch out. Before long, you might be running on empty, too.

Lord, I'm so tired! I've taken on too much. My heart was in the right place, but somewhere along the way I got off-track. Redirect me, Father. Show me what to give up and what to stick with. Amen.

A Hospitable Heart

*After [Lydia] was baptized, along with everyone in her household,
she said in a surge of hospitality, "If you're confident that I'm in this with
you and believe in the Master truly, come home with me and be my guests."
We hesitated, but she wouldn't take no for an answer.*

Acts 16:15 msg

Lydia, a dealer in purple cloth, worked hard at her trade. The
Bible does not tell us much else about her except that she was a
worshipper of God.

One day during their travels, Paul and his companions
stopped to pray by the river outside the city gate of Philippi. They
met a group of women there that included Lydia. She listened to
Paul's message and accepted Jesus. After Lydia was baptized, she
insisted the men come home with her and be her guests. As was
customary for a hostess, she likely prepared and served them food
and gave them a place to rest and pray. She showed hospitality in
the name of the Lord.

You can follow Lydia's lead. Whether your home is small or
large, you can choose to be hospitable. Invite a friend who needs
a pick-me-up to join you for a meal during the week. Ask a single
mom and her children to come over for a pizza and movie night. If
elderly neighbors are unable to get out, take your hospitality to them!
Bake them some cookies or take them flowers from your garden.

*Father, give me a heart for hospitality. May I always serve others in
Your name. Amen.*

CONTENTMENT

A peaceful heart leads to a healthy body;
jealousy is like cancer in the bones.
PROVERBS 14:30 NLT

Dawn was never happy. Just when she would get her apartment decorated the way she wanted it, a friend would purchase a new piece of furniture or paint a room, and suddenly Dawn wanted to have something similar. She would search online and in catalogs and stores for the perfect outfit, coat, or handbag, and when she finally purchased it, she second-guessed her decision.

Dawn's problem was that she was never at peace. She was constantly comparing herself to other people and comparing her things to their things. In the comparison game, Dawn and her stuff never won. What other people had was always so much better.

Proverbs warns us against falling into this dangerous trap. When we compare ourselves to others we become jealous, and this jealousy has a way of growing like cancer—quickly and out of control. It can wreak havoc with our inner lives because we are never satisfied, never at peace.

The quickest way to avoid the comparison trap is to adopt an attitude of thankfulness, to focus on what we have rather than what we don't have, and to make peace with the idea that there is nothing in this world that can truly satisfy our souls. For true satisfaction, we must look to God and God alone.

Heavenly Father, thank You for all You provide for me. Guard my heart
against comparing myself to others. Help me to be at peace. Amen.

MAKING FRIENDS

*A man of many companions may come to ruin, but there is a
friend who sticks closer than a brother.*
PROVERBS 18:24 NIV

Having friends to share your life with is a rich blessing.
If your life is full of close friends, appreciate the intimacy
and companionship that these relationships provide. But if
friendships are lacking in your life, don't give up in despair. You
can do something about it. Although it may require stepping out
of your comfort zone, the rewards will be well worth it.

Consider your interests and hobbies. If you're into sports,
sign up for a tennis team or exercise class. If computers are your
niche, enroll in a class to improve your skills. Join a book club,
Bible study, garden club, or quilting class. Then, when you go,
strike up a conversation with someone around you. You may be
surprised to find that you are not alone; everyone is looking for
a friend. To have a friend, you need to be a friend. Take the first
step, and friendship will soon be yours.

*Dear Lord, give me the courage to take the first step
in making new friends. Amen.*

I'VE GOT THE JOY, JOY, JOY, JOY...

You have made known to me the path of life; you will fill me with joy in your presence, with eternal pleasures at your right hand.

PSALM 16:11 NIV

It's one thing to be single. It's another thing to be *happy* single. Maybe you read those words, cringe, and ask, "How can I ever be happy single?" Oh, daughter of God, you can! In fact, your singleness puts you in the perfect spot for happiness because you've got time to pour into your relationship with your heavenly Father—the very giver of happiness.

Our Creator God is a joy-giver, and He pours it out when you need it most. At your very lowest point, He's there, ready to fill you with that bubbling-over kind of joy. And how wonderful to know that in His right hand there is happiness forever. Forever! That's a mighty long time. Longer than any earthly relationship, for sure!

Today, spend time with the Lord. Give Him your frustrations and fears. Ask Him to replace them with His overwhelming joy. Then begin to live out that joy in every other area of your life.

O Lord, I need Your bubbling-over joy today. Thank You for the reminder that You are a joy-giver and that You want me to be happy, not just in my singleness, but in every aspect of life. Pour out Your joy, Father!

HIS GOOD WORK CONTINUES

I am certain that God, who began the good work within you, will continue his work until it is finally finished on the day when Christ Jesus returns.
PHILIPPIANS 1:6 NLT

Look back to the time when you decided to let God begin working in your life. For many of us, that was a time of joy and excitement. We recognized that the very One who had created us was personally directing our lives.

Perhaps accomplishments aren't what you have expected them to be at this point in your life. Maybe you hoped to be married by now. You may have imagined that you would be more financially stable at this time. You may have anticipated being further along in your ministry. When you compare your life to the lives of others, you might think that God has forgotten you or that He was only interested in you when you began your relationship with Him.

Be at peace and be filled with joy. God has promised to continue working a great work in us until Jesus returns. Ask God to give you a vision of His plans for your future, and wait expectantly for Him to fulfill them. He has not forgotten you.

Dear God, thank You for calling me to a life spent with You. Show me how You are daily working in my life. Amen.

KNOWN BY GOD

But if anyone loves God, he is known by God.
1 CORINTHIANS 8:3 ESV

How do we show that we love God? Is it by church attendance? Giving? Doing good deeds? Prayer? These may be manifestations of our love for God, or they may be things we do out of a sense of duty; but loving God is first and foremost a response to being known and loved by God. We can't muster emotion or feeling toward God, nor do we love Him simply by willing ourselves to acts of obedience. We begin to love God when we grasp what it means to be known by God.

He knit us together in our mothers' wombs.

He knows the number of hairs on our heads.

He accepts us as we are because of Christ's sacrifice for us.

He has compassion for our weakness.

He forgives our sins.

He longs to commune with us.

He delights to hear our prayers.

He desires to help us, strengthen us, and bless us.

He has given us the Holy Spirit as our comforter, our helper, and our teacher.

He wills all this for us before we ever turn to Him in repentance. We need to reacquaint ourselves with the gospel often, to meditate on what Christ has done for us, and to remember that He first loved us.

Lord, renew my love for You. Help me to remember that You knew me and loved me before I ever knew You.

No Worries

*"So don't worry about tomorrow, for tomorrow will bring its
own worries. Today's trouble is enough for today."*
Matthew 6:34 NLT

What thoughts keep you up at night? Finances?
Relationships? Work? Health or family concerns? We women are
worriers by nature, but living in a constant state of dread isn't
what God wants for us, His beloved daughters.

If we're honest with ourselves, we admit we sometimes hold
on to our worries, thinking that keeping them close somehow
keeps us in control of the situation. In reality, most of our worries
concern things completely out of our hands.

Instead, Jesus offers us freedom from our chains of worry.
"Trust Me instead of relying on yourself. Give Me the things that
you fret over and stress about," He says. "How can you doubt
that I'll take care of you when you mean so much to Me?"

Today, trust Jesus' assurance that He will take care of you.
Ask Him to help you let go of your worrying nature and replace
it with a spirit of praise and thanksgiving. It won't happen
overnight, but soon you'll feel the true freedom from worry that
only Jesus can supply.

*Jesus, You know the toll my worries take on my heart and mind. I don't
want to hold on to these negative thoughts, but it's hard to let go of them!
Help me to place all my concerns in Your capable hands so that I can be free
to praise You as You deserve!*

THE ULTIMATE
BEAUTY TIP

*Charm is deceptive, and beauty is fleeting; but a woman
who fears the LORD is to be praised.*
PROVERBS 31:30 NIV

We live in a beauty-conscious world. Magazine covers,
billboards, commercials, and TV shows try to tell us what we
women need to look our best. The compulsion "I've got to be
beautiful" propels us to purchase makeup, clothes, shoes, and
other "necessities."

There's nothing wrong with looking your best. In fact, it's a
good thing. But if you've become obsessed with your appearance,
then your priorities are out of balance. Remember, true beauty
comes from the inside out. What's the point of going through the
motions of having your hair and face done if you still have a sour
expression? Besides, outward beauty is fleeting. Sooner or later
the hands of the clock catch up with us.

Look to the Word of God for the definition of true beauty.
It comes from the innermost places and is developed by spending
time in the Word and in close relationship with the Lord. Even the
plainest woman glows with the radiance of God when she's spent
time with Him. There's no facial cream that even comes close.

*Lord, I want to be seen as a beautiful woman—not just on the outside
but especially on the inside. Teach me Your beauty tips, Father. Give me a
heavenly radiance that only comes from above.*

LEND A HAND

*"What do you think? Which of the three became a neighbor
to the man attacked by robbers?"
"The one who treated him kindly," the religion scholar responded.
Jesus said, "Go and do the same."*
LUKE 10:36–37 MSG

The woman pushed the button on her garage door opener
and drove her car inside. Before she climbed out, she closed the
garage door, intent on getting inside for her evening meal. She
never noticed the bicycle lying in the grass or the boy who had
tumbled onto the asphalt. Enveloped in the cocoon of her own
home, she went about her business.

Too often we follow a similar pattern. Our lives are busy—
work, church, exercise, entertainment—and we never even meet
our neighbors, much less get to know them.

While it's good to be cautious, the parable of the Good
Samaritan tells us to help one another. Not only does becoming
involved provide someone needed assistance, it expands our
heart-reach. We become Jesus to others, spreading love and
kindness, increasing our witness.

Let's keep our eyes peeled for occasions when we might help
a neighbor. We want to be wise, select carefully, and love openly.

*Father, thank You for Your loving-kindness. Give me an opening to share
Your love with others. Amen.*

OUR REFUGE IN TIME OF PAIN

Be gracious to me, O God. . .for my soul takes refuge in You.
PSALM 57:1 NASB

The voice on the other end of the phone told Jill that a dear friend had been killed in a freak accident. Jill shook her head in disbelief and began to wail.

When her tears were exhausted, her eyes fell on a family Bible on the coffee table. She reached for it, and the pages opened to Psalm 57. Haltingly, Jill read the verses out loud. They comforted her soul as she mourned the loss of her childhood pal.

When death takes someone dear, the world's very foundation seems to shake. The color of the air around us looks different, and we wonder why everyone else is going about their everyday lives as if nothing had changed. We question God, asking why He couldn't stop the situation causing our pain.

His Word doesn't always answer our questions, but it is a place we can run to for comfort. Though the books of the Bible are ancient, they are timeless. Just as the psalmists poured out their anguish, joys, doubts, and fears to God, so can we. And as we commune with God—not holding anything back—He tends to us gently, giving us the scriptures we need at just the right time.

When the world around you breaks loose, don't lose your hold on God. And rest assured, He won't let go of you.

Father, thank You for Your words of comfort when I am wracked with grief and pain. Help me to never forget that You are there for me.

It's Not My Fault

*Someone who lives on milk is still an infant and doesn't
know how to do what is right.*
HEBREWS 5:13 NLT

When Sara was a little girl, she found the perfect alibi for
her every crime. Whether she unrolled a brand-new roll of toilet
paper throughout the house or wrote her name in crayon on the
wall, Sara's imaginary friend, Ella, took the blame.

"Sara, who spilled orange juice all over the floor?" her mother
would ask.

"Ella did it," Sara would always reply.

Sara never outgrew her penchant for blaming others. As an
adult, whether she bounced a check or showed up late for work,
she always found a way to pin her failures on others.

This pattern started in Eden. When Adam ate the fruit,
he blamed Eve. Then Eve blamed Satan. When we fail to take
responsibility for our choices, we tend to make the same bad
ones over and over again. Accepting responsibility for our actions
tells God that we want to learn from our mistakes so they don't
happen again. It also tells Him that we are willing to do what it
takes to make them right.

Are you using the shortcomings of someone else to justify
your own actions? Take a moment to ask God to examine your
heart in this important area.

*Lord, as hard as it is to admit when I am wrong, teach me to
humbly accept responsibility for my choices. I pray for growth
and maturity in my Christian walk. Amen.*

APPRECIATE
WHAT YOU HAVE

*"You shall not covet your neighbor's house; you shall not covet your
neighbor's wife, nor his male servant, nor his female servant, nor his ox,
nor his donkey, nor anything that is your neighbor's."*
EXODUS 20:17 NKJV

The dictionary defines the word *covet* as "having a strong
desire to possess something that belongs to somebody else."

It is okay to want something. The danger comes when we
want *what someone else has*. You probably don't struggle with
coveting a neighbor's donkey, ox, or servant as the commandment
suggests. But could it be a friend's husband that you wish were
your own? A neighbor's swimming pool? A sibling's talent? A
star's fame?

When God tells us that we "shall not," we must pay
attention. His commandments are for our good. Catch yourself
when you sense a desire for that which is not yours. Appreciate
your own gifts, blessings, and belongings. An even higher calling
is to be happy for others in their accomplishments and as they
acquire possessions.

*God, You have poured out so many blessings on me. Protect my heart from
desiring that which belongs to others. Amen.*

A Powerful Voice

The voice of the LORD is powerful;
the voice of the LORD is full of majesty.
PSALM 29:4 NKJV

Julie found herself pulled this way and that by the voices of the world. Magazine covers, TV shows, movies—they all cried out to her that she needed to be or look a certain way. And other voices hollered in her ear, too: her boss, parents, friends, and coworkers. Julie found herself inundated with messages, and none of them matched each other. A few even conflicted with her own voice, the one that came from her innermost being.

Maybe you know what it feels like to struggle with mixed messages from the media and people in your life. Yet in the midst of the chaos, there is a voice that rises above all others. The voice of the Lord is powerful. It's full of majesty.

You would think a voice like that would be nearly impossible to miss, right?

So why do we have such a hard time hearing the Lord's voice above the others? It's probably because we're not tuned in. We're distracted. And perhaps we're so busy responding to the chatter going on around us that we lose our bearings. Today, spend time tuning out the voices of the world—and tuning in to God.

Lord, there are so many messages out there! Help me tune my ears to hear
Your words. Your thoughts. Your plans. Rid me of any distractions and help
me to focus solely on You.

REMEMBERING

Behold, I have engraved you on the palms of my hands;
your walls are continually before me.
ISAIAH 49:16 ESV

A phone number, a homework assignment, an item to pick up at the grocery store—we might jot any of these reminders on our hand if a piece of paper isn't available. We know if we write something on our hand we will see it. How can we not? We use our hands all day, every day. They are always in front of us.

When the Lord said He has engraved us on the palm of His hands, He was telling us that He remembers us. All day, every day, He remembers us. We are of utmost importance to Him. We cannot be forgotten. When He submitted Himself to Calvary's cross and allowed nails to be driven through His hands, He was remembering us. Our names are in those scars.

Romans 8:34 (NIV) says, "Christ Jesus, who died—more than that, who was raised to life—is at the right hand of God and is also interceding for us." Jesus is remembering us in constant prayer to the Father. His eyes never close and His memory never fails. God remembers us.

Father, thank You that through Christ You have brought me to
Yourself, You reign over my life, and You always remember me.

LIGHT VS. DARKNESS

*But if we walk in the light as He is in the light, we have fellowship with
one another, and the blood of Jesus Christ His Son cleanses us from all sin.*
1 JOHN 1:7 NKJV

Our world offers us endless choices. There are a multitude
of dark paths to walk down, but only one that truly offers light.
When we choose to walk with Jesus—the light of the world that
casts away darkness—He will provide the illumination we need
to make each day's choices.

At times you may be tempted to take a detour into darkness.
It may not appear to make a big difference. Satan can convince
you that doing something "just this once" will be of no real
consequence. He tricked Adam and Eve that way in the Garden
of Eden when he offered them fruit from the one tree that God
had declared forbidden.

How do we remain in the light? We ask the Holy Spirit to
guide us, and when we get an uneasy feeling regarding a choice,
we pay attention to it. It may be hard to say no, but the payoff
for obedience will be great.

Walk with others who walk with Christ. If you don't have
Christian friends, take the initiative to attend a church small-
group Bible study, and you'll probably make friends as a side
benefit. Christian friends can make all the difference in avoiding
wrong paths.

*Father of Light, help me to be sensitive to Your Holy Spirit.
Shine Your light into my life. Amen.*

Church

And let us not neglect our meeting together, as some people do, but encourage one another, especially now that the day of his return is drawing near.

Hebrews 10:25 nlt

Do you ever find yourself making excuses to skip church? "I stayed up too late Saturday night. . . . The weather is bad. . . . I don't have anyone to sit with." The list of excuses is endless. We rationalize our decision by saying we're going to watch a TV sermon or worship the Lord by being in nature.

Attending church every Sunday takes effort. That's why the writer of Hebrews reminds us of the importance of meeting together. But why is corporate worship so necessary?

Believers are strengthened as we focus on the Lord together. Praising the Lord with one voice in song is powerful. Being reminded of God's truth is crucial. Fellowship encourages us in our spiritual walk. We've each been given at least one spiritual gift to benefit the church body, and that gift is exercised as we are connected to each other.

Church worship gives us a glimpse of what heaven will be like—believers of every nationality and background worshipping the Lord together. We will acknowledge His holiness. We will bow before Him in adoration. Why wait until heaven? Go to church this week. The blessings will be yours!

Dear Lord, I need to worship You with other believers. Help me to be consistent in church attendance. Amen.

SIN NO MORE

"Then neither do I condemn you," Jesus declared.
"Go now and leave your life of sin."
JOHN 8:11 NIV

John 8 paints one of the most beautiful portraits of grace in all of scripture. The woman was dragged from the bedroom and paraded before the men in the temple courts. Can you imagine the humiliation? The man who had likely declared his love for her only moments before was nowhere to be seen. Only the woman was dragged into the temple—already tried and declared guilty of adultery. It was all over except for the stoning.

Until Jesus stepped in. He didn't say anything for what probably seemed like an eternity. Then, "If any one of you is without sin, let him be the first to throw a stone at her" (John 8:7 NIV). With that one sentence, the crowd dispersed. The only man on earth qualified to stone this woman offered grace.

The Pharisees knew the letter of the law like the backs of their hands: adultery meant stoning. But in His gentle and loving way, Jesus brought to light the spirit of the law. Sin begins in the heart. Oh, what freedom is found in the Spirit!

Now, Jesus didn't let this woman off the hook; sin is sin. But under the Spirit, condemnation is no longer necessary. Just a cleansed heart—filled with grace and gratitude for the gift of freedom and forgiveness.

Jesus, thank You that I am not condemned. Thank You that I am forgiven. Free. Help me to live a life of purity to honor You. Amen.

PRIDE. . .BE GONE!

Pride ends in humiliation, while humility brings honor.
PROVERBS 29:23 NLT

Linda struggled with pride—and didn't even know it! She worked hard, made a decent income, found just the right home to live in, and picked out exactly the right clothes to wear. Nothing wrong with any of those things, right? Unfortunately, every time Linda talked about her accomplishments, she used the "I" word. "I've" done this, or "I've" done that. She forgot that her many blessings came not from her own hand, but the Lord's.

It's hard to remember that everything is a gift from God. Yes, we work hard. And yes, there are some wonderful accomplishments along the way. But if we're not careful, we can begin to think we've brought about those things ourselves. Nothing could be further from the truth. Every detail of our lives is orchestrated by God, and every blessing is a gift from heaven.

So, you have a great job? Praise Him! Working your way to the top of the corporate ladder? Driving a nicer car? Looking for a bigger home? Remember to keep it all in perspective. It's all from Him, after all.

Lord, in this "me first" time I'm living in, it's easy to forget that I'm not responsible for the blessings in my life. Remind me daily, Father, that every good and perfect gift comes not from my hard work, but from You.

CALL ON GOD

"Call to me and I will answer you and tell you great and unsearchable things you do not know."
JEREMIAH 33:3 NIV

W here do you go when you need answers? Friends, the Internet, a parent, a boyfriend, or a minister?

All of these resources can be great blessings to our lives. We all need Christian fellowship and godly counsel, particularly when we are puzzled or unsure about what to do. But the next time you are depressed or unsettled—when you find your mind racing with questions and the future seems far too big to face—call on God.

He is sovereign. He is before and after all things. He is Spirit. Yet He is accessible to each of His children at any time. He will not force His ways upon you. Our God gives us a lot of choice in this life, a lot of free will. But He does want to reveal His ways to us. He wants us to know His answers for our lives.

God may not give you all the answers you are seeking at once. He knows that some things you are not ready to know or able to comprehend. Nonetheless, call on Him. Trust in Him. He will unfold the unknown to you as He sees best.

God, teach me to call on You when I am tempted to call on others instead. Thank You for being a Father who longs to reveal Himself to me. Amen.

KEEPING ON

Blessed is the man who perseveres.
JAMES 1:12 NIV

A child played with an inflatable superhero toy. When he punched the towering figure, it flopped over, then bounced back upright on its round base. Despite constant pummeling, nothing the child did could keep the superhero flat on its back.

We can feel like the superhero toy: we get knocked down by situations we cannot control. We're off balance, our breath thumped out of us. At these times, we need to adopt our own ability to bounce back.

The book of James encourages us to persevere so we might attain "the crown of life that God has promised to those who love him" (James 1:12 NIV). He reminds us that God is with us. When Satan attacks, finds our Achilles' heel, and knocks us over, we need to dig deep into reservoirs of faith, tap into God's Word, and pop back up, fighting the fight He's put before us. We can't be passive, or we will be demolished.

Perseverance means staying in the fight and refusing to give up. This attitude empowers us and makes the victim mentality dissipate. It builds confidence, one fight at a time. Keep on keeping on—it's a powerful life tool.

Lord, give me the strength to get up from the mat and continue.
I choose to believe in Your promises. Amen.

A WELL-STOCKED PURSE

We can make our plans, but the LORD determines our steps.
PROVERBS 16:9 NLT

Have you ever noticed how a woman will carry a purse, a diaper bag, a work satchel, a beach bag, and other totes appropriate for the occasion while men go empty-handed? She'll stuff everything from snacks to sewing kit to toilet paper in her bag. He'll shove his wallet in his pocket and is good to go.

Women want to be prepared for any and every crisis that may arise, while most men figure they will find, make, or otherwise produce whatever they need should an emergency cross their path. Women don't understand what seems to be neglect on the part of men, but that is just the way it is.

We women can plan every move we are going to make, but all the planning we do will not keep trouble away. We can hoard all the things on our persons, in our cars, and in our houses that we think will make a problem manageable, but they cannot dam up the flood of emotions that come with a crisis.

Only God knows what tomorrow brings, and only He knows the tools we will need to get through any given situation. No packet of tissues or pocket-size scissors is going to be more useful than a spirit that is calm and trusts in the Lord.

Lord, help me to carry a peace-filled spirit with me at all times, and I will trust You to guide me and to provide for my needs along any path You may take me.

What to Give God

Through Jesus, therefore, let us continually offer to God a sacrifice of praise—the fruit of lips that confess his name.
HEBREWS 13:15 NIV

What can we possibly give God for what He has done for us through Christ? The only real gift we have to offer is praise.

Implicit in Hebrews 13:15 is a reminder of our identity as sinners in desperate need of the precious gift of righteousness through Jesus' sacrifice for us. Our own righteousness, consisting of our own human efforts, was as filthy rags to God. Only Christ's righteousness could satisfy the divine justice of a holy God.

Jesus was willing to live among us, suffer, and die on the cross for us. He exchanged His life for ours. He took our filth and our punishment and gave us His righteousness and eternal life. God receives us based on this exchange.

How do we respond? With a sacrifice of prayer and praise. God desires to hear us praise Jesus, to speak of Him with gratitude or to acknowledge our great need of Him. Pray in His name. Ask for the things Jesus promised. Pray Jesus' own words back to His Father in heaven. God is pleased with our faith in Jesus and our sacrifice of praise.

Father, I praise You for clothing me in the righteousness of Christ. May my life reflect His transformative grace.

A "KEPT" HEART

Keep your heart with all diligence, for out of it spring the issues of life.
PROVERBS 4:23 NKJV

When you read the words "keep your heart," what comes to mind? Godly women keep many things: their purity, their word, and even their relationships. They are careful to guard these things from the evil one who seeks to steal them. Still, there is something far more important we should keep—something we often forget.

The Lord wants us to diligently guard and protect our hearts. Why? Because everything we are or ever will be comes from that very vulnerable place. In many ways, the heart is like a tiny spring that feeds a big river; out of it flow the issues of life. The heart is the hub, the center of our being. It's a place we often forget to protect, and the enemy knows it. He seeks to break our hearts or bring discouragement at every opportunity, particularly when we let our guard down.

Today, make a commitment to keep your heart with all diligence. Don't let past relationships, loneliness, or untapped dreams weaken you. Instead, stand strong against the enemy's attacks. And don't allow your heart to become tainted by the things of this world. Guard it. Protect it. Keep it.

Lord, I know You're interested in matters of the heart. Who I am in my innermost being concerns You most. Today I commit to "keep" my heart with all diligence. Strengthen me from the inside out.

PRESENT HELP

*"For I, the LORD your God, hold your right hand; it is I who say to you,
'Fear not, I am the one who helps you.'"*
ISAIAH 41:13 ESV

We shake hands to greet each other; it's a sign of welcome.
We reach for the hand of a child when we're walking in a crowd
or near a street; it helps protect and comfort the child. In times
of great emotion or anticipation, we grab the hand of a nearby
friend or family member; it says, "I am with you." By a hospital
bed, we clasp the hand of a sick loved one; our hand tells them
we are present, suffering with them. With every gripping of
another's hand, we are bearing witness to God.

He holds your hand. He welcomes you into His kingdom.
He protects you. He comforts you. He is with you in your most
anxious moments and in your darkest hours. With the clasp of
His hand comes courage for any situation. He tells you not to
fear, for He is your ever-present help in times of trouble. He has a
hold of you.

*Almighty God, I am grateful that You hold my hand. Forgive me for
the times I have forgotten this and let fear reign in my life. Help me to
remember I am never alone. Grant me the courage that comes
from knowing You as my helper.*

LET IT SHINE!

Let your light so shine before men, that they may see your good works,
and glorify your Father which is in heaven.
MATTHEW 5:16 KJV

Have you ever noticed the stadium lights at a sporting event? They not only illuminate the field, but they also put off a radiant glow that lights up the sky for miles.

The Bible says that Christians are the light of the world. As followers of Christ, we get to share the light of Jesus with those who may be living in darkness. How do we keep our lights shining bright? By staying connected to the true source of light, Jesus Christ, through prayer and Bible study.

Loving the unlovable, giving to the needy, forgiving the unforgivable, being honest, and striving to be Christlike are all perfect ways to share the light of Jesus. Let your life be a beacon of light and hope to all you meet. You are the light of the world, so let it shine and bring glory to Jesus Christ.

Dear Lord, thank You for bringing light to my darkness. Help me to
spread the light of Jesus to those who don't know You. Amen.

WITH EVERY BREATH!

I bless GOD every chance I get; my lungs expand with his praise.
PSALM 34:1 MSG

We humans are a self-centered bunch. Even those of us who have a personal relationship with the Creator often neglect to give Him the praise that He deserves. Instead, we choose to focus on our own problems and selfish desires. If we try to place praise high on our list of priorities, it's often difficult to follow through; praise isn't something that comes naturally to most of us.

So how can we develop a spirit of praise every day? First, amp up the amount of time you spend in prayer. As you go throughout your daily routine, find new reasons to offer thanks to the Father: the refreshment of a hot shower, a job to do, coworkers to interact with, food to satisfy hunger, the smile of a friend, the change of seasons. . .the list is endless!

Next, sprinkle your conversations with the hope that your faith gives. Verbally acknowledge God's goodness and provision in your life and in the lives of others. Call a coincidence what it really is—the hand of the Father. Don't be afraid to let your newfound praise bubble over to every area of your life!

Father, You are my God, my almighty Redeemer and Friend! I praise You because of the wonderful things You do in my life every day. I praise You for being You! Let everything within me praise the Lord!

WHAT ARE YOUR GIFTS?

*There are different kinds of gifts, but the same Spirit. There are different
kinds of service, but the same Lord.*
1 CORINTHIANS 12:4–5 NIV

A woman felt called by God to help out at her church, but
she couldn't figure out which ministry best suited her. While
some people were clearly Bible teachers, she was not. And
while some could sing, she didn't feel that was her gifting. After
spending time praying and seeking the Lord, she finally opted to
work in children's ministry. She'd always done well with children,
and she realized she could bless the little ones and fulfill her
calling, all at the same time.

Maybe you know what it's like to search for your place.
Perhaps you've tried different ministries and still haven't figured
out your best place of service. Be patient. God has placed specific
gifts within you, and you are needed in the body of Christ.
Although your gifts may be different than someone else's, they are
all from the same Spirit.

Today, thank the Lord for entrusting you with spiritual gifts.
If you're struggling to know where you fit, ask Him to give you
opportunities to minister in different areas until you find just the
right spot.

*Lord, thank You for pouring out Your Spirit on me, and thank You for the
gifts You've placed within me. I want to reach others for You, so place me in
the very spot where I can be most effective.*

God's Blessings

*The LORD bless thee, and keep thee; the LORD make his face shine upon thee,
and be gracious unto thee.*
NUMBERS 6:24–25 KJV

Once we have a relationship with God the Father through Jesus Christ, we are in line for a multitude of blessings. Billy Graham said, "Think of the blessings we so easily take for granted: life itself; preservation from danger; every bit of health we enjoy; every hour of liberty; the ability to see, to hear, to speak, to think—and to imagine all this comes from the hand of God." Without realizing it, we were blessed when we opened our eyes this morning. Some of us can add friends, family, freedom, and possessions to that blessing list.

Why do we not recognize all of our blessings? Because it's human nature to zero in on what's wrong and miss what's very right. We overcome that habit by praise and fellowship with Him. When we bless God in faithful praise and He blesses us, the result is a renewed strength for daily living.

God's love for us is eternal, as are His gifts. We need to open our arms and become thankful recipients for all He's given. Praise Him and bless His holy name.

*Lord, You have given me so much, and I am thankful.
Let me give thanks for Your gifts. Amen.*

In God We Trust

*Moses summoned all the Israelites and said to them, "You have seen with
your own eyes everything the LORD did. . . . For forty years I led you
through the wilderness, yet your clothes and sandals did not wear out. . .so
you would know that he is the LORD your God."*
DEUTERONOMY 29:2–6 NLT

Each election season, political candidates tickle the ears
of listeners by vowing to take care of their constituents. One
promises to cut taxes. Another promises to fix health care and
give the middle class relief.

But there is a graveyard where political promises typically
go to die. When in office, many politicians get distracted by
lobbyists or their party's leaders. And we are disappointed again.

Still, it's our duty and privilege as citizens to vote. But
whether we line up with the conservative or liberal side of
politics, we must not trust in government—or any politician—to
save us. Jesus Christ is the only Savior. And He never breaks any
of His promises.

When the children of Israel suffered under their Egyptian
oppressors, God freed them with signs and wonders. Then for
forty years they wandered in the desert, and each day they had
just enough food and water to sustain them.

God will do the same for us. He will clothe, feed, shelter, and
rescue us from those who try to oppress us. What government
can't—or won't—do, God will. Put your trust in Him.

*Lord, thank You that You promise to take care of us.
Help us not to put too much trust in men or agencies.*

COMFORT THE TROUBLED

All praise to God, the Father of our Lord Jesus Christ. God is our merciful Father and the source of all comfort. He comforts us in all our troubles so that we can comfort others. When they are troubled, we will be able to give them the same comfort God has given us.

2 CORINTHINS 1:3–4 NLT

Comfort is often associated with couches and cushions, leather seats of luxury automobiles, and mattresses that adjust to fit the contours of our bodies. There is comfort food like chicken potpie, potato soup, and mac and cheese.

If you have ever suffered a loss or an unbearable hurt in your life, then you know the deeper meaning of the word *comfort*. You needed it, and hopefully you received it.

God is the greatest source of comfort the human spirit will ever encounter. God listens. He provides. At times, you can almost feel His hand stroking your brow as He blesses you with sleep after many sleepless nights.

As God comforts us, we can comfort others. We particularly ought to reach out to others who are facing a challenge we have faced ourselves. There is something about the empathetic comfort of someone who has been in our situation that means even more than the sympathy of someone who hasn't experienced it.

Is there someone in your life who could use some comfort? Offer it in any small way that you are able. The God of comfort has comforted you. So comfort others in His name.

Merciful Father, comfort me in my times of need and show me those that I might comfort. Amen.

THE TEMPLE OF GOD

*"The God who made the world and everything in it is the Lord of heaven
and earth and does not live in temples built by hands."*
ACTS 17:24 NIV

When Betsy was little, her parents and other adults taught
her well that the church building was God's house, so she couldn't
run or yell or do anything to disrespect where He lived. As she
grew, she revered the man-made building even as her physical and
emotional body broke down from neglect.

These same adults teaching Betsy to respect the church
building failed to tell her how to protect her body from heart
disease, diabetes, and other common diseases. They were too
embarrassed to give her much insight into the sexual dangers
involved in dating. They sent her off to movies that should have
been screened for content. They offered her no special counseling
when her parents divorced.

In other words, the adults were more worried about the
building in which God did not physically live than the body
and soul in which Betsy had invited Him to dwell. Too many
Christians have shifted their priority to things built by hands and
money and away from souls that have been bought by Christ's
blood. That needs to change.

*Lord, draw us back to focusing on You and teach us to care for the temples
in which You dwell. Help us to nurture our bodies and souls, protecting
them as You would have us guard Your home.*

TOSS THOSE
BOXING GLOVES!

Avoiding a fight is a mark of honor; only fools insist on quarreling.
PROVERBS 20:3 NLT

A woman struggled in her relationship with a particular friend. Though they'd known each other for years, they often found themselves disagreeing on things, sometimes even arguing. Whenever they got together, their quiet conversations evolved into heated discussions. Their personalities were vastly different, and they both tended to be a little stubborn. Neither wanted to give in, even though the things they argued about were sometimes silly. Would they ever just get along?

Maybe you're in a complicated relationship with a friend. Perhaps she brings out the worst in you. She gets you stirred up. And yet, you love her. You don't want to see the friendship come to an end. What can be done to salvage it?

As with any relational issue, you approach it with a servant's heart. You've got to follow the golden rule—doing unto others as you would have them do unto you. And you've got to love others as you would love yourself. This is tough to do when you're arguing. But just how important is it to prove your point—in the grand scheme of things? Important enough to sacrifice a friendship? Surely not.

Lord, I ask You today to be at the center of my friendships, especially the difficult ones. Show me what to say and what not to say to avoid strife. Give me Your heart toward my friends.

SPURRING ON

*And let us consider how we may spur one another on
toward love and good deeds.*
HEBREWS 10:24 NIV

W hen Peter walked on water, no one pushed him out of the
boat. Peter decided to get out and take the necessary steps of faith
to walk to Jesus. Have you ever thought about what the other
disciples might have been saying to Peter? "You can do it!" "Go
ahead, Peter, we're with you!" Or perhaps, "You're crazy, Peter,
you're going to sink!"

By stepping out of the boat, Peter's faith grew by leaps and
bounds. He came to know Jesus in a way that he never would
have experienced if he had stayed in the boat. Peter learned
firsthand the saving power of Christ, even though he lost his
focus on the Savior. Jesus is always faithful, even when we're not.

Let's encourage one another to take steps of faith—to get
out of our comfortable boats. Through our own example, we can
inspire others to desire to follow Jesus, too. Don't push. Let's root
for and cheer on one another. Let's pray that the Lord gives us
courage. As we experience life together, let's spur one another on
toward love and good deeds!

*Dear Lord, help me look for ways to encourage others in their
Christian walk. May my words and life inspire
them to follow Jesus. Amen.*

ALL-EMBRACING
WORSHIP

I'm asking GOD for one thing, only one thing: To live with him in his
house my whole life long. I'll contemplate his beauty; I'll study at his feet.
PSALM 27:4 MSG

Sunday isn't the only day that God wants us to spend time
with Him. Sure, it's a great thing to meet with other believers in
corporate worship, but our worship shouldn't be limited to one
place or time.

In addition to corporate worship, begin to seek God in your
everyday life. Start by making a special quiet place in your house
where you can spend time alone with God for Bible reading and
devotions. While you are at work, open the window to enjoy
God's creation or put an image of one of your favorite places
on your computer's desktop. During your lunch break, work
on memorizing a scripture and meditating upon it. When you
get home in the evening, go to a local park and praise God for
the plants and animals that He has created. As you go to bed at
night, put your MP3 player on to relaxing worship music so that
you may praise Him as you drift off to sleep.

Ask God to help you find other ways to grow closer to Him.
You will be blessed as you pursue a greater amount of quality
time with God.

Dear Lord, let me be in Your presence all of my life.
Let me see Your beauty as I daily seek You. Amen.

THE WAITING GAME

I wait for you, O LORD; you will answer, O Lord my God.
PSALM 38:15 NIV

Some researchers have estimated that Americans spend as much as two to three years of their lives waiting in line. We wait at the bank, the supermarket, the theater, and the airport. We wait for our paychecks, for Friday, and for vacation. It seems we are always waiting for something.

Waiting on God is just as hard. What are you waiting for today? Perhaps it's for financial deliverance, for a spouse, to finish school, or for your next big break. Perhaps you're waiting for the results of a medical test or news from your loved one in the military. Waiting can be downright agonizing. But God's Word tells us to wait patiently—with peace. Easier said than done, right? Rather than sighing with impatience, try praying, reading scripture, and making your waiting time productive and meaningful.

God's timing is certainly not ours. But as we wait on Him, we can be confident that He is never too early and never too late. Wait patiently and with confidence. God *will* come through.

*Heavenly Father, when the waiting seems unbearable, remind
me that Your timing is always perfect. Amen.*

DAILY BREAD

Give us each day our daily bread.
LUKE 11:3 NIV

Jesus taught us how to pray by giving us the Lord's Prayer. It is a prayer that most of us are familiar with. The words roll off our tongues, memorized as children and still there, somewhere in our minds, regardless of how often we use them.

Think about this line from the Lord's Prayer: *Give us this day our daily bread.* Do we truly ask Him just to sustain us through one day, to provide nourishment and protection for a mere twenty-four-hour period?

Often we ask Him for much more. We look into the future, and with fearful hearts we plead with God concerning our needs. We don't give God the chance to show us that He will provide day by day. We wish to see a year at a time. We want assurance of much more than daily bread, don't we?

When the Israelites were in the desert, they were provided with manna from heaven. Their daily bread was literally poured out from God's hands. But it wasn't enough. The people hoarded some of the food just in case it did not come the next day. Don't you imagine this hurt our generous, heavenly Father's heart?

This week, try to rely on God for daily provision without asking for more. Put into practice the old advice of "taking it one day at a time."

God, give me this day my daily bread. Let me trust You for this day, believing You are a God who knows my needs. Amen.

God Has Left the Building

And the curtain of the temple was torn in two.
LUKE 23:45 NIV

On the day of Christ's death on the cross, all of creation was affected as the earth shook and the skies turned black. Inside the Jerusalem temple, the thick curtain separating the people from the inner room was split in two by a power unknown to man.

God, who had dwelled in the temple, the holy of holies, and had talked to Zechariah there (Luke 1), left the building when the curtain ripped on crucifixion day. He left a man-made structure to go and make a new home inside each individual who would invite Him in.

No longer did people have to physically move to Him to offer sacrifices and pray. Now God came to each individual on a personal level that was never known before. He made Himself accessible to anyone in any country on any continent.

God is an unchanging God who seeks relationship with us just as He did throughout biblical history. But we no longer have to walk the streets of Jerusalem to find God's Spirit. He comes to us and finds us just where we are.

Holy God, I invite You to make Your temple within me.
I pledge that all I do will show honor to You and give You praise.

A HOPE AND A FUTURE

"For I know the plans I have for you," declares the LORD, "plans to prosper you and not to harm you, plans to give you hope and a future. Then you will call upon me and come and pray to me, and I will listen to you. You will seek me and find me when you seek me with all your heart."

JEREMIAH 29:11–13 NIV

Deb struggled with financial issues. She fought to keep her head above water. When the rent came due, or an unexpected bill arose, she scraped the bottom of the financial barrel to cover the costs. There were instances when she went without medical care. And socializing with friends? Out of the question. At times, Deb wondered what sort of future she might have. Would the stresses ever end?

Perhaps you can relate to Deb's story. Maybe you've gone through seasons of financial lack. Perhaps you're in one now. How wonderful to realize that God promises to give you not just hope, but a future. He longs for you to call out to Him, even from your need, your lack. Begin to see your future as He sees it, full of hope.

Today, give your future to God. He already owns it, anyway. Release it. Stop worrying about it. Don't fret over it. And remember to seek after the Lord with all of your heart, even when times are tough.

Lord, sometimes financial issues scare me. They can be overwhelming. In those moments, I lose heart. Remind me, Father, that You've got plans for my hope, my future.

WELL OF SALVATION

With joy you will draw water from the wells of salvation.
ISAIAH 12:3 ESV

In biblical times, wells were of great importance. Digging a well meant you planned to stay at a place. Owning a well meant your family possessed the surrounding countryside. Wells were gathering places and landmarks. People went to the well daily to get water for drinking, cooking, and cleaning. A well was essential to life for man and beast.

Our salvation is also a well. In it is not only our eternal life, but also our abundant life while we live on earth. Christ is the living water, continually refreshing and nourishing us, giving life to our bodies and souls. He is strength when we are weak, wisdom when we are foolish, hope when we are despondent, and life when we are dying.

Just as a bucket is lowered into a deep well, what begins as a descent into unknown darkness and depth becomes the means by which we draw up the water of life. Colossians 2:12 (CEV) says, "When you were baptized, it was the same as being buried with Christ. Then you were raised to life because you had faith in the power of God, who raised Christ from death." We have died with Christ and now we live, but daily we need to go to the well of our salvation, remembering our need for Jesus' life and drawing out the living water with joy.

Lord, thank You for saving me. Thank You for being the living water, my continual source of peace, comfort, strength, and joy. Cause me to remember that my life is hidden in Yours.

WAIT TRAINING

The LORD is good to those whose hope is in him, to the one who seeks him;
it is good to wait quietly for the salvation of the LORD.
LAMENTATIONS 3:25–26 NIV

Life provides all of us with wait training—waiting in line,
waiting for traffic, waiting to hear about a new job, waiting for
a medical report from the lab. Patience is more than a virtue in
today's hypersonic world—it is an essential survival tool for a
happy life. And we have so many opportunities to practice, we
should be really good at it by now! But we seldom are. We want
answers *now*.

Scripture records that miracles unfold on God's timetable,
not ours. Sarah at a baby shower, pregnant in her nineties. David
hiding in a cave, waiting to become king.

Paul exhorts us in Hebrews to run with endurance and
stamina even when we don't immediately see results. God's hand
is at work in our lives when we are totally surrendered to His
clock. He longs for His children to quit fretting and just wait
patiently.

Today let's choose to give up our rights and yield to God's
calendar. The rewards will be great. His Word promises it.

Dear Father, I'm not good at waiting patiently.
Help me learn to lean on You. Amen.

LETTING GO

*As God's chosen people, holy and dearly loved, clothe yourselves with
compassion, kindness, humility, gentleness and patience. Bear with each
other and forgive whatever grievances you may have against one another.
Forgive as the Lord forgave you.*
COLOSSIANS 3:12–13 NIV

Christine knew she needed to forgive her friend Susie. She
valued the relationship and wanted to make things right. But she
couldn't stop rehearsing her grievance in her mind. How could
Susie have been so thoughtless? The harder Christine tried to
make herself forgive, the further away forgiveness seemed.

A short time later, Christine was preparing a meal for Susie
after her father died. She began praying for Susie, and her heart
broke in grief—she knew how it felt to lose a parent. The feelings
of injustice that seemed so deep-rooted were replaced by feelings
of kindness and compassion. By the time Christine delivered the
meal, she realized she'd forgiven Susie.

We talk about "working toward forgiveness," but this effort
can be counterproductive. Instead, Jesus wants us to show His
compassion for others, to think of ways to treat them with
kindness and patience, to pray that God would help us to see the
person through His eyes. As we do these things, patiently and
consistently, one day we will wake up and realize that forgiveness
has replaced our pain.

*God, I cannot express how grateful I am that You have forgiven me for the
many things I've done to hurt You. Please help me to see the person who's
wronged me through Your eyes and to bestow on them the same gift
You've given me. Amen.*

DAUGHTER OF THE KING

You are all sons of God through faith in Christ Jesus.
GALATIANS 3:26 NIV

Galatians 3:26–29 is packed with statements about who you are as a Christian. You are Abraham's seed. You are an heir according to God's promise. And best of all, you are a *child of God*. Galatians reminds us that there is no male or female, race, or social status in the Lord's eyes. Believers are truly *one in Christ*.

You may have had a wonderful upbringing with loving parents. Or you may not have been as fortunate. You may have spent years in the foster system or had abusive parents.

Whether your childhood reflected love or abandonment, there is good news! As a Christian, you are a daughter of the King of kings, the Lord of lords, the sovereign God. He is the One who hung the stars in the sky, and yet He knows the number of hairs on your head. You are not just God's friend or distant relative. You are His *daughter*!

If you have a child of your own, consider the unconditional love you feel for him or her. As intense as that love is, because you are human, you are limited in your ability to love. In contrast, God loves us in a way we will not fully understand until we reach heaven. He is our Abba Father, our "Daddy."

Thank You, Father, for adopting me through Christ as Your daughter.
Teach me to live as a reflection of my Father's love. Amen.

THE HEART TEST

You have tested my heart; You have visited me in the night;
You have tried me and have found nothing; I have purposed
that my mouth shall not transgress.

PSALM 17:3 NKJV

Y ou've probably heard a voice on television announce,
"This is a test. For the next sixty seconds, this station will be
conducting a test of the emergency broadcast system." Then the
screen would go black and a high-pitched tone would come over
the airways. Well, life conducts its own tests sometimes. Some we
pass; others we struggle through.

If you're in a season of emotional testing—of heartbreak or
disappointment—don't allow your heart to become hardened.
Don't allow bitterness to creep in. Do your best to pass the test,
even if it's a hard one.

Let God do the work He wants to do in you—purging,
purifying, and penetrating. Listen to His *"This is a test"* whisper,
then stand firm. Don't yield to the temptation to give up or to
say it's not worth it.

Take another look at today's encouraging scripture. How
amazing to realize you really can come through the trials of life
transgression-free. What a wonderful—and realistic—goal.

Lord, sometimes I feel like my heart is being tested by circumstances,
relationships, or even by You. I want to make it through the testing period
without falling apart. Help me to stand strong in what I know to be true.

Fear of the Lord

*The fear of the LORD leads to life: then one rests content,
untouched by trouble.*
PROVERBS 19:23 NIV

Eight-year-old Elizabeth had a healthy fear of her father. Oh, she loved him, called him "Daddy," and climbed up into his lap for hugs and kisses each day when he came home from work. But she also knew that when Daddy said to do something, he meant business.

Once, when playing in the front yard, Elizabeth lost her ball. It went bouncing into the street, and she ran after it. Just then, her father yelled out, "Stop!" Because of training and discipline her parents had poured into Elizabeth from a very young age, she heeded the warning and stopped at the curb just as a car sped by.

To fear the Lord is to respect Him and acknowledge that His ways are best for us. Our Abba Father, a gracious and loving God, is also a just and mighty God who is saddened, and even angered, by continuous, deliberate sin.

Proverbs sums it up in one verse: "Fear the Lord. Live. Rest content, untouched by trouble." Consider the alternative. Which will you choose?

*Lord, I respect You. Help me to acknowledge that You are God,
You know best, and You have given me guidelines by which to live. Amen.*

THE BLAME GAME

And he said, "Who told you that you were naked? Have you eaten from the tree that I commanded you not to eat from?" The man said, "The woman you put here with me—she gave me some fruit from the tree, and I ate it."
GENESIS 3:11–12 NIV

Maria was on a business trip, and she arrived after a delayed flight to discover her hotel room had been cancelled. She fumed and asked for the manager before remembering that she'd made her reservation online and never checked her printed confirmation.

"It was my fault," Maria admitted when she finally fished the information out of her overnight bag. "I'm so sorry," she told the desk clerk.

Embarrassed, Maria resolved not to let fatigue get the best of her the next time she traveled. And she determined to always check her confirmation e-mails—twice.

When was the last time you owned up to a mistake? Are you like a petulant child, telling God, "It wasn't my fault!" when the Holy Spirit convicts you of sin? Or do you humble yourself and confess your wrongdoing? If you long to be like Christ, determine today not to play the "blame game" anymore. When confronted with sin, ask God for His mercy and accept His forgiveness.

Lord, help me not blame others when I mess up. Give me the strength of character to admit when I'm wrong and ask for forgiveness.

NEVER ALONE

For I am persuaded, that neither death, nor life, nor angels, nor principalities, nor powers, nor things present, nor things to come, nor height, nor depth, nor any other creature, shall be able to separate us from the love of God, which is in Christ Jesus our Lord.
ROMANS 8:38–39 KJV

Everyone experiences loneliness sometimes. If you're a single woman who longs for marriage someday, you may feel that loneliness is a constant companion. Maybe your once-single friends are now married, and family gatherings seem to consist mostly of couples with children. Maybe you feel shut out as married friends engage in more couples-only activities, leaving you on the sidelines.

We can feel cast off, rejected, by life's circumstances. We want a soul mate, a forever companion. Although we know intellectually that even our married friends feel deep loneliness at times, it's a realization that doesn't help when we're feeling unloved and alone.

As a daughter of Christ, God promises that He will never leave you or forsake you. You can have full confidence in knowing that with God's love, you'll never, ever be alone.

Dear God, according to Your Word, if I dwell in love, I dwell with You. Remind me that nothing can separate me from Your wonderful love, not even feelings of loneliness. Amen.

KEEP RUNNING

Let us run with perseverance the race marked out for us.
HEBREWS 12:1 NIV

Karen began the marathon filled with confidence. She had been training for months. She knew the course well and trusted her body. The weather was perfect. But ninety minutes later, she was overcome with a fatigue like none she had ever known. Not only was she exhausted, she was nauseated. Her feet and legs screamed for mercy. She paused at a water station and considered giving up completely. She was about to step off the course and call it a day when a seasoned runner approached her. "Looks like you're having a hard time," she said cheerfully. Karen mustered a weak smile.

"Come on—I'll run with you for a while. See that sign up ahead? Think you can make it at least that far?" Karen willed her body to continue. For the next few miles, her companion slowed her own race to keep pace with Karen's. Every half mile or so she pointed out a goal to reach—mailboxes, stoplights, street signs. Thirty minutes later, Karen felt her strength return, buoyed by her new friend who clearly knew the value of a traveling companion. Finally Karen made it to the finish line. She was exhausted and overwhelmed, but grateful. Grateful she had endured and grateful for a friend who helped her along the way.

Father, when the race is too much for me, give me strength for the journey. Thank You for the friends I have along the way. Help me to finish with confidence. Amen.

LAYING DOWN YOUR LIFE

This is how we know what love is: Jesus Christ laid down his life for us.
And we ought to lay down our lives for our brothers.
1 JOHN 3:16 NIV

Jesus displayed the ultimate love for us when He gave His life on Calvary to pay for our sins. He truly laid down His life. And He asks us to do the same. But what does that mean? Can we really lay down our lives for others? If so, what does that look like?

We lay down our lives for others when we put their needs before our own. This can happen in a number of ways. First, we need to get past any selfishness in our lives and begin to adopt the "others first" attitude that Jesus taught. That means we won't always get our way. It also means we have to have a servant's heart—even when it's difficult.

Today, take a close look at the people God has placed in your life. Is there someone you should be laying down your life for? What can you do to place that person's wants and needs above your own? Ask the Lord to help you implement His "others first" mentality. No, it won't be easy; but yes, it will be worth it.

Lord, it's not easy to have a servant's heart. But You expect no less from me.
This is how we know what love is, Father. You showed us by example. Today,
please show me who I can lay my life down for.

Day
104

READY FOR BATTLE

Be prepared. You're up against far more than you can handle on your own.
Take all the help you can get, every weapon God has issued.
EPHESIANS 6:13 MSG

A fireman must be well-equipped before he enters a burning building. His protective gear includes a helmet, an insulated coat, a tool belt, and boots. A firefighter without this equipment would be in extreme danger. So will we be as Christians if we are not vigilant and prepared with the whole armor of God.

Evil abounds in our fallen world, and there are temptations around every corner. The devil never takes a day off. Be wary. We need to turn away from the lure of evil and place our lives in the center of God's will. In Ephesians 6, Paul lists the armor needed to battle the enemy: a breastplate of righteousness, boots of peace, the shield of faith, the helmet of salvation, and the sword of the Spirit.

Yield to God in prayer and call on His powerful presence. He'll be right beside you, ready for battle.

Lord, help me to keep my armor and obey Your Word so the
ultimate victory will be Yours. Amen.

SCARED TO DEATH

So do not fear, for I am with you; do not be dismayed, for I am your God. I
will strengthen you and help you; I will uphold you
with my righteous right hand.
ISAIAH 41:10 NIV

Living alone had become a nightmare for Liz. Fear had taken over. Before crawling into bed at night, she obsessively checked the lock on the front door—over and over and over. She turned on every light in the house and barricaded her bedroom door with a piece of furniture. Lying awake for hours, she heard every creak that rose above her pounding heart. Something had to change. She knew she could not continue living like this.

Even if you live by yourself, you're never completely alone. God is with you. Pick up the love letter He has written—the Bible. Read it aloud. Read it over and over. Meditate on the Psalms. Let God speak to your heart. Grasp the unfailing love He has for you. Ask Him to bring peace to your fearful heart.

Fear reigns when faith is not exercised. Because you are God's precious child, He who watches over you will not slumber nor sleep. He will protect you as a shepherd protects his sheep. He will guard you with His presence. So do not fear. Exercise your faith, believing that God is with you. Fear will flee. Sleep will come.

Dear Lord, may I experience Your presence. Grant me peaceful
sleep as I trust You. Amen.

A CHILD IN NEED

"For all those things My hand has made, and all those things exist," says the LORD. "But on this one will I look: on him who is poor and of a contrite spirit, and who trembles at My word."
ISAIAH 66:2 NKJV

When a teacher looks across a room full of students working quietly at their desks, which one gets her attention? The one with a raised hand—the one with an immediate need.

Like the student, a humble child of God with a need catches His eye. Though He is always watching over all of us, He is drawn to a child who needs Him. We may need forgiveness, wisdom, courage, endurance, patience, health, protection, or even love. God promises to come to our aid when He sees us with a hand up, reaching for His assistance. He will not ignore a contrite heart and spirit. God's grace rushes to one who cries out for mercy, and He offers restoration to the repentant heart.

What needs do you have in your life today? Raise your hand in prayer to God. He'll take care of your needs and then some—blessing your life in ways you can't even imagine!

Father, thank You for caring about the needs of Your children.
Help me to remember to always seek You first.

CORE STRENGTH

He gives strength to the weary and increases the power of the weak.
ISAIAH 40:29 NIV

A regular exercise program is essential to keep our bodies functioning the way God designed them to. One of the components of an effective exercise regime is the development of core strength. These muscles—the abdomen, trunk, and back—are responsible for strength, stabilization, and balance. Strong core muscles protect our spines, enable us to stand and move gracefully, and prevent the development of chronic pain. Investing the time and energy in developing and maintaining core muscles pays enormous dividends.

The same is true for our spiritual core muscles. Our spiritual core consists of foundational elements from which our lives move. It can include core beliefs—about who God is and the role of the Father, Son, and Holy Spirit in our daily lives.

We can exercise our spiritual core by reading God's Word every day, praying about everything, and spending time in fellowship with other believers.

A strong spiritual core will help ensure that you remain stable and secure in a changing world. That you are able to keep from falling and that you are able to move and live gracefully. As you exercise your physical body, also make a commitment to regularly exercise your spiritual core as well.

Father, help me to return again and again to the core
foundations of my spiritual health. Amen.

HELP IS COMING!

*That clinches it—help's coming, an answer's on the way,
everything's going to work out.*
PSALM 20:6 MSG

Have you ever found yourself in need of rescuing? Been so far down in the pit that you wondered if anyone even heard your cries? Maybe you looked for answers but couldn't seem to find them. Perhaps you exhausted every resource. Oh, there's such wonderful news for you today! God has an answer for any problem you face. *Any* problem, big or small. Help is coming; the answer's on the way. Everything is going to work out.

So, what do you do while waiting for that answer? How do you deal with problems when they look like they couldn't possibly work out? Trust Him. Sounds easy, but it's tough when you're facing the unknown without clear answers. Still, God longs for you to remain faithful during these times, to remember help really is coming.

If you're going through a particularly stressful time, if you need answers and they don't seem to be coming, recommit yourself to trusting God. Don't try to figure things out on your own. Instead, trust in the King of kings, the Lord of lords, the One who created you and has the perfect solution.

Lord, this whole trust thing is hard when I can't seem to find the answers I need. Today I recommit myself to trusting—not in myself or my answers— but in You. Thank You, Father, that an answer is on its way.

THE WHITE KNIGHT

Then I will rejoice in the LORD. I will be glad because he rescues me.
PSALM 35:9 NLT

Ever since she was a little girl, Alex had dreamed of someday playing the part of a damsel in distress who is heroically rescued by a white knight.

Reality soon set in.

"How long am I supposed to wait for him?" she lamented to a friend over lattes. "My white knight apparently has a problem with punctuality."

We're all waiting for someone to rescue us. Maybe you're waiting for a soul mate to fill a void in your heart. Or perhaps you're waiting for a friend to come through in your time of need. It could be that you're waiting for your mom to finally treat you like an adult or for a prospective employer to call back with a job offer. We wait and wait and wait for a rescuer to come.

The truth is, God doesn't want you to exist in a perpetual state of waiting. Live your life—your whole life—by seeking daily joy in the Savior of your soul, Jesus Christ. And here's the best news of all: He's already done the rescuing by dying on the cross for our sins! He's the *true* white knight who secured your eternity in heaven.

Stop waiting; seek His face today!

Jesus, I praise You because You are the rescuer of my soul. Remind me of this fact when I'm looking for relief in other people and places. You take care of my present and eternal needs, and for that I am grateful. Amen.

OVERCOME EVIL
WITH GOOD

Do not be overcome by evil, but overcome evil with good.
ROMANS 12:21 NASB

Martina loved her job, but her coworkers were another story. Ever since Martina had refused to gossip about a fired employee, her fellow worker bees had swarmed against her. They talked about her, excluded her from conversations and social events, and even sent her anonymous, hateful e-mails.

Martina thought about quitting and going somewhere else, but as she prayed and considered her options, God seemed to plant Romans 12:21 in her heart. *Help me overcome evil here, Lord*, she prayed. *Give me the strength to be lonely.*

Do you have a situation in which you could overcome evil with good? After all, you were placed at this point in history for a reason. God has a job—a specific purpose—for you. You are a believer in Jesus Christ in a world that is increasingly hostile to Him in order that you might shine the light of His love.

What has God prepared for you to do? It might be something uncomfortable—like standing up for Jesus in a public setting. Whatever He asks you to do, be assured that He *will* enable you to do it.

Lord, I know You want me to overcome evil with good.
Give me the courage to do just that.

A Comfortable Place

Don't you realize that your body is the temple of the Holy Spirit, who lives in you and was given to you by God? You do not belong to yourself.
1 Corinthians 6:19 NLT

Sandra spent the day picking up her apartment. She purchased a new bedspread for her guest room. On the coffee table, she placed a vase of fresh wildflowers. She got a magazine and set herself to work finding some new recipes for dinner.

Why did she take the time to do all these things?

Sandra's friend from out of state was coming to stay the weekend. She knew that her home was a reflection of herself. The effort that she took in preparing it for her guest would show that she cared enough to make her friend feel at home.

We take the time to make our homes comfortable and beautiful when we know visitors are coming. In the same way, we ought to prepare our hearts for the Holy Spirit who lives inside of us. We should daily ask God to help us clean up the junk in our hearts. We should take special care to tune up our bodies through exercise, eating healthful foods, and dressing attractively and modestly.

Our bodies belong to God. They are a reflection to others of Him. Taking care of ourselves shows others that we honor God enough to respect and use wisely what He has given us.

Dear Lord, thank You for letting me belong to You. May my body be a comfortable place for You. Amen.

ANSWERED KNEE-MAIL

The prayer of a righteous man is powerful and effective.
JAMES 5:16 NIV

We communicate with others in our cyberspace world at
lightning speed—an e-mail, instant message, text messaging—all of
these provide quick results. But prayer is even faster than the digital
world. We have God's attention the moment we focus on Him.

The concept of the power of prayer is familiar, but
sometimes we forget what it means. Prayer is a powerful tool for
communicating with God, an opportunity to commune with
the Creator of the universe. Prayer is not something to be taken
lightly or used infrequently. Yet, in the rush of daily life, we
often lose sight of God's presence. Instead of turning to Him for
guidance and comfort, we depend on our own resources.

But prayer isn't just a way to seek protection and guidance;
it's how we develop a deeper relationship with our heavenly
Father. We can access this power anywhere. We don't need a Wi-
Fi hotspot or a high-speed modem. We just need to look up. He's
connected and waiting.

Father, thank You for being at my side all the time.
Help me to turn to You instantly, in need and in praise. Amen.

REBOUND!

Persecuted, but not forsaken; cast down, but not destroyed.
2 CORINTHIANS 4:9 KJV

Jasmine struggled with her boss. He made it plain she was not to talk about her faith in the workplace. She honored his wishes but continued to share the amazing stories of what God had done in her life with her friends and coworkers in the break room during lunch. The boss became angry and took the matter to his superior. To Jasmine's relief, the "big boss" upheld her right to do as she pleased on her own time.

Have you ever felt persecuted for what you believe? Maybe you have a coworker or acquaintance who goes out of his or her way to put you down or make fun of you. Or maybe you've been ostracized by family members because your faith is in direct contradiction to theirs. The truth is that when it feels like everyone is turning against you, God is still right there.

Today's scripture verse is clear. God promises that even though we may be persecuted at times, He will never forsake us. That means He's right there, walking us through the pain. And even when we're cast down—at our lowest point—we will never be destroyed. If we stick close to Jesus, we are buoyed by His faithfulness.

Father, thank You for Your promise that I will never be forsaken.
When I go through seasons of persecution, I know You'll
walk with me. I will never be destroyed!

LONELY NO MORE

God places the lonely in families.
PSALM 68:6 NLT

Kate moved to a new, unfamiliar town and soon found herself spending her Friday evenings alone with her cat, television, and a carton of double chocolate fudge ice cream. After one particularly lonely Friday, she planned ahead and found a local soup kitchen that needed volunteers. Instead of drowning her sorrows in ice cream, Kate found a whole new community of amazing people to love.

We've all endured a few depressing Friday nights, but that's not what God desires for us. In Genesis 2:18 (MSG) God said, "It's not good for the Man to be alone; I'll make him a helper, a companion." We were created to live in community. We often apply this verse to marriage, but singles weren't meant to be alone either.

Before the next lonely Friday night sneaks up on you, consider some creative acts of service that can bring new community into your life. Is there a homeless shelter that needs your help? Perhaps you know a shut-in who would like some company. Nursing homes and retirement communities are always looking for volunteers to brighten the lives of their residents.

Being lonely is no fun. But the world is also full of lonely people—people who can experience the love of the Father by spending an evening with you.

Father, thank You that You created us to live in community. When I am lonely, help me to resist the urge to feel sorry for myself. Instead, help me to think of creative ways to share myself with others. Amen.

MAGNIFYING LIFE

My soul makes its boast in the LORD; let the humble hear and be glad.
Oh, magnify the LORD with me, and let us exalt his name together!
PSALM 34:2–3 ESV

To magnify is to make larger, more visible, more easily seen. When the angel of the Lord appeared to Mary telling her she would be the mother of the Messiah, her response was to quote the psalm, "Oh, magnify the Lord with me." Mary knew she was the object of God's favor and mercy. That knowledge produced humility. It is the humble soul that desires that God be glorified instead of self.

Try as we might, we can't produce this humility in ourselves. It is our natural tendency to be self-promoters, to manage the impressions others have of us, and to better our own reputations. We need the help of the Spirit to remind us that God has favored each of us with His presence. He did not have to come to us in Christ, but He did. He has chosen to set His love on us. His life redeemed ours, and He sanctifies us. We are recipients of the action of His grace.

Does your soul make its boast in the Lord? Does your life make Christ larger and easier for others to see? Maybe you can't honestly say you desire this. Start there. Confess that. Ask Him to remind you of His favor and to work humility into your life, to help you pray like Mary did.

Christ Jesus, help me to remember what You have done for me
and desire for others to see and know You.

FOCUS ON
PLEASING GOD

*Am I now trying to win the approval of men, or of God? Or am I trying
to please men? If I were still trying to please men, I would not
be a servant of Christ.*
GALATIANS 1:10 NIV

We all have those days when it seems we are disappointing
everyone around us. Your coworker expected you to drop your
projects and help you with hers, but you had hoped she would
be able to do the same for you. Your best friend let you borrow
her favorite handmade scarf for a date, and you accidentally
spilled your café mocha on it. Your sister called to ask if you'd
watch your niece while she takes your nephew to a doctor's
appointment, but you've already made plans for the afternoon.
There are even days when we feel that we have been doing almost
more than we can do and still we have people displeased and
angry with us.

Praise God that He sees us as valuable, even though we don't
always do things perfectly. Thank God that He doesn't expect us
to say yes to every request that we receive. Focus your time on
listening to how God wants you to serve Him and the people in
your life, but don't be discouraged when you discover you can't
please everyone.

*Dear God, help me to know that You see me as valuable.
Help me to realize that my value comes from You alone. Amen.*

SPIRIT OF POWER

*So shall they fear the name of the LORD from the west, and His glory from
the rising of the sun; when the enemy comes in like a flood, the Spirit of the
LORD will lift up a standard against him.*

ISAIAH 59:19 NKJV

Hurricane season comes every summer, and many of us
watch weather reports and marvel at the damage wind can do.
Strong winds stir the water and move it inland, causing storm
surges, rainstorms, and flooding. The power is in the wind,
picking up water and moving it for miles.

God's Spirit is like that wind having its way in a hurricane.
His Spirit is more powerful than anything that comes into
our lives. Health concerns, finances, and an uncertain future
can threaten our peace of mind. Floods can come as anger,
fear, depression, or despair. Uncontrolled emotions, addictive
behaviors, anxiety, and loneliness can overwhelm us. In times
like these, knowing the power of the name and glory of the Lord
is essential. His name is above every other name; none has more
authority than the One who spoke the world into being. His
glory fills the whole earth.

When we cry out to God in the storms of our lives, we are
calling on the most powerful force of all, the One who has the
power over death.

*Lord, forgive me for forgetting how powerful You are and that
Your glory is displayed throughout the whole earth.
Help me remember who my God is.*

UNDERSTAND. . .
THEN ACT

*Make the most of every opportunity in these evil days. Don't act
thoughtlessly, but understand what the Lord wants you to do.*
EPHESIANS 5:16–17 NLT

An older woman found herself acting on impulse—a lot. When
things would go wrong, she'd react, and not always in a good way.
She would blurt out things she didn't really mean. Sometimes
she even made issues out of nonissues. Then later—in the quiet
times—she would wonder why. If she'd just taken the time to think
before speaking, so many problems could have been avoided.

Can you relate to this woman? Do you ever act or speak
without thinking first? If so, you are certainly not alone. Women
are emotional creatures and often knee-jerk, based on emotions.
We're especially vulnerable when our feelings are hurt. We don't
always take the time to understand what the Lord wants us to do
before implementing our own plan of action.

Are you an actor or a reactor? Are you a thinker or a knee-
jerker? The Lord longs for us to think before we act or speak—to
act on His behalf. To react takes little or no thought, but to live a
life that reflects the image of Christ takes lots of work!

*Lord, I don't want to be a reactor. I want to be an actor—reflecting You in
my life. Today, I give You my knee-jerking tendencies. Guard my words and
actions, Father. Help me to think before I speak.*

Open the Door!

*"Look! I stand at the door and knock. If you hear my voice and open the
door, I will come in, and we will share a meal together as friends."*
REVELATION 3:20 NLT

Let's face it, living the single life can be lonely. Deep inside
each of us is a longing for connection with another. We may
search high and low for the perfect soul mate. We yearn for an
intimate relationship in which we are loved simply for who we
are rather than for our accomplishments or physical beauty. If we
could find someone who loves us like that, loneliness would be
gone forever!

Look no further. There is One standing at your door. He
knows all about you and loves you unconditionally. His name
is Jesus, and He will never leave you or forsake you. He will be
forever faithful and true. When He enters your life, loneliness
will depart. But Jesus is a gentleman. He does not force Himself
into our lives. Instead, He waits patiently for us to invite Him in.

Do you hear Him knocking? Go ahead, open the door. Invite
Him in. Exchange loneliness for a constant companion. Enjoy
His sweet fellowship. Embrace the closest friend you'll ever have.
He is waiting. Open the door!

*Dear Lord, You alone are my antidote to loneliness.
May I daily invite You in. Amen.*

Put On a Happy Face

He restoreth my soul: he leadeth me in the paths of
righteousness for his name's sake.
Psalm 23:3 kjv

Sometimes we become discouraged with the direction of our lives. Circumstances are not of our choosing, not the plan we laid out. God's timetable isn't meshing with ours. But to keep others around us pacified, we paste on a smile and trudge through the murky waters.

Be encouraged. The Lord has promised He hears our pleas and knows our situations. He will never leave us. Our God is not a God of negativity, but of possibility. He will guide us through our difficulties and beyond them. In *Streams in the Desert*, Mrs. Charles E. Cowman states, "Every misfortune, every failure, every loss may be transformed. God has the power to transform all misfortunes into 'God-sends.'"

Today we should turn our thoughts and prayers toward Him. Focus on a hymn or a praise song and play it in your mind. Praise chases away the doldrums and tips our lips up in a smile. With a renewed spirit of optimism and hope we can thank the Giver of all things good. Thankfulness to the Father can turn our plastic smiles into real ones, and as the psalm states, our souls will be restored.

Father, I'm down in the dumps today. You are my unending source of
strength. Gather me in Your arms for always. Amen.

LOVE, NOT DUTY

I will take away their stony, stubborn heart and give them a tender, responsive heart, so they will obey my decrees and regulations. Then they will truly be my people, and I will be their God.
EZEKIEL 11:19–20 NLT

Rules—we live by them every day. We obey the rules of the road (don't drive too fast) and the rules created by our bosses (no personal work on company time). We abide by society's rules, too—we turn off our cell phones during movies and don't talk on elevators.

And as believers, we try to obey God's rules. We attempt to do God proud by not taking His name in vain and by going to church and giving money to ministries. We speak of Him when the opportunity arises, listen to godly music, and even wear Christian T-shirts!

But how much of our obedience is out of a sense of duty? After all, God wants us to obey Him *not* because we're afraid He'll punish us if we don't, but because we love Him.

If you obey out of a sense of obligation, ask God to change your heart. Consider all He's done for you—given you His Son, forgiven your sins, answered your prayers. Remind yourself that He gave of Himself freely, with no strings attached.

When You meditate on His character and are convinced of His love for you, obedience will become not a duty but a delight.

*Father, I praise You for the love that left heaven behind.
Help me to love You more.*

STAND STRONG!

A final word: Be strong in the Lord and in his mighty power.
EPHESIANS 6:10 NLT

Have you ever thought about how strong God is? With the strength of His Word, He spoke the planets and stars into existence. That same strength pushed back the Red Sea so the Israelites could cross over. It was His strength that gave David the courage to face Goliath. It was His strength that helped Joshua face his enemies at Jericho. His strength invigorated Naomi and Ruth, and it resides inside every believer who calls on the name of Jesus.

How wonderful to realize we have such power at work within us. The very God of the universe strengthens us with His might, not ours. If it were up to us, we'd make a mess of things, wouldn't we? Oh, we might muster up a little strength on good days, but what about the bad ones?

Perhaps you've never fully understood what it means to tap into God's strength. Maybe you still don't feel strong. Begin to memorize scriptures like the one above. Put notes on your mirror, your refrigerator, and your bedside table as a reminder. Then begin to quote those scriptures on a daily basis and watch His strength within you begin to grow!

Lord, in myself I'm weak. I'm totally dependent on You. Thank You that the same strength that resided in David, Joshua, Naomi, and Ruth lives in me. In Your mighty power, I am strong!

ONE STEP AT A TIME

*With your help I can advance against a troop; with my
God I can scale a wall.*
PSALM 18:29 NIV

Sandi returned home from the doctor feeling discouraged and
defeated. She knew she had put on a few pounds since her last
visit, but was shocked when she saw the number on the scale. Her
shock turned to humiliation when the doctor frankly addressed
it. "Sandi, your health is on the line. If you don't lose at least
seventy-five pounds, the next time I see you you'll be in a hospital
bed. Your heart simply cannot take the strain of the excess weight
you're carrying."

Seventy-five pounds! It seemed like an insurmountable goal. But
a year later, when Sandi returned to the doctor for her annual check-
up, she beamed when he looked at her chart. "Congratulations on
your weight loss," he said. "How did you do it?"

Sandi smiled, "One pound at a time."

We often become discouraged when we face a mountain-size
task. Whether it's weight loss or a graduate degree or our income
taxes, some things just seem impossible. And they often *can't* be
done—not all at once. Tasks like these are best faced one step at a
time. One pound at a time. Chipping away instead of moving the
whole mountain at once. With patience, perseverance, and God's
help, your goals may be more attainable than you think.

*Dear Father, the task before me seems impossible. However, I know I can do
it with Your help. I pray that I will trust You every step of the way. Amen.*

SILENCE

*He was oppressed, and he was afflicted, yet he opened not his mouth; like
a lamb that is led to the slaughter, and like a sheep that before its
shearers is silent, so he opened not his mouth.*

ISAIAH 53:7 ESV

Jesus fulfilled Isaiah's prophecy by remaining silent before
His accusers prior to His crucifixion. This fact is surprising to
read because it goes against everything in us as humans—we
can't imagine being falsely accused and not seeking to vindicate
ourselves.

Jesus' silence can teach us important lessons. Underneath
His silence was an implicit trust in His Father and His purposes.
Christ knew who He was and what He had come to do.

Perhaps He was praying silently as He stood before Pilate. It
is often in the stillness of our lives that we hear God best. When
we take time to think, meditate on scripture, pray, and reflect,
we find that we can indeed hear the still, small voice. Many of us
avoid quiet and solitude with constant noise and busyness. But
important things happen in the silence. The Father can speak; we
can listen. We can speak, knowing He is listening. Trust is built
in silence, and confidence strengthens in silence.

*Lord Jesus, help me to learn from Your silence. Help me to trust You more
so that I don't feel the need to explain myself. Give me the desire and the
courage to be alone with You and learn to hear Your voice.*

DELIGHTFUL STUDY

*Great are the works of the LORD; they are pondered by all
who delight in them.*
PSALM 111:2 NIV

An accomplished pianist and a skilled tennis player both
know that the more they practice, the more enjoyment they get out
of their skill. Someone who has studied furniture design can value a
fine antique that another person sees as a plain brown chest. A chef
can taste and enjoy flavors the average palate cannot identify.

Have you ever thanked God for the pleasure of an orderly
column of numbers in a balanced ledger? Ever noticed the
shelves at the pharmacy and thanked God for all the research
and discovery that led to such life-saving medications? Have you
picked produce from your own garden and praised God for the
delight of harvesting?

Your delight in God's creation is a gift from Him and an
offering of praise back to Him for what He has done. To be
thankful for the interest God gives you in creation brings glory to
Him and leads to knowing and appreciating Him more.

*Great God of all creation, Giver of all good things, thank You for the
endless beauty and wisdom in the world around me that speaks of You.*

REJOICE WITH FRIENDS

*"Then he calls his friends and neighbors together and says,
'Rejoice with me; I have found my lost sheep.'"*
LUKE 15:6 NIV

Gathering with friends and family can be so much fun,
especially when you have something to celebrate. Birthday
parties, weddings, and anniversaries are a blast when you're
celebrating with people you love. There's just something about
being together that adds to the excitement.

God loves a good party, especially one that celebrates family
togetherness. Just like the good shepherd in today's verse, He
throws a pretty awesome party in heaven whenever a lost child
returns to the fold. Celebrating comes naturally to Him, and—
since you're created in His image—to you, too!

Think of all the reasons you have to celebrate. Are you in
good health? Have you overcome a tough obstacle? Are you
handling your finances without much grief? Doing well at your
job? Bonding with friends or family? If so, then throw yourself
a party and invite a friend. Better yet, call your friends and
neighbors together, as the scripture indicates. Share your praises
with people who will truly appreciate all that the Lord is doing in
your life. Let the party begin!

*Lord, thank You that I'm created in the image of a God who knows how to
celebrate. I have so many reasons to rejoice today. Thank You for Your many
blessings. And today I especially want to thank You for giving me friends to
share my joys and sorrows.*

DESPERATE FAITH

And He said to her, "Daughter, your faith has made you well.
Go in peace, and be healed of your affliction."
MARK 5:34 NKJV

When Jesus healed the woman with the hemorrhage, He commended her faith. She had exhausted all her resources on doctors to no avail. Without addressing Jesus at all, she simply got near Him in a crowd and touched His clothes. Instantly His power healed her, and He knew that she had reached out to Him in a way no one else in the pressing throng had. What was unusual about this woman's touch? Why would Jesus commend her faith?

Maybe in her touch He felt her complete emptiness and need. She had nowhere else to turn. He was the source of healing power. Her faith was an act of utter dependence; it was Jesus or nothing.

Proverbs 3:5–6 tells us to trust in the Lord with all our hearts and not lean on our understanding. This is hard to do, since we prefer to trust in the Lord along with our own understanding of how things should work out. Though we are given minds to read, think, and reason, ultimately our faith comes from abandoning hope in ourselves and risking all on Jesus.

Lord, I am often blind to my own weakness and my need of You.
Help me to trust You the way this sick woman did.

FEAR VS. TRUST

*Fear of man will prove to be a snare, but whoever trusts
in the LORD is kept safe.*
PROVERBS 29:25 NIV

We all experience fear. It creeps up on us like a shadow
in a dark alley when we are least expecting it. A relationship
ends. Suddenly you fear. You lose your job. Fear raises its ugly
head again. Someone close to you dies. Fear. Your bills pile
up. Fear. Perhaps it is a diagnosis, an entangling sin that seems
unconquerable, or even a person that you fear.

Fear has an enemy called Trust. When Fear senses Trust
trying to break into any situation, it puts on its boxing gloves
and sets in for a fight. You see, Fear is from Satan, and the
father of lies does not give up his attacks on you easily. Trust is
an archrival. Fear knows it will take all it's got to beat Trust and
remain standing strong when the bell rings.

When you are afraid, speak the name of Jesus. Speak it over
whatever problem or uncertainty is on your mind. Speak it over
medical results, financial worries, and even unreasonable fears
such as phobias or paranoia.

Fear is a snare, but trusting in the Lord brings safety. Fear is
not as tough as it thinks it is. It will be knocked right out of the
ring when you tackle it with Trust.

*Lord Jesus, help me to trust in You more each day. When I feel afraid,
remind me to speak Your name over my worry. Amen.*

JOY NOW AND LATER

*I would have lost heart, unless I had believed that I would see
the goodness of the LORD in the land of the living.*
PSALM 27:13 NKJV

While it's true that God has planned for us a life of joy in eternity with Him in heaven, He also has excellent plans for us here and now. God wants us to enjoy His goodness each day of our lives.

You can compare your earthly life to going on a cruise vacation or a road trip with your best friends. When you go on a trip, it shouldn't only be fun when you've reached a particular destination, but you should be enjoying yourself all along the journey. You plan to enjoy spending time with your friends as you participate in the activities provided on the ship or as you stop to see the sights that you pass as you drive. You expect to enjoy yourself along the way.

In the same way, God's goodness isn't just for when we get to heaven. God wants us to enjoy ourselves and Him all along the journey. Remember that He cares about your job, your family, your emotions, and the things that you care about. Look for the good that He is doing in your life and find joy in knowing that your Friend on the journey deeply cares for you.

*Dear Lord, thank You for allowing me to see Your goodness each day.
Help me to enjoy the life You have given me. Amen.*

WHOLLY DEVOTED

*An unmarried woman or virgin is concerned about the Lord's affairs: Her
aim is to be devoted to the Lord in both body and spirit.*
1 CORINTHIANS 7:34 NIV

A young woman watched her friends get married. One after
another, they made the march down the aisle. She played the role
of bridesmaid several times and wondered if her big day would
ever come. After a while, she became so consumed with finding
Mr. Right that she almost forgot the *real* Mr. Right had already
come for her.

Can you relate to this woman's story? Have you been on
a quest to find a mate? If so, have you—even on occasion—
forgotten that the King of kings and Lord of lords calls you His
bride? That He gave His very life out of love for you? He is your
beloved and you are His! And He longs to spend time with you,
telling you just how much He loves you.

Today, loosen your grip on the "I've got to find a mate"
dream. Give it to the Lord. Turn your devotion to the One who
gave you life and who has every answer for every question you
might face; the One who, in His walk up the hill to the cross,
proved His love for you in a way like no other. Then trust that
He has great plans for you.

*Lord, please forgive me for forgetting just how much You love me! Turn
my focus away from my earthly love life and toward my heavenly love life.
Thank You for proving Your love on Calvary.*

WHAT DO YOU KNOW?

Hold on to instruction, do not let it go;
guard it well, for it is your life.
PROVERBS 4:13 NIV

We learn valuable lessons from every experience God gives us; it's preparation for a future that only He can see. God will use the talents He has given us and what we have learned and will stretch us further—sometimes out of our comfort zones. Following the unknown path that God has prepared leads us to a greater obedience, obedience that helps us to learn more of Him. This newfound knowledge will ultimately lead to happiness and contentment.

All of us have talent; we can prepare ourselves and make the most of opportunities when they arise. Our greatest challenge is not the lack of opportunity to respond to God's leading, but being ready when that opportunity comes.

Seek the Lord's face by prayer and study of His Word. Then hold on to His promises and trust in Him. When our focus is set on His face, we are open and ready to learn whatever He wants to teach us. We are prepared.

Father, guide me on Your path to success. Help me to learn of
You and use what You teach me for Your glory. Amen.

WHAT'S THIS THING IN MY EYE?

"Why do you look at the speck of sawdust in your brother's eye and pay no attention to the plank in your own eye?"
LUKE 6:41 NIV

Whether we admit it or not, we judge others. Maybe it's how they look ("Just how many tattoos does a person need?") or their political leaning ("How can you call yourself a Christian and vote for a president from *that* party?"). Sometimes we pigeonhole others because of an accent ("What an ignorant hillbilly!") or an achievement of some kind ("Mr. Smarty Pants thinks he's better than everyone else because of his PhD.")

Our Father God urges us not to judge others in this way. After all, He doesn't look at our outward appearance. He doesn't pay attention to our political affiliation or anything else in our lives that is open to interpretation. He looks at the heart and judges by whether we have a personal relationship with Him.

In Luke 6:41, Jesus reminds us through His sawdust/plank analogy that none of us are blameless. It's important to put our own shortcomings into perspective when we face the temptation to judge others. Today, work on removing the plank from your eye and praise God for His gift of grace!

God, please forgive me for the times that I have judged others. Help me to develop a gentle spirit that can share Your love and hope in a nonjudgmental way. Amen.

FOLLOW THE LORD'S FOOTSTEPS

"Come, follow me," Jesus said, "and I will make you fishers of men."
MATTHEW 4:19 NIV

The beach was empty except for one lone walker near the water's edge. With every step she took, her feet left an impression in the sand. But as the waves lapped upon the shore, her footprints quickly vanished. Following her footsteps would have been impossible unless someone were walking close behind.

Jesus asked His disciples to follow Him, and He asks us to do the same. It sounds simple, but following Jesus can be a challenge. Sometimes we become impatient, not wanting to wait upon the Lord. We run ahead of Him by taking matters into our own hands and making decisions without consulting Him first. Or perhaps we aren't diligent to keep in step with Him. We fall behind, and soon Jesus seems so far away.

Following Jesus requires staying right on His heels. We need to be close enough to hear His whisper. Stay close to His heart by opening the Bible daily. Allow His Word to speak to your heart and give you direction. Throughout the day, offer up prayers for guidance and wisdom. Keep in step with Him, and His close presence will bless you beyond measure.

Dear Lord, grant me the desire to follow You. Help me not to run ahead or lag behind. Amen.

IDOLATRY

The idols of the nations are silver and gold, the work of men's hands. They have mouths, but they do not speak; eyes they have, but they do not see; they have ears, but they do not hear; nor is there any breath in their mouths. Those who make them are like them; so is everyone who trusts in them.

PSALM 135:15–18 NKJV

We use the word *idol* loosely in modern life, referring not to golden statues, but to celebrities or people we admire. Yet real idolatry is a serious matter. Wealth, beauty, power, freedom, control, or security can become idols to us.

Idols can be made from good things like relationships, families, religion, or work. When the psalmist says our idols are the work of our hands, he is telling us to look at our own lives, the things we spend our time, energy, thoughts, and resources to achieve. Anything we love and desire more than Christ becomes an idol.

Idols cannot speak transforming words to us. They can't see all that happens to us, past, present, and future, and they can't hear our cries for help. The psalmist warns us that those who spend themselves to make idols will become like them, powerless and lifeless.

Spend time in prayer and ask God to reveal any powerless idols you serve.

Gentle Savior, who died to set me free, please show me the things I love more than You.

LIFT UP YOUR HEAD

*But You, O LORD, are a shield for me, my glory and the
One who lifts up my head.*
PSALM 3:3 NKJV

Anna felt overwhelmed. In the wee hours of the night she
sensed her aloneness more than at other times. And during the
daylight hours, she worked to provide her own needs, often
feeling sorry for herself because she had no one else to ease the
burden. More often than not, Anna found herself looking at the
ground in defeat.

If you've been single for any length of time, it's likely you
know what it feels like to be overwhelmed. Problems can pile
up and can even seem unmanageable at times. And then, just
when you think things can't possibly get any worse, something
comes along out of the blue—an unexpected bill, a flat tire, an
emotional wound. During those times, you wish you could curl
up in a ball and pretend the problems didn't exist.

There's a huge difference between pretending everything is
okay and dealing with issues head-on. Today, lift your head. Look
your problems squarely in the eye. Don't hide from them and
don't run from them. Tackle them directly, one by one. But don't
do it alone. Ask the Lord to give you the wisdom you need to
handle each one.

*Lord, sometimes it's easier to stay in a head-down position, hiding from
problems instead of facing them. Today I ask for Your courage to lift my
head. Give me wisdom to deal with the issues that need to be dealt with.*

ANNUAL OR PERENNIAL?

They are like trees planted along the riverbank, bearing fruit each season.
Their leaves never wither, and they prosper in all they do.
PSALM 1:3 NLT

Emily and Lisa had a lot in common, but their gardening preference was not one of them. Every spring, Emily ran to the garden center at her local home improvement store to purchase cartloads of beautiful flowers. Soon her yard would be a riot of color—from daisies to zinnias and everything in between.

While Emily was busy at the home improvement store, Lisa patiently waited. The majority of her planting had been done in the fall and in prior years, so each spring she simply waited. Nothing inspired hope in Lisa like the little green shoots poking their heads out of ground that had been cold for far too long.

Annuals or perennials? Each has its advantages. Annuals are inexpensive, provide instant gratification, and keep boredom from setting in. Perennials require an initial investment, but when properly tended, faithfully provide beauty year after year—long after the annuals have dried up and withered away. What's more, perennials generally become fuller and more lush with each year of growth.

The application to our lives is two-fold. First, be a perennial—long lasting, enduring, slow growing, steady, and faithful. Second, don't be discouraged by your inevitable dormant seasons. Tend to your soul, and it will reward you with years of lush blossoms.

Father, be the gardener of my soul. Amen.

GIVE AND BE BLESSED

"Give, and it will be given to you. A good measure, pressed down, shaken together and running over, will be poured into your lap. For with the measure you use, it will be measured to you."
LUKE 6:38 NIV

Every day you encounter opportunities to serve others. You may have a sick friend who needs help cleaning her house. An elderly person at your church may need assistance with her shopping. A coworker could use some help meeting a deadline. The list of possibilities is endless.

The Bible tells us to help carry each other's loads. You may think you have nothing to give, but as a child of God, your supply is greater than you imagine. You can serve others by giving of your time, a kind word, a listening ear, financial aid, or even physical work. Give, not because you have to, but because you want to. God appreciates a gift given with a servant's heart.

There's someone out there who needs your help. Ask God to show you that person and what you can do to help meet their needs. Giving to others will always bring an abundance of blessings back to you. So what are you waiting for? It's time to give!

Dear God, help me to give to others in a way that will bring glory and honor to Your name. Amen.

FORGIVEN MUCH

She began to wet his feet with her tears. Then she wiped them with her hair, kissed them and poured perfume on them.
LUKE 7:38 NIV

Imagine as a theatrical production.

The stage is set. It's dinnertime in the home of Simon, a Pharisee well-versed in the law. Two main characters recline at the table—Simon and Jesus. Others are there as well.

Suddenly a woman with a questionable reputation bursts onto the scene. She was not invited and is poorly dressed. As she weeps, her tears fall upon Jesus' feet. Breaking custom, she lets down her hair. She wipes Jesus' feet, kisses them, and pours perfume on them. Gasps are heard. Such indiscretion! But Jesus smiles.

The horrified host mutters that if Jesus were truly a prophet, He would know this was a sinful woman.

Christ shares a story: "One man owed much, and another man little, but neither could pay their debts. The moneylender canceled both debts. Which will love the moneylender more?"

"Naturally," answered Simon, "the one who owed the greater debt."

Simon had not washed Christ's feet. In contrast, this woman of ill repute was beside herself with appreciation. The woman loved much because she was forgiven much.

Extravagant forgiveness and extravagant love were displayed that day. Christ tells her to go in peace. Another life changed by the Master.

Lord, teach me to love You more. I have been forgiven much. Amen.

THE DESIRES OF MY HEART

Delight yourself in the LORD and he will give you the desires of your heart.
PSALM 37:4 NIV

Do you delight in something? Maybe it's your job. Or perhaps you take great joy in your friendships or your family members. Maybe you're delighted with a potential relationship with someone of the opposite sex. These are all fine things that single women around the globe also enjoy. Just remember, delighting yourself in God takes precedence over anything or anyone else.

When you spend time with your heavenly Father, it brings joy to His heart and to yours. Curled up on His lap, you're in the ideal place to share your joys, sorrows, fears, and concerns. You're also in the best possible place to receive the secret desires of your heart. Only He truly knows those desires, anyway.

If you're struggling with putting other things—or people—above the Lord, make a conscious decision to turn it around. Allow your joy to be found in Him. It starts with confession. Tell Him that you've been delighting yourself in the wrong things. Then spend some time delighting yourself in Him.

Father, there are so many things in this world—even good things—that can woo me away from You. Today, I come into Your presence, putting You first. I find my joy—my delight—in You, Lord.

Truth in Love

O L<small>ORD</small>, I know the way of man is not in himself; it is not in man who walks to direct his own steps. O L<small>ORD</small>, correct me, but with justice; not in Your anger, lest You bring me to nothing.
<small>JEREMIAH 10:23–24 NKJV</small>

A good friend will tell you the truth. "No, those pants do not flatter you." "He's not the right guy for you." "Yes, you need to update your hairstyle." Hopefully, she will go even further and gently help you see your missteps. Are you a gossip? A grumbler? Even when it is painful to hear, the truth is liberating.

Though confrontation is difficult, if we love someone, it is good and right to speak the truth in love. Jeremiah 17:9 tells us that our own hearts are wicked, and we can't understand our own feelings and actions. Our tendency is to rationalize our sinful behavior. Thankfully, God has given us the gift of the Holy Spirit to help us on our journey. If we ask, the Lord is faithful to His Word and He will reveal our motivations to us. We can use Jeremiah's words as our prayer, asking God to correct us, to show us what is true and how to live in light of it.

Thank You, Father, that You are the discerner of hearts, that You gently show me my sin, and that You have given me Your Holy Spirit to help me.

POWER OF THE WORD

The Spirit gives life; the flesh counts for nothing. The words I have spoken to you are spirit and they are life.
JOHN 6:63 NIV

While waiting for a phone call regarding lab results from a recent blood test, Lisa meditated on Psalm 56:3 (NIV), "When I am afraid, I will trust in You." When Lisa was a little girl, her mother taught her to recite it in times of fear: a barking dog as she rode her bike, a dark room at bedtime, a first piano recital. Even now, it calmed her to remember how this verse had helped her conquer those childhood fears. She knew the Spirit gave life to those same words and stilled her anxiousness.

Jesus told His followers that His words were Spirit and life. How He works through His Word is a mystery, but He does. When we hear it, meditate on it, pray it, memorize it, and ask for faith to believe it, He comes to us in it and transforms our lives through it. Once the Word is in our mind or before our eyes and ears, the Holy Spirit can work it into our hearts and our consciences. Jesus told us to abide in His Word. That's our part, putting ourselves in a place to hear and receive the Word. The rest is the beautiful and mysterious work of the Spirit.

Thank You, Jesus, the Living Word, who changes my heart and my mind through the power of Your Word.

CHOOSE

" But as for me and my household, we will serve the LORD."
JOSHUA 24:15 NIV

Under God's mighty hand, Joshua led the Israelites into the Promised Land. Toward the end of his life, he assembled the people together and shared the story of the Lord's deliverance. Then he laid out the choice that was before them. Joshua set an example by emphatically proclaiming his allegiance to the Lord.

We, too, must choose whom we will serve. The truth is, we all serve something. We may serve careers, money, appearance, or even relationships. Although we may not admit it, we become slaves to whatever we choose to serve. Jesus warns us in Matthew 6:24 that we cannot serve two masters. We will hate the one and love the other, or we will be devoted to the one and despise the other. Here Jesus was referring to money, but our idol could be anything.

Who or what captivates your thoughts, motivates your actions, or inspires your passions? Whom do you love with all your heart, soul, mind, and strength? What has your heart's allegiance? Let's get more specific. What keeps you from attending church? What gets in the way of reading the Bible? What prevents you from obeying the Lord? The answer to these difficult questions reveals what we have chosen to serve. Let's follow Joshua's example by choosing to serve the Lord with all that we have!

Dear Lord, forgive me for choosing to serve anything other than You. Help me to faithfully love You. Amen.

TAKING A REAL SABBATH

By the seventh day God had finished the work he had been doing; so on the
seventh day he rested from all his work.
GENESIS 2:2–3 NIV

One of the Ten Commandments was to honor the Sabbath and keep it holy. God gives the example we can follow. In Genesis 2, He rested after His work was done.

What does honoring the Sabbath look like for women today? Some churches practice a literal Sabbath on Saturday and others take Sunday as their day of rest. Some Sabbath-keeping women rest from shopping and cooking, and many women who have to work on Sunday take another day as their personal Sabbath.

But too often we let our Sabbath day become as packed as the other six. We rush to get ready for church, then sing in the praise team, teach Sunday school, and (whew!) go to a meeting over lunch. The afternoon is for running errands, and our evening is spent in a discipleship group.

All those activities are fine in themselves. But when we overextend ourselves every single day, we run the risk of burning out—and forgetting why God created the Sabbath. He did it not so we could have another commandment to keep, but for our own good. Our bodies, minds, and emotions need rest. The Sabbath gives us a chance to take a breather. As we slow down our schedule and quiet our hearts, we can more easily hear from Him.

God, forgive me for taking Your commands too lightly. Help me to
remember the Sabbath and keep it holy, just as You did.

MY HELPER

*So we say with confidence, "The Lord is my helper; I will not
be afraid. What can man do to me?"*
HEBREWS 13:6 NIV

Remember when you were a kid and you had a school project
due? The whole thing seemed overwhelming until your father
said, "Let me help you with that." He listened to your ideas, then
helped you make the necessary purchases. Finally, the day arrived
to put together your project. Instead of doing the work for you,
your father simply made his presence known as you worked—
encouraging you with, "That's great, honey!" and "Wow, I can
hardly wait to see this when it's done!" His words boosted your
confidence and spurred you on.

Your heavenly Father is a "That's great, honey" kind of
encourager. Talk about building your confidence! When you're
up against a tough situation, He's standing right there, speaking
positive words over you, telling you you've got what it takes to
be the best you can possibly be. And while He won't take the
reins—He wants you to learn from the experience, after all—He
will advise you as you go.

What are you facing today? Do you need a helper? God is
the very best. Just knowing He's there will ease your mind and
invigorate you for the tasks you face.

*Father, I'm so glad You stand nearby, whispering words of encouragement.
You're the best helper possible. Thank You for taking my fears and replacing
them with godly confidence.*

First Things First

*Before daybreak the next morning, Jesus got up and went
out to an isolated place to pray.*
MARK 1:35 NLT

Jana was packing an overnight bag for a weekend trip. It didn't
seem like she had that much stuff, but as hard as she tried,
she just couldn't fit everything into the luggage. Finally her
roommate, Lisa, came to the rescue. Within minutes, Lisa had
the bag packed and ready to go.

"How on earth did you do that?" Jana asked, amazed at her
efficiency.

"Simple," Lisa replied, "I just put the big things in first. Once
the larger items are in place, it's much easier to stick the small things
in the space that's left. You just have to start with the big stuff."

This concept works for our lives as well, and no one modeled
this better than Jesus during His earthly ministry. His days were
packed with urgency—no matter where He was or what He did,
someone wanted something from Him. And yet He never seemed
to be in a hurry and always accomplished everything that needed
to be done. His secret? Jesus' priorities were clearly in order. He did
the important things—like spending time with His Father—first.

If you're having trouble fitting everything into your life, take
a moment to unpack your bag and reassess your priorities. Do the
big things first, and everything else will fall into place.

*Father, there's no denying that I'm busy and there's much to be done. Order
my priorities; help me to put You first and to trust You to
help me to do the rest. Amen.*

GOD IS NEAR

The LORD is near to all who call on him, to all who call on him in truth.
PSALM 145:18 NIV

Have you ever come home to an empty house and just wished someone were there? It is not necessarily that you want to carry on a deep conversation or even sit down to a meal at the kitchen table. You just wish there were someone moving about, living life with you in that place. You wish there were someone to ask you how your day was or give you a hug good night.

We read in Psalms that our God is near. He is always looking after His children, and He delights when we call upon Him.

The next time you find yourself in a lonely spot, call on God. He does not require fancy words or prayers of great faith. Just talk to Him. Just tell Him that you need Him to put His arms around you and fill the empty places in your heart.

Sometimes we need to neglect our cell phones and e-mail when we are hungry for companionship. We need to call on the name of the Lord.

*Father, help me to remember this promise in Psalm 145 when
I feel alone. Draw near to me even now, I pray. Amen.*

GOD'S FRIEND
IS NEVER ALONE

*And the scripture was fulfilled that says, "Abraham believed God, and it
was credited to him as righteousness," and he was called God's friend.*
JAMES 2:23 NIV

Amber's eyes filled with tears as she hung yet another
bridesmaid dress in her closet. Another one of her close friends
had just gotten married.

Amber knew she should feel happy for her, but she had been
through enough weddings and baby showers that she knew how
her relationship with this newly married friend would change.
Sometimes she felt so lonely.

Instead of caving in to her first instinct to head to the
freezer to fill up on some chunky triple-chocolate ice cream, she
remembered a conversation from her small-group study at church
about Abraham being God's friend. She sat down in her favorite
armchair and began praying to God and telling Him how she
felt. She told God of her melancholy feelings and asked for Him
to comfort her. She told Him she believed He had good plans for
her, but she asked for His continued help in times like this when
she was tempted to doubt Him.

It wasn't long before she felt God's closeness, comfort, and
reassurance. Her loneliness disappeared as she was reminded of
God's love.

*Dear heavenly Father, thank You that You are my friend and
that You never leave me to be alone. Amen.*

TROUBLE OR TRUST?

"Don't let your hearts be troubled. Trust in God, and trust also in me."
JOHN 14:1 NLT

Trouble or trust? Which will you choose today? We women tend to be troubled in our hearts, worrying about our relationships, our appearance, our finances, our work, and perhaps especially about the future.

The disciples were worried about their future as well. Jesus had told them He would be going away from them. He was preparing them for His death, resurrection, and ascension into heaven. They were saddened when they heard Him say that they could not come with Him at that time, although they would follow later.

So Christ spoke these words to them in John 14:1, reminding them to trust in God and to trust in Him. He told them not to let their hearts be troubled. Sometimes we feel as if we can't control feeling troubled. But when we focus on the Lord and meditate upon His promises, we can gain control of our worries and replace them with trust.

You do not know what your future holds, but God does. He asks you to stop worrying. He asks you to trust in Him. He is faithful to provide for His own.

Father, please replace trouble with trust in this heart of mine that is sometimes lonely and unsure of the future. Thank You, Lord, that I can trust in You. Amen.

STAND BY ME

"Never will I leave you; never will I forsake you."
HEBREWS 13:5 NIV

A woman ended a long-term relationship with feelings of rejection and betrayal. She felt abandoned. Forsaken. In fact, she was so badly wounded by the experience that she wondered if she could ever trust again. Why should she put her heart out there again—only to have it broken? In an attempt to protect herself, she eventually shied away from personal relationships.

Have you ever experienced the pain of rejection? If so, then you know just how difficult it can be to pick up the pieces and begin again. Looking toward the future is painful. Maybe you struggle with trust issues. Perhaps you've even closed your mind to the idea of close relationships.

How wonderful to realize that God will never leave us or forsake us. Sure, we'll go through rejections from friends, family, coworkers, or members of the opposite sex. However, we can rest assured God will never abandon us. He'll never decide He's had enough of us. In fact, it's just the opposite. He longs to spend time with us, and the more time, the better. He longs for those walls to come down, and for barriers of distrust to be broken.

Lord, the pain of rejection is a tough one. I want to trust again, but it's so hard. Today, Lord, I give any pain from past relationships to You. Help me tear down the walls I've built up in my heart.

GODLY BEAUTY

Like a gold ring in a pig's snout is a beautiful
woman who shows no discretion.
PROVERBS 11:22 NIV

Today's society has redefined beauty, and it certainly does not include discretion.

Some of the most attractive female stars fail to use discretion in their choices regarding their apparel, child-rearing, materialism, drugs, and relationships with men. Yet these women are teenage girls' role models. " What happened to modesty?

We are called to honor the Lord by demonstrating discretion. In doing so, we also guard our hearts. The Bible calls the heart the "wellspring of life." It is difficult to live a pure life for Jesus while lacking modesty in choices of clothing, language, and lifestyle.

A gold ring is a thing of beauty, but in a pig's snout, it quickly loses its appeal! A beautiful woman without discretion may attract a crowd, but not the right one. She may appeal to a man, but not a godly one. She will receive attention, but sadly it will come in the form of shock, rather than respect.

As a single Christian woman, no matter your shape or size, your height or hair color, you are *beautiful*. Beauty is in the heart first. It shines forth through attitudes and actions that honor God. This is true beauty.

Lord, when I am tempted to use beauty to attract the world to
my body, remind me that a godly woman uses modesty to point
the world to You. Amen.

A New Perspective

But do not forget this one thing, dear friends: With the Lord a day is like a thousand years, and a thousand years are like a day.
2 Peter 3:8 niv

Imagine that your workday was five minutes long. You'd hardly have time to clock in and get settled at your desk. You'd maybe have a minute or two to check e-mail, and suddenly the day would be over. The time would fly.

But what if you spent five minutes sitting at a stoplight? It would seem like an eternity. Five minutes can fly by, or it can drag on forever. It all depends on your perspective.

For Jonah, spending a few nights in the belly of a fish changed his perspective from doing whatever he could to avoid God to doing whatever he could to follow Him obediently. For Job, losing everything changed his perspective from enjoying life's luxuries to falling on his knees and begging God to deliver him. For Saul, a blinding light changed his perspective from investing his life in hunting down Christians and persecuting them to pouring out his life at the foot of the cross.

If you are feeling worried, burdened, or overwhelmed, take a step back and look at the big picture. Ask God to give you some of His perspective. Maintaining a biblical perspective on our circumstances can mean the difference between peace and anxiety, between sorrow and joy.

Father, I admit that I often become discouraged by my circumstances. Please give me a fresh perspective and help me to see my life through Your eyes. Amen.

MASTERPIECE

*You made all the delicate, inner parts of my body and
knit me together in my mother's womb.*
PSALM 139:13 NLT

At the moment of your conception, roughly three million decisions were made about you. Everything from your eye color and the number of your wisdom teeth, to the shape of your nose and the swirl of your fingerprints was determined in the blink of an eye.

Now consider that there are approximately six billion human beings alive on this planet today, and each of *them* was as individually crafted as you. If that thought isn't staggering enough, think about this: It's estimated that as many as 100 billion people have walked the earth at one time or another—and each of *them* was uniquely made. Wow. How can we even begin to fathom the God who is responsible for all that?

He is a big God. Unfathomable. Incomparable. Frankly, words just don't do Him justice. And He made *you*. You were knit together by a one-of-a-kind, amazing God who is absolutely, undeniably, head-over-heels crazy-in-love with you. Try to wrap your brain around that.

*Heavenly Father and Creator, thank You for the amazing gift of life,
for my uniqueness and individuality. Help me to use my life as a
gift of praise to You. Amen.*

His Strength, Not Mine

I can do all things through Christ who strengthens me.
PHILIPPIANS 4:13 NKJV

If you've been walking with the Lord for any length of time, you've probably quoted Philippians 4:13 . Maybe you even memorized it during a rough season as a reminder. We know—in our heads, anyway—that we can do anything through Christ Jesus who strengthens us. But knowing this and believing it are two separate things.

Do you really believe you can do all things through Christ Jesus? All things? If not, then it's likely you're still relying on your own strength to get things done. It's human nature to try to handle things on our own, after all. But the same God who created the heavens and the earth stands ready to work through you. Talk about power! It's above and beyond anything we could ever ask or think.

If you're struggling to believe God can and will work through you to accomplish great things, spend some time in prayer today. Acknowledge that you've been trying to do things on your own. Change your "I can't" attitude to "I can!" Then prepare yourself to be infused with strength from on high. Fully submit yourself to the One who longs to do great things—both in you and through you!

Lord, I'll be the first to admit, I try to do things on my own. I often leave You out of the equation. Today, I lean on Your strength. Remind me daily that I can do all things through You.

SPRING CLEANING

*Soak me in your laundry and I'll come out clean, scrub me
and I'll have a snow-white life.*
PSALM 51:7 MSG

Traditionally the time when the snow melts and the daffodils
bloom is when we turn our thoughts toward spring cleaning.
Women of old would hang the quilts outside to air, throw the
rugs over the fence to beat out the dust, wash the ceilings and
walls to remove traces of wood and coal smoke, and tackle a
never-ending list of necessary springtime chores.

Today our homes are more efficient and don't require quite as
heavy a cleaning each spring, but we still tend to cull out the clutter
of too much stuff and redecorate to refresh our environment.

When we look within our hearts, we can always see places
where a good annual cleaning is in order. In the dark corners of
the heart are dust bunnies of envy and fear. On the floor and
furniture is the clutter of stress and strife. Hanging from the
ceiling are cobwebs of worry and confusion. And buried and
forgotten under all of that is the joy and peace God intended for
us to enjoy in life.

Though it takes time, focus, and sometimes a bit of pain, a
spiritual inventory is well worth the effort to lighten our burdens
and refresh our outlook.

*Dear Lord, help me to take the necessary time to do
some spiritual housecleaning. Help me to sweep out the
collection of junk so my soul is renewed.*

CHRIST,
OUR SANCTUARY

O God, You are my God; early will I seek You; my soul thirsts for You; my flesh longs for You in a dry and thirsty land where there is no water. So I have looked for You in the sanctuary, to see Your power and Your glory.
PSALM 63:1–2 NKJV

T he word *sanctuary* may make you think of a church, an altar, a place of quiet beauty, a place to worship. You may also think of a place of rest and safety where animals may live protected. At various times in history, a sanctuary was a place of refuge where even accused criminals could seek shelter.

Christ Himself is our sanctuary. The psalmist speaks of hungering and thirsting, both body and soul. What is he looking for? He is searching for God. Clearly he did not find salvation in the dry, thirsty land where there was no water, and neither will we. The world's offerings, its counsel, and its substances have nothing to sustain us. Satisfaction can only be found in relationship with Jesus Christ, the One who called Himself living water and bread of life. The power and glory of God are manifest in Him. In Matthew 11:28 Jesus tells us to come to Him and we will find rest for our souls. Christ Himself is the sanctuary, the place of rest, protection, and shelter.

Lord Jesus, forgive me for seeking rest and satisfaction in the desert of this world. Thank You for being my sanctuary.

GOD'S DEPOSIT
OF THE SPIRIT

Now it is God who makes both us and you stand firm in Christ. He anointed us, set his seal of ownership on us, and put his Spirit in our hearts as a deposit, guaranteeing what is to come.
2 CORINTHIANS 1:21–22 NIV

You probably make regular deposits in at least one bank account. You trust the bank. You are fairly sure your money will be there when you need it, that it will draw interest, and that no one else will have access to it.

Enter: Economic crisis

Enter: Identity theft

Enter: Doubt about those deposits

God placed His Holy Spirit in our hearts as a deposit. When we accepted Christ, we received the Spirit as our guide and comforter. God's deposit guarantees a day when Christ will come again.

Financial troubles are a reality for many. You may lose money on the stock market or even have to suffer through untangling a web of confusion due to identity theft. When you face such trials, recall God's promise in 2 Corinthians. His deposit is His Spirit. He is always with you. And He is preparing a place for you even now in heaven.

Father, we face times of economic crisis and uncertainty even about financial institutions. Thank You that Your deposit of the Holy Spirit in my heart is secure. Amen.

THE SPIRIT INTERCEDES

And the Holy Spirit helps us in our weakness. For example, we don't know
what God wants us to pray for. But the Holy Spirit prays for us with
groanings that cannot be expressed in words. And the Father who knows
all hearts knows what the Spirit is saying, for the Spirit pleads for us
believers in harmony with God's own will.
ROMANS 8:26–27 NLT

Prayer is a mystery. The Bible says that the prayers of a righteous
person are powerful and effective (James 5:16), but how?

We bring our needs before God and ask for His help,
acknowledging our utter dependence on Him. This is a
beginning, but prayer goes much deeper.

It is not about changing God's mind to get what we desire.
It's about allowing the Holy Spirit to change our minds to agree
with God's will. The secret to prayer is praying in accordance
with God's will.

How do we know God's will? Much of it is revealed in the
Bible, but not everything is clearly spelled out. Sometimes we
find ourselves so confused that we don't really know what to pray.

Be encouraged! The Lord has given every believer the gift of
the Holy Spirit as a guide, counselor, and prayer warrior. Romans
8:26–27 assures us that the Holy Spirit intercedes for us in
accordance with God's will, even when we're at a loss for words in
our prayers. Believe that truth. Walk in that knowledge. Pray and
let the Holy Spirit intercede.

Dear Lord, thank You for providing the Holy Spirit to intercede
for me when I have no idea how to pray. Amen.

PLANTING SEASON

Farmers who wait for perfect weather never plant.
If they watch every cloud, they never harvest.
ECCLESIASTES 11:4 NLT

Life is all about priorities, isn't it? We do our best to figure
out the proper order of things: God, family, church, job, friends,
social life, but sometimes things get out of whack. We get
confused by the seasons we go through. We struggle to figure out
what we should be doing now and what we can put off till later.
And when things don't go our way, we give up, shake our head,
and say, "What's the point?"

Sometimes it's hard to know when to move forward and
when to sit still. But if the Lord has called you to a particular
task, you can't let lack of understanding of the details keep
you from doing what He's called you to do. Hesitation and
procrastination tend to keep us from achieving our goals. But we
can't let them defeat us.

Are you in a planting season in your life? Is it time to step
out and do something—even something a little frightening?
Are you hesitating, wondering if you should make your move?
Better watch out! If you wait too long, you might just miss your
opportunity. Make the best out of the time you're given. Pick up
that shovel and start planting!

Lord, sometimes I procrastinate. I get confused about what I should
be doing—and when. Help me get back on track, Father. Remove my
hesitation and propel me forward!

No Other Gods

"You shall have no other gods before me."
Deuteronomy 5:7 niv

After twenty-five years of marriage, Beth found herself alone. The pain of divorce left her searching for answers. They were hard to come by. She had fulfilled her life's ambition by marrying and raising children. As a devoted wife and mother, she had poured herself into the lives of her family. What went wrong?

Picking up the pieces of her broken life was humbling. What could she learn from the past? Beth asked the Lord for wisdom. Through the devastation of divorce, the Lord showed her that over the years she had allowed her family to become her idol. As she started over, she vowed to put the Lord first.

What place does God have in your life? Although it may be unintentional, we can allow many other gods to take His place: friends, work, money, power, or even ourselves. It's subtle. It's gradual. It's sinful.

The Lord knows that when we put Him first, our lives will be fruitful and fulfilling. Worshipping anything else eventually leaves us empty.

God is the Alpha and Omega—beginning and end. He was before all and will exist forever. He is worthy of our undivided worship. Let's allow the Lord to reign in our lives. Let's not permit anyone or anything to overtake His rightful place on the throne of our hearts.

Dear Lord, You alone are God. May my allegiance be to
You and You alone. Amen.

JUST REST IN ME

And He said to them, "Come aside by yourselves to a deserted place and rest a while." For there were many coming and going and they did not even have time to eat.

MARK 6:31 NKJV

Pastor Kevin Turner served as president of the Strategic World Impact, a mission traveling around the world to help those in need. In one country, a riot broke out, trapping Turner and his team in an extremely dangerous situation. After he returned home, Turner became depressed and overanxious. His doctor's diagnosis: post-traumatic stress disorder.

While we might never travel to another country and face riots, there are times in our lives when stress becomes overwhelming and our emotions raw. A state of anxiety might persist. How do we cope? We follow the model of our Savior. Even Jesus and His disciples needed a break. He told them to withdraw to a quiet place for a time of restoration and communion with the Father.

In our hurry-scurry world, a failure to find quiet time might result in poor choices and damaged relationships. A seaside vacation might be nice, but not always practical. Short periods of time garnered throughout a week might suffice. The front seat of your car, your bedroom, a park bench. All places where conversation with God can restore your soul.

Dear Lord, grant me peace during this hectic time. Amen.

FINDING CONFIDENCE
IN CHRIST

Let us then approach the throne of grace with confidence, so that we may
receive mercy and find grace to help us in our time of need.
HEBREWS 4:16 NIV

Celebrities have it. So do CEOs, professional athletes, and
musicians. No, not money—confidence. So how can we modern
women cultivate confidence in a world that rewards thinness,
talent, and tabloid-readiness over character and virtue?

First, we can take our eyes off the world and focus them on
God. The world says that you have to be beautiful and successful
to be worthy—but God says we are worthy because He created us
and He loves us.

Second, we can resolve to put our confidence in Christ,
because He is trustworthy. His Word says all the promises of
God are "yes" in Christ Jesus. He will never leave or forsake us,
and since He lives in our hearts, He will give us the peace and
contentment we need to follow Him. We can take our requests
to God, knowing that He hears us and approves them because of
Jesus Christ. What freedom there is in that!

So when you wonder why in the world God placed you here,
remember: We can approach His throne with confidence, finding
all we'll ever need to live—and thrive.

Lord, help me to remember that Your arms are open wide,
and I need only to walk into them.

YOUR FUTURE IS BRIGHT

*"No eye has seen, no ear has heard, no mind has conceived what
God has prepared for those who love him."*
1 CORINTHIANS 2:9 NIV

The interview for Mary Ann's dream job couldn't have gone
better. She wore the perfect suit with the perfect matching
pumps. She was poised, witty, and articulate. It would only be a
matter of time before she was climbing her way up the corporate
ladder, complete with full-time salary and benefits. It seemed too
good to be true.

But a few days passed, and Mary Ann hadn't heard anything.
At first this didn't worry her—she knew big companies often
moved slowly. A couple weeks later, a letter arrived in the mail.
We appreciate your interest in our open position; however. . . She
skimmed the rest of the letter and promptly threw it in the trash.

We make plans, set our hopes high, and then, without
warning, our dreams collapse. Often, when plans don't go our
way, it's because God has something better for us down the road.
Sometimes He puts those plans on hold so that our character can
be molded, refined, and made ready for what He has in store.

When our hopes are dashed, we have a choice. We can
wallow in anger and disappointment and cling tightly to the past
and our lost dreams. Or we can look toward the bright future
that God promises to every believer. It is a choice, and that choice
is always ours.

*Lord, even when plans don't go my way, help me to trust in the
future that You have planned for me. Amen.*

WAIT!

*Wait on the LORD; be of good courage, and He shall strengthen
your heart; wait, I say, on the LORD!*
PSALM 27:14 NKJV

As a little girl, you probably heard your mother repeat
herself—a lot. "Pick up those dirty clothes off the floor." (Then,
after a few minutes. . .) "Pick up those clothes *now*!" Yes, parents
often repeat themselves when distracted children aren't listening.
How else would they get our attention?

God is the most amazing parent of all. His love for us is
without question. So is His patience. And sometimes—like
our mothers—He finds Himself having to repeat something.
Today's verse is a great example. "Wait on the Lord. Wait, I say,
on the Lord!" When our heavenly Father takes the time to repeat
Himself, it must be important. He longs to strengthen your heart
and to give you courage. How does He do that? He asks you to
wait—and wait again.

Maybe you're weary with waiting. Perhaps your courage is
waning. The Lord promises that He will strengthen your heart
if you can just hang on. And here's the best news of all: God has
an answer for whatever you're going through. And that answer is
coming in His time. So, hurry up and wait!

*Father, I need You to strengthen my heart while I'm in waiting mode.
Sometimes I just don't think I can keep up my courage. I give up hope.
Today I recommit myself to trusting You with the things I'm waiting for.*

DESIRES

The eyes of all look to you, and you give them their food at the proper time.
You open your hand and satisfy the desires of every living thing.
PSALM 145:15–16 NIV

Anita pulled into her driveway to be greeted by her two dogs, standing side by side and staring into the driver's side window. The young black mutt's tail frantically wagging and the old yellow Lab's slower wag showed their excitement for their mistress. When Anita stepped out of the car, the two pets knew that within minutes food would be in their bowls.

The dogs' eager and trusting faces made Anita consider her own trust in God. He made every creature. He designed their appetites and their tastes. He provides in the earth all that is needed for their fulfillment. Will He not satisfy them?

We can give to God every desire of our heart, every longing, and every appetite. He can satisfy them. Prayer is the link. Start by telling Him what you long for and what you desire. As you commune with Him, you will find your desires are either fulfilled or they begin to change to the blessings He wants to give you.

Lord, help me to be open and honest before You with all my yearnings.
Enable me to trust You to fulfill or change the desires of my heart.

ANGER WITHOUT SIN

*Be angry, and do not sin. Meditate within your
heart on your bed, and be still.*
PSALM 4:4 NKJV

Swept up in a flurry of anger, words sometimes fly from our
mouths in a tone that injures others. Maybe we go so far as to
slam doors, yell and scream, even throw things. Anger, at times, is
inevitable; but does it have to be sinful and destructive?

The psalmist tells us to be still when we feel anger well up
inside, to meditate on our beds when we're staring anger in the
face. When we pause to meditate, to go to a quiet place to get
alone with God and be still, we are choosing to let Him have
control in the situation. We are acknowledging our weakness
and giving Him the opportunity to display His strength in us. In
going to God about our anger, we open the door for Him to calm
us and to reveal to us the truth of the situation that angered us.
In handing over our feelings of anger, we make room for peace.

What situations in your life cause anger to flare up in your
heart? Before you're experiencing the heat of the moment, give
these problems over to God. He'll prepare your heart to deal with
the situations the way He wants you to.

Lord, enable me to trust You wholly with my anger and keep me from sin.

A GODLY GUEST LIST

"But when you give a banquet, invite the poor, the crippled, the lame, the blind, and you will be blessed. Although they cannot repay you, you will be repaid at the resurrection of the righteous."
LUKE 14:13–14 NIV

You may not host banquets, but what about barbeques? Dinner parties? Pizza and movie nights? Now we're talking.

It is tempting to carefully select a few people to invite to a dinner party. You know the routine—a close girl friend, a guy she thinks is attractive, a guy you are interested in, and then a couple of "fillers" just so that the plot isn't obvious.

The Bible admonishes us to get more creative with our guest lists. You may read the words *crippled* and *lame* and think they sound like old-fashioned Bible words. In actuality, there are those all around us with physical limitations. Their eyes, ears, or legs that don't work properly do not make them any different on the inside.

Expanding our guest lists requires us to consider others, not just ourselves. Reaching out to someone who looks or seems a bit different than you will feel good. Likely you will notice that you have more in common than you'd imagined.

There is certainly reward in heaven for believers who demonstrate this type of kindness. The reward on earth is sweet as well. It may provide you with an unexpected new friend.

Father, remind me to reach out to others and to
be a friend to all types of people. Amen.

WHEN I THINK
OF THE HEAVENS

When I consider your heavens, the work of your fingers, the moon and the stars, which you have set in place, what is man, that you are mindful of him, the son of man that you care for him?
PSALM 8:3–4 NIV

Do you ever spend time thinking about the vastness of God? His greatness? His majesty? When you ponder His creation— the heavens, the moon, and the stars—do you feel tiny in comparison? Do you wonder how, in the midst of such greatness, He even remembers your name, let alone the details of your life or the problems you go through?

Daughter of God, you are important to your heavenly Father, more important than the sun, the moon, and the stars. You are created in the image of God, and He cares for you. In fact, He cares so much that He sent His Son, Jesus, to offer His life as a sacrifice for your sins.

The next time you look up at the heavens, the next time you *ooh* and *aah* over a majestic mountain or emerald waves crashing against the shoreline, remember that those things, in all of their splendor, don't even come close to you—God's greatest creation.

Oh, Father, when I look at everything You have created, I'm so overwhelmed with who You are. Who am I that You would think twice about me? And yet You do. You love me, and for that I'm eternally grateful!

A Heavenly Party

"I tell you that in the same way there will be more rejoicing in heaven over one sinner who repents than over ninety-nine righteous persons who do not need to repent."
Luke 15:7 NIV

God is a major party animal. Want proof? He throws the biggest bash in all of creation every time a baby Christian is born into His family. Can't you just imagine it? Angels and saints join together at the foot of the throne in sheer praise and celebration over one more soul saved for all eternity!

The Father threw your very own party on the moment you accepted His Son as your Savior. Did you experience a taste of that party from the response of your spiritual mentors here on earth? As Christians, we should celebrate with our new brothers and sisters in Christ every chance we get.

If you haven't yet taken that step in your faith, don't wait! Heaven's party planners are eager to get your celebration started.

Father, I am so grateful that You rejoice in new Christians. Strengthen my desire to reach the lost while I am here on earth. Then, when I reach heaven, the heavenly parties will be all the sweeter! Amen.

THIN ENTERING WEDGE

Joyful are those who obey his laws and search for him with all their hearts.
They do not compromise with evil, and they walk only in his paths.
PSALM 119:2–3 NLT

It started out small. Every few months or so, Kara would go to the library and check out a couple romance novels. Occasionally a chapter would contain a steamy love scene, and she would just skip over those pages. One afternoon she read one in its entirety and was surprised at how much she enjoyed it. She began stopping by the library more often, and soon she was reading several novels a week. She'd long since stopped skimming through the steamy scenes. The steamier the better. She would often stay up all night on the weekends to finish her latest reads.

One Sunday morning Kara woke up late again and was shocked when she realized that it had been two or three months since she'd been to church, and even longer since she'd picked up a Bible. It happened so gradually. . .she couldn't believe this was where she was.

Most people don't set out to become addicted to romance novels, rack up thousands in credit card debt, or get caught in a cycle of unfulfilling relationships. These things generally happen gradually—often with one compromise at a time. This is why we must continually be on guard against making small compromises. Many small compromises can lead to devastation. Be on guard and live wisely.

Father, help me to stay connected to You regularly. Help me to stay on the wise path and to guard myself against compromise. Amen.

GOD'S WORKING IT OUT

*And we know that all things work together for good to them
that love God, to them who are the called according to his purpose.*
ROMANS 8:28 KJV

A minor car accident landed Tracy in the emergency room.
While taking routine X-rays, the doctor noticed a spot on one of
her kidneys unrelated to the accident.

After several follow-up visits with her physician, she was
diagnosed with kidney cancer. Tracy came out of surgery, and
the doctor was confident the cancer had not spread, since it was
caught early.

Tracy soon realized that if she hadn't been in the car wreck,
the kidney cancer might not have been diagnosed until it was too
late. She knew God didn't cause her car wreck, but He used it to
save her life.

God can take any bad experience and turn it into something
good—something that will fulfill His plan. He has called you and
has a divine purpose for your life. He'll make all things work out
according to His plan for your good and His glory. Thank Him
for His mighty plan today!

*Dear God, thanks for working all things out according to
Your purpose for my good. Amen.*

Amnon and Tamar

And Tamar lived in her brother Absalom's house, a desolate woman.
2 Samuel 13:20 niv

Second Samuel 13 tells the tragic story of Amnon and Tamar. Amnon, one of King David's sons, raped his half-sister Tamar.

Absalom, Tamar's other brother, was kind to her and took her into his home. Although she lived with him, scripture says that Absalom never said a word about her pain. The last time we read of Tamar is in 2 Samuel 13:20, "And Tamar lived in her brother Absalom's house, a desolate woman." Unfortunately, because of the culture of the time, Tamar would no longer be considered marriageable. The stigma of rape would remain with her, and this one event would shape the rest of Tamar's life.

Many women today have also been victimized. After experiencing pain and victimization, they, like Tamar, live desolate lives, allowing the experience to define them and determine their future. This does not have to be. Unlike Tamar, women today have choices.

No matter how dark your circumstances, God can redeem them. He can weave your pain into the tapestry of your life and provide hope, help, and healing. You can begin by speaking of the pain, then refusing to carry it. Open your heart to God today and receive the gift of healing.

Father, thank You for offering me hope and healing. Help me to let
go of the pain of my past so that it does not define me.
Redeem it for Your glory. Amen.

LOVE DEFINED

*Love is patient, love is kind. It does not envy,
it does not boast, it is not proud.*
1 CORINTHIANS 13:4 NIV

There's really only one true test for love: the 1 Corinthians 13 test. It's easy to say you love someone—a friend, a family member, a coworker. But does your brand of love pass the test?

Today, think of a particular friend. Ask yourself, "Am I patient with her? Do I treat her with kindness? Am I ever envious of her? Do I ever try to outshine her in any way? Do I ever let my pride get in the way?"

These are all issues we battle. And sometimes they get the better of us. Our patience wears thin. We have a bad day and kindness flies out the window. We think of ourselves first or sing our own praises instead of focusing on others. In short, we slip up.

If you struggle with any of these issues, then you might want to focus on that particular area. As you hand these areas over to God, your friendships will be strengthened. Spend some time studying God's plan for friends, then do your best to pass the test in every relationship the Lord places in your path.

Lord, I want the best possible relationships. I know You want that for me, too. Give me Your patience, Your kindness. Help me see beyond my pride and to let go of any envy. Help me to pass the 1 Corinthians 13 test, Father.

A HIDING PLACE

You are my hiding place; you will protect me from trouble
and surround me with songs of deliverance.
PSALM 32:7 NIV

We all need a place to rest. Life is busy and stressful. Look around you and designate a place to rest. It may be in your bedroom, your living room, at a park, in your backyard, on a patio or deck, or even on a tiny apartment balcony.

When you have found the physical place of rest, then look to Jesus. He is your hiding place, a haven, a quietness, a hug from God Himself. Give the Lord your worries, your troubles, and your questions. Give Him your praise and thanksgiving, too. When your day has been especially long, when you feel alone and empty and hopeless, ask your Savior to sing over you. He promises to sing songs of deliverance over you.

Like a mother sings lullabies and rocks her baby to sleep, so your Redeemer longs to hide you from the pressures of this great big world and give you peaceful rest. Hold onto Jesus. All the days of your life He will be a hiding place for you.

Jesus, be my refuge, my place of rest. Sometimes I feel so alone
and so weary of trying, trying, trying. Lift my burdens.
Sing songs of deliverance, over me
I ask. Amen.

ORDINARY TRANSFORMED

*Now when the Sabbath was past, Mary Magdalene, Mary the mother of
James, and Salome bought spices, that they might come and anoint Him.*
MARK 16:1 NKJV

Mary Magdalene, Mary the mother of James, and Salome
bought burial spices and headed to Jesus' tomb to perform an
ordinary task after the death of a loved one. In their darkest hour,
as they grieved, they went about doing the job at hand. What a
surprise they had in store when they got to the tomb and found
that Jesus had risen from the dead!

A sleepless woman got up from bed, her mind troubled
with a problem. Wandering around her house, she saw a stack
of wrinkled clothes on the ironing board, a tiresome task she
had left unfinished. As she prayed and asked for God's help, she
remembered a phrase she'd heard on the radio earlier that day:
"Do the next thing." In the middle of the night, with a heart
heavy with care, she began the repetitive chore. Pressing shirt
after shirt, her head cleared and she found a solution to her
problem. Soon her ironing was finished and she went to bed.

That night the sleepless woman learned what Christian
monks have known for centuries: There is spiritual value in the
monotonous tasks essential to our lives. Often it's in these times
that we are surprised by the Lord, just as the women at His tomb
were. As we engage our bodies in work, our minds are free to feel
His presence and sense His leading.

*Lord, help me to look and listen for You during the
ordinary moments of my daily work.*

CHRIST'S LOVE FOR YOUR DATE

Dear friends, let us love one another, for love comes from God. Everyone who loves has been born of God and knows God.
1 JOHN 4:7 NIV

Of course Wendy asked Trent about himself and his job, but mostly she spent their first date telling him about her personal and professional accomplishments.

Trent knew Wendy would answer his calls because she had spent a quarter of her time answering her ringing cell phone on their date. When the evening ended and he dropped her off at her condo, she made sure to give him her phone number and asked for his. She let him know that she was often busy, but that if he'd give her at least a week's notice she could usually fit him into her schedule.

If Trent is seeking a relationship with someone characterized by God's love, then he probably won't find it in Wendy. The way we show that we've experienced God's love is by loving one another. God gave no better example of love than when He sent His Son to live a life of service and to die as a sacrifice for our sins. We ought to put the feelings and needs of others—including those we are dating—before our own as we imitate Christ and His sacrificial love.

Dear God, thank You that true love comes from You.
Let me show the one I date Your love. Amen.

SURRENDER

Then David got up from the ground. After he had washed, put on lotions and changed his clothes, he went into the house of the LORD and worshiped.
2 SAMUEL 12:20 NIV

The pain must have been agonizing. Not only was David burdened over his sin with Bathsheba, but now his beloved son was ill and not expected to live. It was the kind of grief that knocks you to the floor and takes your breath away. When his son finally died, David's servants were afraid to deliver the news. They worried for his emotional well-being and feared that he might do something drastic in the face of this loss.

David's response surprised them. He washed, put on fresh clothes, and then worshipped the Lord. This does not mean that David handled this news flippantly. Instead, it indicates a heart of surrender. David experienced the sadness then moved to a place of acceptance.

In the New Testament, Mary understood this when the angel told her she would experience the humiliation of an out-of-wedlock pregnancy. No doubt she imagined the disgrace and shame, but instead of resisting, she chose to accept God's plan. "I am the Lord's servant," she whispered. "May it be to me as you have said." Then she worshipped.

Acceptance isn't denial, and it isn't acting as if nothing has happened. It is a quiet surrender, opening ourselves to the Lord's work in our hearts.

Heavenly Father, help me to accept what You offer me—the good and the bad. Help me to worship You in my pain. Amen.

Late-Night Counseling

*I will praise the LORD, who counsels me; even at night
my heart instructs me.*
PSALM 16:7 NIV

For us women, the nighttime hours are often difficult. When the chaos of the day settles down and our head hits the pillow, we're free to think. . .about everything. Problems. Relationship issues. Job concerns. Decisions. The "what ifs." The "I should haves." Sometimes our thoughts wander for hours. We toss and turn, and sleep won't come.

If you're like this, if you find nighttime difficult, then it's time for a change of thinking. Instead of looking at the night as problematic, look at it as your one-on-one time with the Lord. He longs to meet you in the wee hours of the night. He wants to chase away any unnecessary worries and give you everything you need to sleep like a baby.

How encouraging to know that God longs to counsel us—to advise. And He's fully aware that nighttime is hard. So, instead of fretting when you climb into bed, spend that time with Him. Use the nighttime as your special time with God. Meet with Him and expect to receive His counsel.

*Lord, nighttimes are hard sometimes. I want to trust You. I want to put my head on the pillow and fall fast asleep. But the cares of the day overwhelm me. Father, I trust Your counsel. Speak to me in the night.
Instruct my heart.*

HOLD ME

My soul clings to you; your right hand upholds me.
PSALM 63:8 NIV

David spoke the words of Psalm 63:8 to God when he was in the desert. Annie spoke them last night in her third-floor condo in Dallas, Texas. Through her tears, she laughed as she prayed, asking God to go ahead and hold her up with His left hand as well. She needed both!

Many jokes about women and their relationships with men center on a woman's request: "Hold me." It may bring laughter in a humorous context that compares the needs of men and women. For a lonely woman, however, the words are no laughing matter. The desire is universal. We want to be held.

You may not have an earthly relationship right now that meets this need. In fact, you will never have one that *fully* meets your emotional needs. Only God, your Maker and Savior, can meet the deepest needs of your heart.

God promises to uphold you when your soul clings to Him. Loosen the tight grasp you have on other things in your life—aspirations, reputation, friendships, or family. Even good things can hinder your "soul-walk" with Christ. In order to cling to Him, you must release other things that you are holding onto for your strength. Then you will know the peace of being upheld by the right hand of Immanuel—*God With Us*.

Jesus, Immanuel, my Savior, my Comforter, will You hold me?
Just hold me. I feel secure in Your arms. Amen.

JESUS, OUR ARBITRATOR

If only there were someone to arbitrate between us. . .
so that his terror would frighten me no more.
JOB 9:33–34 NIV

Penny took her daily walk, trying to clear her thoughts. Her sister Susie had been diagnosed with stage 3 breast cancer. . .not a death sentence, but a serious and frightening diagnosis, nonetheless. Not only that, but Penny's job was in jeopardy, her parents had needs of their own, and Penny's car was in the shop—again. "I don't know how much more I can take," Penny said out loud. "God, help—if You're even listening!"

When our world caves in, it's tempting to blame God and push Him away. Though such a reaction is all-too-human, God longs for us to seek Him during times of struggle. We may never know this side of heaven why He allows certain things to happen, but we can be sure that He loves us and will never leave us.

As Job noted, God knew of our need for someone to bridge the gap between us and our perfect heavenly Father. So He sent Jesus to be our arbitrator and the perfect sacrifice for our sins. Because of His death, we don't have to fear God's wrath.

Today, instead of looking at your circumstances, lift your head and look to Jesus. He wants to spare you the terror you are experiencing. When you surrender your situation to Him, He will comfort you with His presence.

Lord, thank You for sending Jesus to be the bridge between us. Help me to turn to Him—and not run away—in times of fear and doubt.

KNOCKED DOWN,
NOT OUT

The spider taketh hold with her hands, and is in kings' palaces.
PROVERBS 30:28 KJV

Have you ever watched a spider spin a web? Everything the spider needs is within its own body. Knock down the spider's web, and it reaches inside and weaves a strand of silk, slides down, and lands in another safe spot.

God has placed within us all we need when we get knocked down, brushed aside, or cast away. Scripture records in 2 Peter 1:3 (NIV), "His divine power has given us everything we need for life and godliness." Everything. With the power of prayer and praise, we can stand on God's Word and draw forth what we need to rise again. He has promised the Helper inside of us will lend a hand.

Life might have knocked us down, but it hasn't knocked us out if we summon what God has put within. With His grace, we will be able to return steadfast and true to the path He has determined for our lives. As a child of the King, our worth far exceeds that of a lowly spider.

Father, this is a difficult path I'm on. I need Your help to continue. Please allow the Holy Spirit to work in my life. Amen.

DESTINATION
OF THE HEART

The highway of the upright is to depart from evil;
he who keeps his way preserves his soul.
PROVERBS 16:17 NKJV

Type a few words and click your mouse a couple of times and you can find directions to anywhere in the world. With minimal effort, you can have step-by-step instructions, maps, and even satellite images of the places you want to go and the best route to get there. All you need is a starting point and a final destination.

Life is a journey, and we are traveling a highway to a final destination. There is a road that will take us where we want to go, but there are also many opportunities to take detours—sin that distracts us from the path God has laid for us.

But there is direction to be found! In solitude, reflection, and self-examination we often hear God speak. In these times of prayer, He will show us the wrong turns we have taken and give us the opportunity to turn back to Him. He will set us back on the right path.

Ask God what He wants for you. What is the destination for your heart? Are you staying on the right road? Do you need to set some boundaries for yourself so you can better hear His voice? He is ready to show you the way.

Father, help me to be still, to sit in silence and listen for Your voice.
Show me the boundaries I need for my life and give me
grace to repent when I have strayed.

ANXIETY CHECK!

Do not be anxious about anything, but in everything, by prayer and petition, with thanksgiving, present your requests to God.
PHILIPPIANS 4:6 NIV

Twenty-first-century women are always checking things. A bank balance. E-mail. Voice messages. The grocery list. And, of course, that never-ending to-do list. We routinely get our oil, tires, and brake fluid checked. And we wouldn't think of leaving home for the day without checking our appearance in the mirror. We even double-check our purses, making sure we have the essentials—lipstick, mascara, and the cell phone.

Yes, checking is a part of living, isn't it? We do it without even realizing it. Checking to make sure we've locked the door, turned off the stove, and unplugged the curling iron just comes naturally. So why do we forget some of the bigger checks in life? Take anxiety, for instance.

When was the last time you did an anxiety check? Days? Weeks? Months? Chances are, you're due for another. After all, we're instructed not to be anxious about anything. Instead, we're to present our requests to God with thanksgiving in our hearts. We're to turn to Him in prayer so that He can take our burdens. Once they've lifted, it's bye-bye anxiety!

Father, I get anxious sometimes. And I don't always remember to turn to You with my anxiety. In fact, I forget to check for anxiety at all. Today I hand my anxieties to You. Thank You that I can present my requests to You.

CONTENTMENT

I have learned how to be content with whatever I have.
PHILIPPIANS 4:11 NLT

Webster defines contentment as "being satisfied with one's possessions, status, or situation." Many roads lead to the state of singleness: never married, divorced, or widowed. Are you content with being single or do you secretly pine for a husband?

The grass isn't always greener on the other side. Marriage, like money, does not guarantee happiness. The apostle Paul elaborates on the many advantages of singleness in 1 Corinthians 7. Singles are free from family distractions or concerns. Because their interests and loyalty are undivided, the Lord can use their lives in powerful ways.

Paul learned contentment in all circumstances by relying upon the Lord's strength. Like Paul, realize that the Lord has a plan and purpose for your life. You are right where He knows it is best for you. Trust Him. Rather than focusing on what you're missing, decide that your single life will be used to attract others to His kingdom. Take your focus off self and put it on the Lord. As you find your contentment and satisfaction in Christ, He will meet your deepest needs, and you will receive His blessing.

Dear Lord, teach me contentment in my singleness.
May I find satisfaction in You. Amen.

APPROVAL TRAP

Whoever flatters his neighbor is spreading a net for his feet.
PROVERBS 29:5 NIV

We all want to be liked. It is human nature to want validation, especially from those we love and respect. There is a trap, though, in loving the praise of others. Needing to have the approval of people can become a form of idolatry. When this happens, we lose the freedom Jesus intends for us. We make choices based on what another person will say or think about us. We begin to live our lives for the applause and praise of others. Often we compromise who we are and some of the things we should be doing in life.

When you are assured that God loves you and accepts you in Christ no matter what you have done, you will not need the praise of others. You may sometimes get worldly praise—and you may receive it graciously—but you will not need it because your security rests firmly in your approval from God Himself.

*Lord, thank You for accepting me and forgiving all my sins. Show me if I
have become a slave to others' opinions of me and help me to be
free of the need for their approval.*

REAL FREEDOM

"Then you will know the truth, and the truth will set you free."
JOHN 8:32 NIV

Each year we don our red, white, and blue and wave tiny flags in celebration of the freedom we enjoy as Americans. While it's good and right to recognize the blessings we have in the United States, the freedom we honor with barbeques and fireworks is only a tiny glimmer of the freedom we can discover in Jesus Christ.

In John 8, Jesus tells us that truth is the key to real freedom. He *is* the truth—His very existence as God's Son. What kind of freedom is He talking about here? Freedom that breaks us free of the chains of worry, fear, and sin; it's freedom that gives us assurance of our future in heaven. When we know the truth of salvation through Jesus, the burdens of the world that used to be overwhelming are lifted from our shoulders. Real freedom is simply this: God has everything under control.

What is keeping you from experiencing the freedom of Jesus? He can take care of any burden, no matter how heavy. It's time to accept the truth and break free!

Jesus, I long to experience total freedom in You. Show me how to grab hold of Your truth and live a life free from the worries and care of sin. Amen.

HIGH PLACES

For who is God, except the LORD? And who is a rock, except our God? It is God who arms me with strength, and makes my way perfect. He makes my feet like the feet of deer, and sets me on my high places.
PSALM 18:31–33 NKJV

Samantha worked for the same company for years but didn't seem able to climb the corporate ladder. At times, depression set in, and she struggled just to get out of bed and drive to work. What was the point? She could hardly stand to watch others promoted when she'd worked so hard.

Have you ever struggled with feelings of insecurity related to your work? Wondered if you'd ever get the accolades you feel you deserve or the occasional pat on the back? Ever felt you were overlooked for a promotion? We all want to feel needed, especially in the workplace. But we often forget that God is the One with the plan. He's the One who sets us in high places, and He knows just when to do it.

Today, offer your career to the Lord. He knows the desires of your heart and He can be trusted. He's your rock and the One who arms you with strength. He will truly make your way perfect—but only if you don't jump the gun and try to do things in your own strength.

Father, it's so hard for me to watch others promoted and not say anything. Still, I give my desires back to You today. I trust You with every aspect of my career.

PRESERVATIONIST

Preserve my life, for I am holy; You are my God;
save your servant who trusts in You.
PSALM 86:2 NKJV

Historical preservation is painstakingly detailed work. To save an old building of architectural significance requires all kinds of research to carefully restore it in an authentic manner. Specialized craftsmen are often called in to do the work. Custom materials must be ordered to match existing pieces. Construction on these structures usually requires more time and money than building something new. The very act of preservation speaks of the intrinsic value of the building.

Have you ever considered that God is in the business of preservation? He is continually preserving us, His holy and precious children. Our health, our safety, our ability to move, to think, to work, and to play, all of it comes from His power. He is protecting our minds and hearts from evil. He surrounds us with the Holy Spirit. God is aware of every detail of our lives and is carefully tending us. He is deliberate, patient, and focused. We are told in Ephesians 2:10 that we are His workmanship. When thoughts of worthlessness or abandonment strike us, we can pray, "Preserve my life, for I am holy," knowing it is His will to do so.

Thank You, God, for preserving me. Help me to remember that I am valuable to You and You are concerned with every detail of my life.

HEALTHY HABITS

*Since we have these promises, dear friends, let us purify ourselves from
everything that contaminates body and spirit, perfecting
holiness out of reverence for God.*

2 CORINTHIANS 7:1 NIV

Tanya woke up Monday morning with a terrible headache.
She washed down a couple aspirin with a cup of coffee, showered,
and tried her best to go to work with a smile plastered on her
face. By noon the pain lessened, and she grabbed a sandwich
from the vending machine. By 2 p.m. she was ready to call it a
day. Diet soda kept her going through the afternoon. Dinner
was a frozen entrée, eaten over the sink. After some mindless
television she fell into bed, but her sleep was restless. As she
stared at the numbers on her digital clock glowing in the dark,
she knew the next day would be no better than this one.

What Tanya doesn't realize, and what many fail to
understand, is that the way we feel today is directly related to
the habits we practiced yesterday. A weekend of staying up until
all hours of the night and eating junk food will likely produce a
Monday morning of misery. On the other hand, the investment
of exercising, getting enough sleep, and eating properly reaps
countless benefits in helping us be more productive, clearheaded,
and energetic. God created our earthly bodies to be temples, and
we only get one.

*Father, thank You for my temple. Help me to care for it to the best of my
ability and honor You with healthy habits. Amen.*

No Wind-Chasing

I observed everything going on under the sun, and really, it is all meaningless—like chasing the wind.
ECCLESIASTES 1:14 NLT

All Ashley really wanted was some quiet time sitting outside on her porch swing to read her devotions. Just as she sat down, her cell phone beeped, indicating that she needed to check her voice mail. As she listened to her messages, she heard reminders about meetings at work, a vet appointment for her cat, a bridal shower for a close friend, an invitation for a home cookware party, and someone at church asking her to volunteer in the nursery. It was enough to make her heart pound in her chest. She immediately forgot about her reading and began the task of scheduling all of those events on her calendar.

There will always be things that need to be done. There will always be people who want our time. We can become wind-chasers and focus on all of the things that this world is calling us to do. But Christ Jesus wants our time, too. He doesn't want us to feel overburdened or stressed. Ask God to help you see what things in your life are necessary and important as you let Him help you focus on the best things that He desires for you.

Dear God, help me to prioritize the tasks in my life and be able to say no to the activities that take away from what You have planned for me.

A FIRM STANCE

*Therefore, my dear brothers, stand firm. Let nothing move you. Always
give yourselves fully to the work of the Lord, because you know that your
labor in the Lord is not in vain.*

1 CORINTHIANS 15:58 NIV

Twenty-first century women are so easily moved—by
fashions, trends, jobs, attitudes, emotions, jealousies, the opposite
sex. For single women, the pressures can be overwhelming. We
often fall at the very time we should be standing strong.

Don't be moved. Though these words from scripture were
penned thousands of years ago, they are as relevant today as ever.
Don't be moved when others talk about you behind your back.
Don't be moved when your friends have cars, houses, clothes, and
other things you wish you had. Don't be moved when your boss/
friend/coworker is having a bad day. Don't be moved when your
heart is aching over the "what ifs" of life.

It's not only possible to stand firm during tough times, it's
what God expects from His daughters. He doesn't want anything
to move us. Today, if you're facing challenges, resolve to stand
firm—no matter what. Don't give in. Don't back down. Don't
concede. Just stand.

*Father, I'll admit I want to give up sometimes. I'm too easily moved by
things. My emotions get in the way. Lord, give me the spiritual backbone to
stand firm. . .no matter what.*

Reach Out:
Be a Friend

Never abandon a friend—either yours or your father's.
PROVERBS 27:10 NLT

Erica sat alone in her apartment on Friday night. *No one called. I've got nothing to do.* Her isolation caused her heartache. Turning to the Lord, she cried out, "I need a friend." God quieted her heart with the promise He would never leave or forsake her, and in the stillness He gave her peace. She knew Jesus was her friend, yet she longed for a flesh-and-blood person with whom she could talk. But she was shy.

How do you form friendships? By reaching out. In spite of nervousness and timidity, you reach out to another in your sphere of influence.

Friendships don't just happen, they require work on our part. We must choose to focus on the other person's needs, not our own. Our heart may race, and we may think we have nothing to offer another, but when we overcome that shyness and focus on someone else, in time hearts will be knitted together.

Dear Jesus, draw close to me at this time.
Help me find a trusted friend. Amen.

"EVERYTHING I HAVE IS YOURS"

*" 'My son,' the father said, 'you are always with me,
and everything I have is yours.' "*
LUKE 15:31 NIV

Trina couldn't have been happier the day that Aimee accepted
Jesus as her Savior. Trina helped Aimee quickly plug into her
church fellowship, and she saw her friend blossom in ministry,
in her spiritual maturity, and in her Bible knowledge. Soon the
other members of their home Bible study even started asking
Aimee for godly counsel—instead of coming to Trina like they
had always done in the past.

Have you ever experienced jealousy over blessings that you
see in the life of a new Christian? Jesus knew these feelings could
pop up, and that's why He included the prodigal son's brother in
the story. When the father accepted the prodigal son back with
open arms, the faithful son felt the green grip of envy take over.

The father's response is the same response God has to all
of His children: "My daughter, you are always with me, and
everything I have is yours." Take comfort in knowing you have
been with Him since you accepted His gift of grace, and His
blessings are now and forever yours in abundance.

*Father, please forgive me when I am jealous of the blessings I see in the
lives of others. I rejoice in knowing You love each of Your children with an
everlasting love. Amen.*

THE POWER OF
THE WORD

"Heaven and earth will pass away, but My words
will by no means pass away."
LUKE 21:33 NKJV

Every word spoken about Jesus by the Old Testament prophets was fulfilled. Every word that Jesus uttered when He lived on earth was true and powerful. The gospel of John tells us He *is* the Living Word of God.

When God's Word is planted in our lives it can transform us, choking out weeds of distraction, indifference, and unbelief. Because Jesus lives, every word spoken by Him has power today. By the Holy Spirit, God's words can accomplish His will in our lives, just as they did when Jesus spoke to those around Him when He walked on the earth.

Pray for a desire to read the Word and for memory to call it to mind when you need it. Ask God to sink the Word deep in the soil of your heart. Pray to see the transforming power of the Word in your life. Set aside time daily to read the Bible and pray, then watch and see God's faithfulness to work His Word into your life.

Lord Jesus, I have forgotten the power of Your Word and have trusted other
things more than You. Give me a desire to read and hear Your Word and
obey Your voice. Thank You for what You will do in my life.

TRUTH AND LIGHT

*Send out your light and your truth; let them lead
me; let them bring me to your holy hill
and to your dwelling!*
PSALM 43:3 ESV

Who leads you? We all follow others in various areas of our lives. We have political leaders, church leaders, employers, family members, and friends who lead us.

Have you ever considered who your leaders are following? This is an important question to ponder. Are they seeking God, or are they blinded to His truth?

This world is full of darkness and confusion. God's enemies would have us believe there is no such thing as absolute truth, no difference between right and wrong. God's Word tells us otherwise. Jesus said in John 14:6 (NIV), "I am the way and the truth and the life. No one comes to the Father except through me." In John 8:12, Jesus says He is the light of the world.

Truth brings freedom to our lives that in turn produces joy. Only Jesus can give us clear vision and freedom in our lives, because He is light and He is truth. When the psalmist prays for light and truth to lead him, he is asking for the salvation of God, the person of Jesus Christ.

What about you? Is He the light by which you see? Is He the truth who sets you free?

*Jesus, cause me to remember that all truth and all light come
from You. Let me be led by those who love You.*

A Strong Heart

*Whom have I in heaven but you? And earth has nothing I desire
besides you. My flesh and my heart may fail, but God is the strength
of my heart and my portion forever.*
PSALM 73:25–26 NIV

Do you ever feel like you have a weak heart? Feel like you're
not strong? You crater at every little thing? Do you face life's
challenges with your emotions in turmoil instead of facing them
head-on with courage and strength? If so, you're not alone.
Twenty-first-century women are told they can "be it all" and "do
it all," but it's not true. God never meant for us to be strong every
moment of our lives. If we were, we wouldn't need Him.

Here's the good news: You don't have to be strong. In your
weakness, God's strength shines through. And His strength
surpasses anything you could produce, even on your best day.
It's the same strength that spoke the heavens and the earth into
existence. The same strength that parted the Red Sea. And it's the
same strength that made the journey up the hill to the cross.

So how do you tap into that strength? There's really only
one way. Come into His presence. Spend some quiet time with
Him. Acknowledge your weakness, then allow His strong arms to
encompass you. There's really nothing else in heaven or on earth
to compare. God is all you will ever need.

*Father, I feel so weak at times. It's hard just to put one foot in
front of the other. But I know You are my strength. Invigorate me
with that strength today, Lord.*

LOVE DEEPLY

*Above all, love each other deeply, because love covers
over a multitude of sins.*
1 PETER 4:8 NIV

Kate grew up in a small, tightly knit community. Her church
friends were her school friends—until they were in high school
and she made choices they didn't approve of. By her senior year,
Kate had become completely isolated from her lifelong friends.
Hurt and disillusioned with the church, she made a new group of
friends, one that was far more accepting of her new lifestyle.

There was one friend—Shelly—who never shunned Kate.
Although she didn't approve of the choices Kate made, she
continued to treat her with love and respect, something that
deeply affected Kate years later when she finally returned to her
faith.

"Shelly," Kate told her later, "you were the only person who
never gave up on me, and I never forgot that. Thank You for
giving me grace when I didn't deserve it. Thanks for being Jesus
to me."

In our effort to take sin seriously, we often make the mistake
of condemning the sinner with the sin. While it is sometimes
difficult to separate the person from her actions, it is essential
that we make the effort to do so. Jesus models this attitude time
and time again throughout scripture. Sin He cannot tolerate, but
people. . .He always loves them deeply.

Jesus, help me to love others as You do. Amen.

HONOR YOUR PARENTS

Honour thy father and thy mother: that thy days may be long upon the land which the LORD thy God giveth thee.
EXODUS 20:12 KJV

Honoring your parents is a lifelong duty. It looks different at four, fourteen, and forty, but it is a commandment important enough that almighty God chose to include it in a list of just ten.

This commandment may be difficult for an adult woman to know how to obey. You know you should honor your mother and father, and yet it is not always simple. What exactly does honor entail? You are an adult, and yet they are still your parents. What if your parents are unbelievers?

These are not easy questions to answer, but the commandment is fairly cut-and-dried. Honor them, respect them, treat them well, listen to them, and never speak ill of them to others. You may not follow all of your parents' advice. Now that you are an adult, you are not required to do so. It is still admirable to seek it at times. They know you well, and they have lived longer than you have. They may have helpful input.

If your parents are not believers, honor them in every way possible so long as it does not cause you to stumble in your walk with the Lord. We are always called to put the Lord first.

God, help me to honor my parents as You have instructed me to do. Amen.

CHRIST'S LIFE IN US

He who loves purity of heart and has grace on
his lips, the king will be his friend.
PROVERBS 22:11 NKJV

What qualities draw you to a person? What kind of people do you want as your friends? We may settle for faux fur and costume jewelry, but when it comes to human relationships, we want the real thing.

Most of us would list honesty as an important character trait of someone we love. In fact, it is hard to imagine a healthy relationship without it. We are drawn to people who seem pure in heart and transparent in how they live. It is refreshing to have friends who speak the truth. We long for authenticity in others. In their presence, we feel free to be truthful about ourselves.

We are also attracted to compassionate people. A compassionate woman is one who continually knows her need of a Savior. People who have experienced God's grace are gracious to others. They extend the mercy they have received from God and speak kindness out of hearts that have experienced it. The presence of a compassionate friend is a safe place to be.

Are we exemplifying those character qualities we so desire to see in others? Are others drawn to Christ's life displayed in us?

Lord, open my eyes to the areas of hypocrisy in my life. Show me where I
have not been honest with You, myself, or others. Help me to extend the
mercy You have shown me to those around me.

GREEN PASTURES

He maketh me to lie down in green pastures:
he leadeth me beside the still waters.
PSALM 23:2 KJV

Perhaps today's verse brings to mind images of reclining alongside a mountain stream or resting in an open field. Maybe if you close your eyes you can almost hear the sound of the water rushing against the rocks in the creek bed or smell the sweetness of the grass. What a perfect place to meet with God.

Have you ever considered that the Lord "makes" us lie down in green pastures? The verse doesn't say He "leads" us to green pastures, or even that He "hopes" we'll lie down in green pastures. No, it's clear. He *makes* us lie down. But why? What's so important about our quiet time with Him? And if it's truly important, why don't we just do it on our own?

Twenty-first-century women lead busy lives. There's so much to get done, and so little time to do it. Our intentions are good; we intend to meet with God, but we forget. Or we get busy. Or we meet with Him and then get distracted.

When life is at its most chaotic, don't be surprised if God makes you lie down in green pastures. He will woo you from the busyness to rest by a quiet stream. . .so He can have you all to Himself.

Lord, I don't often meet You at the quiet streams. More often than not, I have a quick word with You in the car on my way to work. Today, I commit to meet You in green pastures, to rest at Your feet.

THE PEACE OF GOD

And the peace of God, which passeth all understanding,
shall keep your hearts and minds through Christ Jesus.
PHILIPPIANS 4:7 KJV

Tabitha had been struggling for months over the future of the downtown gift shop she owned. She decided to make a list of pros and cons on closing the business or keeping it open. The final list confused her even more.

Tabitha prayed continually, asking God to show her the direction to take. Soon what should have been a simple decision had turned her life into a state of confusion and turmoil. She decided to seek her mother's advice. After Tabitha explained the situation, her mom said three simple words.

"Follow after peace."

God immediately showed Tabitha that the answer had been there the entire time. Instead of fretting over the business matter, she needed only to put her complete trust in God. Looking to Him instead of at her problem brought calmness to her heart and mind. She finally made a decision that brought her complete peace.

If you're facing a major decision or going through a difficult trial, remember these words of wisdom: Follow after peace. The precious peace of God will put your heart and mind in a state of tranquility and contentment.

Dear God, help me to always follow after peace by
putting my complete trust in You. Amen.

MUCH LOVE

*"Therefore, I tell you, her many sins have been
forgiven—for she loved much."*
LUKE 7:47 NIV

Scripture records the story of Jesus dining with a Pharisee. At
the dinner, a woman of loose morals showed up, kissed Jesus' feet,
and washed them with her tears. The Pharisee was incensed. He
felt Jesus should reprimand the woman; after all, she had sinned
greatly. But Jesus didn't. He stated her sins were forgiven and her
faith had saved her because she poured out everything at His feet.

Often we feel we fall short in our walk with God. We plunge
into the trap of measuring ourselves by another's yardstick. This
isn't what God wants for us. He desires that we fall at His feet
and worship Him—loving Him with an extravagant love. When
sin enters our lives, as it will, we confess that sin and turn to His
face. He's there in the darkest hours.

Others may know what you've done, but Jesus knows what
you can become. Simon the Pharisee saw this woman as a weed,
but Jesus saw her as a potential rose. When you fall in love with
Christ, the first thing He opens is your heart. Be transformed by
the Father's grace. Love extravagantly.

*Dear heavenly Father, I love You. Pour Your love
into my heart this day. Amen.*

KING FOREVER

You, O God, are my king from ages past,
bringing salvation to the earth.
PSALM 74:12 NLT

Sometimes it seems like every part of our lives is affected by change. From the economy and headline news to friendships and family relationships, nothing ever seems to stay the same. Even our leaders are in a constant state of flux. Every election cycle we see politicians come and go. Generation after generation, monarchs succeed their elders to the throne. Ministers move from one church to the next, and bosses get promotions or transfers.

These changes can leave us feeling unsteady in the present and uncertain about the future. With more questions than answers, we wonder how these new leaders will handle their roles.

It's different in God's kingdom. He's the King now, just as He was in the days of Abraham. His reign will continue until the day His Son returns to earth, and then on into eternity. We can rely—absolutely depend on—His unchanging nature. Take comfort in the stability of the King—He's our leader now and forever!

Almighty King, You are my rock. When my world is in turmoil and changes
swirl around me, You are my anchor and my center of balance.
Thank You for never changing. Amen.

ANGER UNDER CONTROL

The beginning of strife is like letting out water,
so quit before the quarrel breaks out.
PROVERBS 17:14 ESV

Water is one of the most powerful forces on earth. Though necessary and life giving, it can also be dangerous and life threatening. To a desert traveler, a canteen of water is a lifeline to avoid dehydration and death. The person who lives in a house in a floodplain lives in terror of the river spilling over its banks. Hurricanes and tsunamis can wipe out entire coastlines.

Proverbs 17:14 compares the beginning of anger to the spilling of water. There is no end to the destruction that can occur once anger runs rampant. Whether it's an explosive tantrum or a seething, quiet resentment that undermines a relationship, anger is as destructive to our relationships as floods are on the earth.

What is it that sets you off? Realize your triggers, and ask the Father to help you stop anger when you feel it welling up inside. He is faithful. He will help keep you from the disasters that can result from a tidal wave of anger.

Lord, I cannot control my anger without Your help any more than
I could stop a river from overflowing. Soften my heart to repentance and
forgiveness when I offend or am offended.

GOING ABOVE
AND BEYOND

*Now to him who is able to do immeasurably more than all we
ask or imagine, according to his power that is at work within us,
to him be glory in the church and in Christ Jesus throughout
all generations, for ever and ever!*
EPHESIANS 3:20–21 NIV

Are you one of those people who goes above and beyond—at
work, in your relationships, and at play? Maybe you like to do all
you've promised to do, and then some. If this is true of you, then
you're more like your heavenly Father than you know. His Word
promises that He always goes above and beyond all that we could
ask or imagine.

Think about that for a moment. What have you asked for?
What have you imagined? It's amazing to think that God, in His
infinite power and wisdom, can do immeasurably more than all
that! How? According to the power that is at work within us. It's
not our power, thankfully. We don't have enough power to scrape
the surface of what we'd like to see done in our lives. But His
power in us gets the job done. . .and more.

Praise the Lord! Praise Him in the church and throughout all
generations! He's an immeasurable God.

*Heavenly Father, You have more power in Your little finger than all of
mankind has put together. Today I praise You for being a God who goes
above and beyond all I could ask or imagine.*

HE IS A PROVIDER

*"For all the animals of the forest are mine, and I own
the cattle on a thousand hills."*
PSALM 50:10 NLT

Friends wondered how Trish did it. Since her injury, she was only able to work part-time. She lived frugally, but still there never seemed to be enough money to cover even her most basic expenses. Somehow she never seemed anxious or upset. And miraculously, month after month, Trish's needs were always met. When asked how she was able to remain at peace in the midst of such financial uncertainty, her reply was always the same: "My God owns the cattle on a thousand hills. There isn't anything He can't provide for me."

Financial certainty is never a guarantee. This isn't a surprise to God. Throughout history He has sustained His children through droughts, depressions, and natural disasters. Though at times our foundations may be shaken, God's remain secure. His resources are vast and He has promised to meet all our needs. Regardless of the circumstances, we can depend on Him to carry us through and provide for us. You do not have a need that God cannot meet. Whatever you are facing today, rest in the knowledge that God *will* take care of you.

*Heavenly Father, thank You for being my Provider.
Help me to trust You to provide everything I need. Amen.*

ONE MORE DEGREE

*Serve wholeheartedly, as if you were serving the Lord, not men, because
you know that the Lord will reward everyone for whatever good he does.*
EPHESIANS 6:7–8 NIV

Sometimes we think we've reached our maximum potential—
we have no more to give or accomplish. Maybe adversity has
struck and we see no purpose or value in life, and we flirt with
the idea of giving up. What more can we possibly achieve?

Motivational speaker Mack Anderson states, "At 211 degrees,
water is hot. At 212 degrees it boils. With boiling water comes
steam. And steam can power a locomotive. One extra degree
makes all the difference in life; it separates the good from the
great."

One degree. One tiny bit more. A push could power great
things. Do we have it in us?

In Romans, Paul exhorts believers to be fervent in spirit,
serving the Lord. Fervent means bubbling or boiling, zealous.
Can we become zealous Christians choosing to serve one another
because Christ asked us to? We can if we allow the Holy Spirit to
guide and direct us.

Reach today for another step, another degree, just a tad
more. It can be done. The Bible has promised us so.

*Dear Lord, at times I feel I have nothing left to give.
Help me, push me one more degree. Amen.*

WORK REVIEW

And we pray this in order that you may live a life worthy of the Lord and may please him in every way: bearing fruit in every good work, growing in the knowledge of God.
COLOSSIANS 1:10 NIV

It had been a typical day in Candace's office. She drove home from work recounting the events that had occurred.

"Lord, did I do Your will today?" she asked God as she waited in traffic.

God answered her by bringing to mind the times when she had shown integrity and worked in such a way that she was working unto Him. God also reminded her when she had encouraged her coworkers and supervisor. Even when she was tempted to be short with a difficult client, she had prayed that God would help her to have the patience she needed.

God also reminded her of some times during the day when she failed to be about His business, but He promised her that there would be new opportunities to follow Him tomorrow.

Have you asked God if you have been about His work today? He spends all day with you. Ask Him to help you grow to know Him better as you please Him more and more, even as you are at your place of employment.

Dear God, help me to please You as I work. Let me remember that I am serving You in my daily tasks. Amen.

A FAMILY BLESSING

*"Bless my family; keep your eye on them always.
You've already as much as said that you would, Master GOD!
Oh, may your blessing be on my family permanently!"*
2 SAMUEL 7:29 MSG

God is completely trustworthy. Think about that for a moment. When we can't trust others, we can trust Him. When we can't trust ourselves, we can trust Him. God keeps an eye on everyone at all times. He's got things under control, especially when we loosen our grip.

Did you know that you can trust God with both your own life *and* the lives of your family members? And that includes every single person in your family. Parents, grandparents, siblings, children, aunts, uncles—everyone. You can trust the Lord with their dreams, their goals, their aspirations, their attitudes, their reactions, their problems. You can trust Him to handle any relationship problems. God's got it covered. All of it.

Today, recommit yourself to trusting God with your family. Don't fret and don't try to fix people. That's not your job, after all. And besides, God's keeping an eye on everyone. He's said it, and you can believe it. It's in His master plan to bless your family . . .permanently!

God, I confess I sometimes struggle where my family is concerned. I want to fix people. I want to fix situations. Thank You for the reminder that You have great plans, not just for me, but for my family members, too.

WRONG MESSAGES

They are not of the world, even as I am not of the world.
JOHN 17:16 NASB

The world sends women messages every day. You should be thin with long, flowing, gorgeous hair. You should be married to a man—tall, dark, and handsome, of course—and on your ring finger there should be a sparkling diamond. You should smell of the finest, most expensive perfume. And if you are to be loved, you should dress a certain way, talk a certain way, and live in a certain neighborhood.

But believers in Christ are not of this world. We are in it, but not of it. We are visitors here, and heaven will be our eternal home. While we are here on earth, we must avoid believing the things the world whispers to us. It is okay if you are not beautiful in the world's eyes. God sees you as a beautiful daughter, important enough to give His Son's life for! Diamonds and perfume are not the definition of a woman. It is the heart that defines her, and if her heart is turned toward Jesus, it will shine brighter than any diamond ever could.

Father, remind me today to tune out the world as I tune into what You have to say about me. Amen.

GOD FIGHTS FOR US

*Then I spoke to the nobles and officials and everyone else: "There's
a lot of work going on and we are spread out all along the wall,
separated from each other. When you hear the trumpet call,
join us there; our God will fight for us."*
NEHEMIAH 4:20 MSG

Alice shuddered as she sat in her car. A few minutes earlier,
her boss had called her into his office and announced that she'd
been accused of impropriety by a client.

She asked tons of questions and got few answers—except
that her firm's lawyers would be in touch. Alice had worked hard
for years to get to the position she held, and she saw it crumbling
into dust in front of her eyes.

The worst part was that as a dedicated believer, she always
took pains to make sure no one could accuse her of any
misconduct. She had always thought God would protect her
from any kind of lawsuit.

Suddenly, Alice realized she hadn't prayed about the
situation. "Oh, Lord," she murmured, "I'm lost here. I'm scared.
Help!"

That night, Alice curled up on the couch with her kitty, her
Bible, tissues, and a cup of tea. By the time she went to bed, she
felt at peace. God would fight for her, she was sure. And whatever
the outcome, He would provide for her. He had always been
faithful to her, and He wasn't going to stop being faithful now.

*Lord, thank You that You promise to fight for me. Forgive me for trying to
wage battles on my own, instead of going to You first.*

DOING OUR PART

Therefore, my dear friends, as you have always obeyed—not only in my presence, but now much more in my absence—continue to work out your salvation with fear and trembling, for it is God who works in you to will and to act according to his good purpose.
PHILIPPIANS 2:12–13 NIV

God is the author of life—both physical and spiritual. He gives us freedom to either cherish or abuse the life we have been given. Healthy bodies do not just happen. Effort and sacrifice are required on our part to assure that we get proper exercise, diet, and sleep. We may jog before work, turn off the television in the evenings to head to bed, or limit our sweets. Taking proper care of our physical bodies enables us to enjoy life on earth to its fullest.

In the same way, we must make the effort to maintain optimal spiritual health. Spiritual growth doesn't just happen—it takes a lot of discipline. Obedience is required. Reading God's Word is a great start, but we must take it a step further. We need to transfer our head knowledge to the heart by applying God's truth in everyday life.

The good news is that we're not alone in our pursuit of spiritual health. Along the way, the Holy Spirit gives us the desire and the ability to follow the Lord. Let's not forget that spiritual growth is not only profitable for this life, but for the life to come!

Dear Lord, may I obediently apply Your truth to my daily life. Thank You for helping me in this process. Amen.

THE WORKER'S TOIL

*What does the worker gain from his toil? I have seen the burden God has
laid on men. He has made everything beautiful in its time.*
ECCLESIASTES 3:9–11 NIV

Most women are hard workers. They spend hours a day
either caring for the needs of others or working at their jobs.
They give tirelessly of themselves and come home at the end of
the day worn out. There's not always much energy left over to
effectively develop a relationship with the Lord.

If you're the type of woman who works especially hard,
you might wonder if you'll ever find the beauty in your labors.
Perhaps it all seems to be in vain—for someone else's benefit.
Take heart! Work is a necessity, but it doesn't have to consume
you. Be on the lookout for telltale signs that you're working too
hard. If your prayer time is suffering or you don't feel as close to
the Lord as you once did, it might be time to reorganize your
schedule.

Keeping things in balance is key. Hard work is good—and
so is rest. And if you're so taxed that you're not effective, then it's
definitely time for a change. Take a look at what drives you to
work so hard. Then, as you are able, work with the Lord to bring
every area of your life into perfect balance.

*Lord, I sometimes think my life is out of balance. I work too hard,
then seem to crash. My down times are too down. Bring order to my life,
Father. Help me to keep everything in perfect balance.*

KNOWING GOD'S PEACE

Search me, O God, and know my heart;
test me and know my anxious thoughts.
PSALM 139:23 NIV

The economy, crooked politicians, terrorist attacks, natural disasters. . .a quick scan of the morning's headlines is enough to make you want to crawl back in bed and pull the covers over your head. As if world events aren't enough, we have bills to pay, jobs to keep, and families to care for. On top of that we're supposed to exercise and eat right and get plenty of sleep. Just how *is* a person supposed to sleep with all that weighing on her mind?

The National Institute of Mental Health estimates that forty million Americans suffer from some kind of anxiety-related disorder in any given year. It's no wonder. In the short-term, anxiety may help us accomplish our goals. Our bodies were designed to cope with anxiety in short bursts, but not day after day.

Jesus offers an eternal solution: Fix your eyes on Him—not your circumstances. Immerse yourself in the truth of God's Word—not the dismal news of the newspaper. It's not about burying your head in the sand; it's about knowing how the story ends. Jesus said this world would bring trouble. But it doesn't have to bring anxiety, because He promises peace.

When I am overwhelmed by life's circumstances, teach me to fix my
thoughts on You. Thank You for the peace that passes all understanding
and that is beyond worldly wisdom. Amen.

JUST ONE

One of them, when he saw he was healed, came back,
praising God in a loud voice.
LUKE 17:15 NIV

Ten men were afflicted with the horrible disease of leprosy.
Ten met Jesus as He passed through their village. Ten called out,
addressing Him by name, "Jesus, Master, have pity on us!" Ten
received healing from the Lord.

Just one man rushed back and threw himself at the feet of
Jesus. He used the same loud voice that had pled for mercy to
offer thankfulness and praise.

We read this passage, and we want to shake our heads at
those other nine. How could they have forgotten to thank Jesus?
They had just been healed of leprosy! How could they go on
about their day, not honoring Him with gratitude?

Before we judge too harshly, we must examine our own hearts.
Do we remember to thank God when a prayer is answered?

Do you give Him glory for answering your prayers for a
friend's marriage to be restored, or do you merely comment that
it's great the couple has decided to reunite? Do you thank Him
for providing a new job after your Bible study group prayed on
your behalf? Or are you too busy picking out the suit and heels
you will wear on your first day?

It takes discipline to react like the one leper, rather than like
the other nine. God delights when He finds a believer with a
grateful heart.

Help me, Lord, to have a grateful heart.

CHANGING HEARTS

The king's heart is a stream of water in the hand of the LORD;
he turns it wherever he will.
PROVERBS 21:1 ESV

Relationships can be difficult at times. Even when communication is good and both people are Christians, there is still conflict when two human beings have a long-term relationship with each other. Children, parents, coworkers, roommates, friends, sisters, former spouses, and in-laws can all frustrate us at one time or another. We have our own desires and goals we want to meet; they have their agendas and needs, and everyone has selfishness in his or her heart. How do we get beyond competing desires that conflict with each other and harm our relationships?

Prayer is a key ingredient in pursuing successful relationships. We can pray for our own hearts to change as well as those we're in conflict with. God can and will shape our affections, and He can change the minds of those for whom we pray. It is not difficult for Him, yet we so easily forget to ask. What relationships in your life need prayer today?

Heavenly Father, there is nothing in my heart and mind or in those
of whom I love that You cannot change. Turn my heart to You,
to desire Your best for my life.

SEEING JESUS
IN THE LAW

Where there is no revelation, the people cast off restraint;
but happy is he who keeps the law.
PROVERBS 29:18 NKJV

T he job of the Old Testament prophet was to speak to people
on God's behalf. Jesus was the perfect prophet, the complete
expression of God's love for man. In Him, God revealed how
much He loves us. When we see and know Jesus, the law of God
becomes real because we understand that love is behind the law.

The law was given for our good, to lead us to Christ and to
instruct us in how to live. Without Jesus, it is impossible to keep
the law of God. And even though we fail daily in keeping all of it,
we have the assurance that Christ has kept it for us. We are seen
as law-keepers in God's eyes. That which we do obey is the work
of the Holy Spirit whom Jesus has given to us as our helper.

When we do not focus on Christ, we will cast off restraint,
rebelling and resisting the very things that are good for us. We
will forget how much we are loved by God and that the law was
perfected for us in Christ. When God's law is not pleasurable to
us, we have lost our focus on Christ, forgotten that the law has
been kept for us, and lost our sense of gratitude.

Father, please keep before my eyes the picture of the risen Son, who
kept the law for me. Thank You for my salvation. Enable me by
Your Spirit to love and keep Your law.

M.I.A.?

GOD, are you avoiding me? Where are you when I need you?
PSALM 10:1 MSG

Do you ever feel like God is Missing in Action? Like He's hard to reach during the very times you need Him most? Have you ever wondered if the Lord is actually avoiding you during your times of crisis? If He even cares at all about what you're going through?

God isn't in the avoiding business. And He cares about you very much. In fact, He loves you deeply and is with you through thick and thin. If you're in a season in which His voice seems to be waning, take the time to listen more attentively. If you still can't hear His voice, remember there are times when He chooses to remain silent. That doesn't mean He's not there or that He doesn't care. Nothing could be further from the truth. Perhaps He's just waiting to see if you're going to act out of what you already know, what He's already taught you.

If God's voice isn't clear right now, think back to the last thing you heard Him speak to your heart. Act on that thing. Just keep walking in consistent faith, love, and hope. And before long, you'll be hearing His voice again. . .crystal clear.

Lord, I'm calling out to You today. Sometimes I feel like You're not there. Until I hear Your voice, I'm going to keep on believing, keep on hoping, and keep on living a life of faith.

A Lesson from Rahab

He fulfills the desires of those who fear him;
he hears their cry and saves them.
PSALM 145:19 NIV

The second chapter of Joshua tells of a woman named Rahab who ran a house of ill repute. The city of Jericho guarded the pass leading to the Promised Land, and the Israelite leader Joshua had been told by God that His people were going to conquer Jericho.

Jericho was a city full of sin. Rahab had been told about Israel's God, as had the rest of Jericho. But Rahab took to heart the miracles she'd heard about. When Joshua sent a couple of spies to survey the town, she offered them protection in her home, risking her life when the king's men came looking for the Israelite spies.

The men agreed to spare Rahab and her family when they conquered the city—and they kept their promise. Her faith provided them escape, and they provided safety for her during the battle for Jericho. Rahab even became part of the lineage of Jesus Christ!

What is your situation? Do you feel walled in, with no escape? Don't give up! God will hear your cry and save you, just as He heard Rahab's cry and saved her, because of her faith in Him.

Lord, help me to not fear my circumstances, but to trust that
You will hear my cry and save me, because I fear You.

How's Your Heart?

"The LORD doesn't see things the way you see them. People judge by outward appearance, but the LORD looks at the heart."
1 SAMUEL 16:7 NLT

Definitions of beauty—of attractiveness—are subjective standards set by a sinful world. Fads come and go (is stick-thin in or is it waif-thin this year?), but God's take on true loveliness is never changing. Where we humans make snap judgments about others by their appearance, God looks deep into our hearts to find real beauty.

So what does the Father see when He finds a woman with a beautiful heart? He sees an individual overflowing with the fruit of the spirit: love, joy, peace, patience, kindness, goodness, faithfulness, gentleness, and self-control. The inner beauty of this person outshines whatever physical appearance she has on the outside, and the people who can look past her outer shell are blessed to know such a lovely woman.

Are you guilty of judging others strictly on their outward appearance? Or maybe you've given in to the temptation to measure your outward appearance by the standards of worldly beauty. In either case, make it a priority to value others—and yourself—for the appearance of the heart. Then you'll experience the true beauty God has given us through His creation!

Dear Father, thank You for being a God who values me for far more than my physical beauty. Help me to always look at others with the same depth that You look at me. I want to cherish others for their loveliness within. Amen.

FAMILY FRUSTRATIONS

Each of you should look not only to your own interests,
but also to the interests of others.
PHILIPPIANS 2:4 NIV

W hy is it that sometimes it is most difficult to show Christ's love to our own family members? Is it because we spend so much time with them? Is it because they seem to expect certain things from us that strangers and even close friends wouldn't? Sometimes it seems as if being single compounds the problems.

Your parents will always be your parents, even if you haven't been living with them for years. It is easy to appreciate their love and caring, but sometimes their advice is tiresome, if not annoying.

If you have married siblings, they may grate on your nerves as well. Whenever you have a disagreement with them, they might be quick to point out that you'd understand things their way if only you were married. On the other hand, as they see it, you are the perfect built-in babysitter of your nieces and nephews because you don't have anything better to do.

What is the solution? Change your perspective and try to find things that you can thank God for about them, even though they sometimes act in ways that are less than ideal. Work on seeing things from their perspective, but kindly let them know when their advice or comments hurt. Ask God to help you to see their needs and to have His help as you minister to them.

Dear God, thank You for each member of my family.
Help me to show my family Your love. Amen.

WRESTLING MATCH

*How long must I wrestle with my thoughts and every day have sorrow in
my heart? How long will my enemy triumph over me?*
PSALM 13:2 NIV

Every day we struggle with thoughts that may not be
pleasing to God. Not everything that flits through our mind or
imagination is edifying to Him, after all. And it's frustrating to
know we fall short of where we think we should be, especially
when it comes to what we think or feel.

When we struggle in our thought life, the enemy is thrilled.
But he needs to take a second look. Those fleeting thoughts are
not sinful unless we act on them. And if we can stop them while
they're just thoughts—if we can bring them under the blood
of Jesus—then the battle is already won! Satan may be gleeful
now, but when we recognize that we are more than conquerors
through Christ, he stops partying and is vanquished.

Your mind is the battlefield. That's why we are advised
to bring every thought captive, because the enemy will try to
defeat us in our mind before actions ever come into it. Instead
of wrestling with your thoughts, make a conscious effort to give
your thought life to the One capable of handling it.

*Father, sometimes I don't like the thoughts that go flitting through my mind.
I know they're not Your thoughts. Today, I give my thought life to You. May
the enemy no longer triumph over me in this area!*

SECURITY

Therefore, there is now no condemnation for those who are in Christ Jesus.
ROMANS 8:1 NIV

Every woman longs for security. But where can security be found—in a large investment portfolio, a job with benefits, or a loyal friend? Placing our trust in these things is like building our house on shifting sand. Investments tumble. Jobs end. Friends move. There are no guarantees. What is here today could easily be gone tomorrow. So is permanent security just an illusion?

Jesus Christ is the same yesterday, today, and forever. He is the Rock, not shifting sand. He is immutable—unchanging. Christ died for us while we were yet sinners. By accepting His gift of eternal life, we will never be condemned. Our security is rooted in Christ's unconditional love for us. It is not based upon our performance but upon who He is. There is nothing that can separate us from that love, including our poor choices or disobedience. Nothing can pluck us from His hand. He is ours and we are His. He has prepared a home in heaven for us and has given us the indwelling Holy Spirit as a deposit guaranteeing that promise.

That is the hope and assurance that we can stake our lives on. Embrace the eternal security that is yours in Christ Jesus!

*Dear Lord, my security comes in knowing You.
Thank You for Your enduring love! Amen.*

BEHOLD JESUS

*And we all, with unveiled face, beholding the glory of the Lord, are being
transformed into the same image from one degree of glory to another.
For this comes from the Lord who is the Spirit.*
2 CORINTHIANS 3:18 ESV

A small boy walks alongside his father, swinging his arms
just the way his dad does. A little girl holds her doll in the same
careful fashion she sees her mother cradle her new baby brother.
Children watch their parents. Without consciously choosing to
do so, they become like the ones they observe.

This same principle can work for our good if we choose
to gaze on the Lord Jesus. Rather than focusing on our own
obedience or our efforts to be holy, we can be like those children,
unconsciously adopting the traits of the One we are watching.

Follow Jesus around. Read His Word. Reflect on His life.
Talk to Him in prayer. As you focus on getting to know the
person of Christ, your sanctification will take place. The Bible
tells us that the Spirit will do this in us. As you look at Jesus, His
glory will transform you, one degree at a time; and slowly but
surely you will begin to look like Him. Don't focus on yourself—
instead, watch Him.

*Lord Jesus, help me to know You as a person. Give me the
desire to follow You around and in doing so to become like You.*

A Fertile Heart

He who tills his land will have plenty of bread, but he who follows
frivolity will have poverty enough!
PROVERBS 28:19 NKJV

It is easy to see the Proverbs' application in our physical lives. Diligence to work yields positive results. One more sales call each day will produce more income. A little more exercise will have added health benefits.

The principle of sowing and reaping also is true in our spiritual lives. The landscape of our souls needs attention.

Our hearts are like a garden, where the ground often gets hard and rocky because of unforgiveness or blindness to some other sin. Diligent prayer and self-examination lead to repentance. This is the spade that breaks up the ground. A soft heart, like soft earth, is ready to receive the seed of God's Word. Once His Word is planted in our hearts, it will grow. The harvest is the life of Christ that grows in us.

Just as one who pursues frivolity will not advance in a career, one whose soul is fed worthless pursuits will have poverty of spirit. Without God's Word, prayer, and worship, there will be no bread of life grown in us. Ask God to show you what to pursue. Ask Him to help you till the ground of your heart. As your heart becomes receptive, He will plant His Word in it, and it will produce much fruit.

Gracious God, give me the desire to sow the things of the Spirit. Enable me
to repent of sowing that which hardens my heart. Produce Your life in me.

LET IT FLOW

"He who believes in Me, as the Scripture has said, out of his heart will flow rivers of living water."
JOHN 7:38 NKJV

Water from the sprinkler arced through the air, casting drops over the grass. Only when it slapped a large oak did it lose its trajectory and dribble to the ground. The water couldn't pass through the oak tree. Yes, the thirsty tree soaked up the needed moisture, but it stopped the shooting sprays.

Do we stop the life-giving water of the Savior from gushing out of our hearts? Is a large oak tree—maybe fear, doubt, anger—rooted within us that keeps the flow of water stilled?

Jesus encouraged us to believe in Him so there would be an overflowing of the Spirit upon others. If we harbor destructive emotions, the Spirit is slapping the oak tree. It's not flowing out of us. While our circumstances might not be perfect, we're still asked to let the river flow.

The Spirit within us is greater than any trouble we might face, any situation we might be in, any obstacle in our paths. We need to acknowledge His promise and obey His commands so God can work in our lives. When we do, streams of water flow.

Dear heavenly Father, help me to ferret out anything that would keep the Holy Spirit from working in my life. Thank You, Lord. Amen.

A SONG OF PRAISE

But let all who take refuge in you rejoice; let them sing joyful praises forever. Spread your protection over them, that all who love your name may be filled with joy.

PSALM 5:11 NLT

Have you ever been so swept away by a great worship service that you wished it would never end? Maybe you sang song after song of praise, your heart ready to burst with anticipation of what God would do. There's great joy in lifting up praises to God. And He loves it when you come into His presence with singing. If you're not convinced, read the book of Psalms!

Today's scripture points out that all who take refuge in God have something to sing about. It's a matter of walking in daily relationship with God, and then—overwhelmed with His goodness, His protection, His joy—coming into His presence with a song in your heart. It's not a song that's drummed up by a worship leader. It's a song that was already there—one ready to spring out the moment you open your mouth.

Has God been your refuge? Has He spread His protection over you? If so, then you have plenty to sing about. Let that joy spill over into a heartfelt song of worship!

Oh, Father! You've been so good to me! You've covered me, protected me, loved me, given me refuge. Today, the song in my heart erupts. I'll make a joyful noise because of Your goodness!

BECOME A
WORLD-CHANGER

*"This is my command—be strong and courageous! Do not be afraid or
discouraged. For the LORD your God is with you wherever you go."*
JOSHUA 1:9 NLT

In the Word of God, women from all professions and
backgrounds are changed by grace, and then, with the Holy
Spirit's help, transform the people around them. In the Old
Testament, God shines the light on a beauty queen (Esther) who
saves an entire generation of people with her bravery. In Exodus,
Moses' sister, Miriam, exhorts her fellow Israelites to worship.
And in the New Testament, Lydia and Tabitha run successful
businesses and invest their profits in ministry to the poor.

God wants you to change your world, too. Does that thought
scare you? Whatever station God has called you to, He will equip
you for the task. Are you a businesswoman? He will guide you
to do your job with integrity and faithfulness. Do you have a
classroom of kids looking up to you? God will give you energy
and creativity to discipline, lead, and teach them. Perhaps you've
felt called to minister, and you wonder whether you've heard God
right. Through circumstances, scripture, and mature Christian
mentors, He will make clear the path He wants you to take.

Don't be afraid to follow God—wherever He leads. Women
in every era have changed the world because they remained
faithful to God and followed His leadership.

*Lord, help me be strong and courageous as I follow You wherever
You lead. I want You to use me to help change the world.*

HANDS THAT HOLD

*My times are in your hands; deliver me from my
enemies and from those who pursue me.*
PSALM 31:15 NIV

Our lives are composed of seconds, minutes, hours, days, weeks, months, and years. We think in each of these increments in different situations. Look at a clock and we think about seconds, minutes, and hours. Our calendar shows us days, weeks, and months. On a birthday or holiday, we reflect on a year. We may think about the era in which we live and the culture around us that inhabits that time frame. We may dwell too much in the past or worry too much about our future. All of these are part of the times that the psalmist places in God's hands.

Think about God's hands that hold our time. These are the hands that fashioned the world. These are the hands that took a rib from Adam and made Eve. These are the hands that healed the blind and the lame. These are the hands that broke bread in an upper room. These are the hands that were nailed to a cross. These are the hands graciously extended to doubting Thomas. Our times, from our moments to our years, are in the hands of the Creator, Healer, Sustainer, Provider, Redeemer, and Lover of our souls. There is nothing He cannot do. Knowing this, the psalmist releases his fears to God—so can you.

*Gracious God who rules and reigns over all my days,
cause me to remember that I am held by Your loving hands.*

Being Alone

On the day I called, you answered me;
my strength of soul you increased.
PSALM 138:3 ESV

Age has its privileges, but it also has its aches and pains. Work responsibilities increase. Life becomes complex. With every year there are added relationships, changed relationships, and lost relationships.

Some of us find ourselves alone at a point in life when we did not expect to be single. Marriage just never happened, or death or divorce has left us without a mate. For many women, the idea of going through the rest of their lives alone is one of their greatest fears.

Psalm 138:3 reminds us of the nearness of God and the holy ear that is attuned to our cry. He does not want us to fear loneliness, but to call out to Him immediately. He will answer our cry because He wants to be near to us. He is the strength of our souls. Many times, He gives us His help through another person. But even if no other human being is there to help, He will give us boldness to face whatever is before us, whether it is loneliness or added responsibilities and challenges as we age. Our strength is in His constant companionship.

Lord Jesus, help me remember that You hear my cry. Even when I am physically alone, You are there with me. Help me to trust You to supply all my needs and embolden me for whatever lies ahead.

THE VALLEY

Yea, though I walk through the valley of the shadow of death, I will fear
no evil: for thou art with me; thy rod and thy staff they comfort me.
PSALM 23:4 KJV

Cyndi walked through a particularly dark valley as she
watched her mother battle a terminal illness. After a lengthy
struggle, her mother passed away, leaving Cyndi with feelings of
anger, pain, and even hopelessness. At times, she felt as if no one
understood the depth of her pain. Who could she turn to?

Slowly the Lord began to do a healing work in Cyndi.
Whenever she saw a rainbow in the sky, she felt a special touch
from the Lord, and it lifted her pain. And rays of sunlight were a
constant reminder of God's presence. She saw beyond the valley
of the shadow to hopeful days ahead. God brought the comfort
Cyndi needed—sometimes in the least likely ways and places.

Daughter of God, if you're going through a grieving season,
if you're walking in the valley of the shadow, look for God to
surprise you with rays of sunshine that break through your dark
days. If you will open your heart to the possibilities, He will send
comfort to mend your brokenness. Your heavenly Father truly
understands your pain. After all, He lost someone He loved, too.

Lord, sometimes I feel like the valley I'm in will never end. Today
I choose to look up to see those rays of sunshine above. Thank
You for Your rod and staff. They bring me comfort.

COME TO HIM

"Come to me, all you who are weary and burdened, and I will give you rest. Take my yoke upon you and learn from me, for I am gentle and humble in heart, and you will find rest for your souls. For my yoke is easy and my burden is light."
MATTHEW 11:28–30 NIV

Making ends meet as a single woman is tough sometimes. Since everything depends upon us, burdens routinely land on our shoulders.

Take heart—there is hope. The Lord never intended for us to go through life alone. Come to Him and pour out your worries in prayer. Tell Him your concerns and lay your burdens at His feet. Ask for wisdom, then listen. Open the Bible and read truth in the Psalms. Be still. Meditate on His many promises: He'll never leave or forsake you; He offers wisdom for the asking; He offers rest for your soul. Learn from Him. Allow the still small voice of the Holy Spirit to whisper encouragement—to build you up—to strengthen you.

As a single woman, you have an advocate. Allow the Lord to carry your burdens and give you the rest you yearn for.

Dear Lord, help me remember that You are there to shoulder my burdens. Give me rest as I come to You. Amen.

WAIT ON GOD

*Do any of the worthless idols of the nations bring rain? Do the skies
themselves send down showers? No, it is you, O LORD our God. Therefore
our hope is in you, for you are the one who does all this.*
JEREMIAH 14:22 NIV

You've already prayed for God to help you, but you won't
wait for His answer. Are you really putting your trust in Him?

Maybe while waiting in the checkout line, you see an article
that boasts "Get a Commitment before Christmas." Instead of
trusting that God is in control of your relationship, you buy the
magazine and plan on following the advice in it step by step. Or
you may have decided that you can't tithe this month because
your finances are too tight. Or perhaps you have had some
medical tests done. Even though you've prayed about the results,
you've spent your free time researching your symptoms on the
Internet and worrying about what the results might be.

Compared to God, the wood and stone idols in the Bible
are useless. Similarly, when we trust someone or something other
than God, then we trust something as useless as wood and stone
idols. God can and will take care of you. After you've sought
His help, then wait for Him to act. He'll do a much better job
providing and protecting you than a magazine, your own ideas,
or even the Internet can.

*Dear God, help me as I wait patiently for You to fulfill my
desires in Your timing. You provide for me and help me. Amen.*

God Will Always Meet Your Needs

*And my God will meet all your needs according
to his glorious riches in Christ Jesus.*
PHILIPPIANS 4:19 NIV

If you're like most people, your want list is long and your budget is tight. Watching the evening news can be frightening for anyone trying to make ends meet. Economic uncertainty is a constant reality. Gas prices fluctuate like a yo-yo. Buying groceries and paying utilities seem like near-impossible tasks. Then there's the unexpected car repair and doctor bills that throw your monthly budget into a tailspin. The paycheck that was once large enough to meet your obligations may now seem like a cut in pay.

As a child of God, it's important to remember that He will supply all of your needs. He is your source for all things—financial, physical, mental, and spiritual.

Keep your anxiety at bay! God's economy is not in a crisis, and it never will be. You can take that straight to the bank!

*Dear God, You know my needs before I even ask.
Thank You for being my provider. Amen.*

THE APPLE OF HIS EYE

Keep me as the apple of Your eye; hide me under the shadow of Your wings.
PSALM 17:8 NKJV

Remember when you were a little girl and you knew what it felt like to be the apple of your mother or father's eye? Maybe you were one of those kids who enjoyed being teacher's pet. Or maybe your swim coach or dance teacher paid extra attention to you, encouraging you with their kind words. Perhaps you enjoyed the admiration of a Sunday school teacher or choir director.

It feels so good to know you're special to someone. How amazing—how completely overwhelming—to know that the God of the universe thinks you're special! You are the apple of His eye. He wants to draw you close, to tell you just how much He loves you. Like that teacher you had in elementary school, He wants to whisper words of encouragement in your ear, to convince you that you can accomplish great things in Him.

Today, spend some time thinking about all of the many ways the Lord has encouraged you over the years. Think back on all of the people He's placed in your life—people who've whispered nuggets of gold into your ear. Those words were God-breathed! They came straight from the heart of your heavenly Father, who longs to let you know you are the apple of His eye.

Lord, thank You for all of the people You've sent to encourage me through the years. They made me feel so special, so loved. Thank You that I am the apple of Your eye, a dearly loved child.

TAKING MATTERS INTO HER OWN HANDS

But the LORD's plans stand firm forever;
his intentions can never be shaken.
PSALM 33:11 NLT

Genesis 27 tells the story of Jacob, Esau, and their meddling mother, Rebekah. This mother was so concerned for her son's future that she took matters into her own hands.

An ailing Isaac instructed Esau to prepare a meal for him so that Esau could receive the blessing reserved for the firstborn son. Rebekah overheard this conversation and quickly hatched a new plan for younger son Jacob to receive the blessing. Rebekah's plan worked, and before Esau returned from his hunt, Jacob had stolen his brother's blessing. Although Romans 9:11 says this was God's plan all along, Rebekah's interference drove a potentially deadly wedge between her two grown sons.

Are you ever impatient for God's plans to unfold? Are you ever tempted to take matters into your own hands and act in a manipulative way? Sometimes this works and our plans succeed, just like Rebekah's. However, when we do this, the consequences can often be disastrous. Learn to wait on God. You can be assured that His plans and His purposes will be fulfilled. And His way is always the best way.

Thank You, Father, that Your plans stand firm, even when I try to intervene.
Help me to wait patiently on You and to trust You to bring about Your plans
in Your way and in Your time. Amen.

JESUS WON'T CHANGE

Jesus Christ is the same yesterday, today, and forever.
HEBREWS 13:8 NLT

Relationships can change. Jobs can change. You may be someone who rearranges your furniture every few months for a new look. You may change your clothes six times before deciding on an outfit. Your hair color may even change like the seasons. Change is everywhere, and although change can be good, not knowing what the future holds can be unsettling.

There is one thing, however, that is unchangeable, and that is Jesus Christ. Today, meditate on these truths about Jesus. Allow His steadfastness to give you peace in an ever-changing world:

His Word will not change (1 Peter 1:25).

His goodness will not change (Psalm 100:5).

His ways will never change (Isaiah 55:8–13).

His provision for His children will never change (Philippians 4:19).

His promises will never change (Hebrews 6:10–12).

His mercy will never change (Psalm 107:1).

His grace will never change (2 Corinthians 12:9).

His love will never change (1 Corinthians 13).

Changes will come, but Jesus will be there through each one, remaining the same always and forever.

Dear Jesus, I take comfort in knowing that You will remain the same through all the changes in my life. Amen.

SPEND WISELY

The wise have wealth and luxury, but fools spend whatever they get.
PROVERBS 21:20 NLT

Kelly's financial problems started innocently enough. Her recent raise made her able to afford to join the trendy gym where many of her friends and coworkers belonged. The three-year service contract didn't seem like that big of a deal at the time.

Shortly thereafter, her car broke down, and she decided to purchase a new, reliable model. Five years seemed like a long time to be making payments, but Kelly felt her job was secure. When her roommate moved out of state and took furniture with her, Kelly decided to purchase some of her own for 0 percent interest over four years.

Six months later, when Kelly was laid off from her job, she stared at her monthly bills in disbelief. There was no savings to fall back on. She was locked into payments for things that she suddenly neither needed nor wanted. Kelly would have given just about anything to turn back the clock and undo many of the foolish spending decisions she had made.

Ouch. Most of us can relate to the temptation to spend more than we have. It takes wisdom and discipline to be able to say no to something we would like to have—or something we feel we deserve to have. But wise spending decisions bring peace and security, especially during tough economic times. Whether or not you're in a predicament like Kelly's, pray for wisdom regarding your finances. Listen to and obey this wise course of action.

Father, help me to spend my money wisely. Amen.

RIGHT BESIDE US

And Jacob awaked out of his sleep, and he said,
Surely the LORD is in this place; and I knew it not.
GENESIS 28:16 KJV

A soldier on patrol trekked through the night, his infrared goggles probing the path for obstacles. He was surrounded by the unseen, yet he was able to detect the invisible with his special equipment and save his squad from danger. His viewpoint kept himself and others safe.

Sometimes we feel alone. But we need to realize we are surrounded by an invisible world. Messengers of God—angels—exert their influence. The Holy Spirit pursues the hearts of people all across the globe. Satan and his powers work to thwart God's plans. Yet we act as though nothing is in sight. Our spiritual eyes are closed. We worry and fret as though the visible world were the only reality. We find it hard to believe what is not before our eyes.

Despite what we see in the natural world, God *is* there. His presence is everywhere. We should view life through a scriptural lens and realize the Lord *is* in this place. Once we're His child, He's beside us forever. He'll never leave us: He promises to be right there.

Lord, help me realize Your moment-by-moment presence in my life. Amen.

JOY COMES
IN THE MORNING

For his anger lasts only a moment, but his favor lasts a lifetime; weeping
may remain for a night, but rejoicing comes in the morning.
PSALM 30:5 NIV

A woman struggled with a broken heart. Though she forgave
the person who hurt her, it seemed as if the pain would never
go away. Every time she thought about him, it would rise to the
surface again and she would find herself hurting.

Maybe you know the pain of a broken heart, too. Perhaps
you've been through low seasons—brought on by a broken heart,
a job crisis, a housing situation, or a relational challenge. If so,
you've probably already learned that times of true mourning don't
last forever. They might feel like it, but they eventually pass. The
pain lessens. Time is a wonderful healer.

If you're battling depression or heartache, hang tight to the
One who can best minister to your broken heart. He feels your
pain. He weeps alongside you. And His hand of favor has not
lifted from your life, though it may seem like it at times. He
wants you to know that your pain and your tears will only last for
a season. Joy is coming, if you will just hang on.

Father, sometimes I feel the pain of a broken heart and wonder if I'll ever
get past it. Thank You for Your healing balm. I'm so grateful that my tears
are only temporary. Joy is coming in the morning.

GRIEVE WITH HOPE

We do not want you to be ignorant about those who fall asleep, or to grieve like the rest of men, who have no hope.
1 THESSALONIANS 4:13 NIV

When Lazarus died and Jesus arrived at the family home, Lazarus's sister Mary ran to meet Jesus. Her grief was palpable as she fell at His feet.

"Why did you wait so long?" she sobbed. "He's gone."

Jesus knew that Mary and her brother would be reunited, very soon, in fact. However, in spite of this knowledge, He was visibly moved by Mary's grief. He wept. His heart ached for those He loved.

Sometimes as Christians we are given the impression that grieving or crying somehow implies that we don't trust God. That we don't believe He has everything under control. However, in 1 Thessalonians 4, when Paul teaches on the subject of death, he is clear: grieve, but not without hope. Perhaps your heart is heavy over a recent loss. Go ahead. Cry your heart out. Jesus feels your pain and your tears are precious to Him. But when you grieve, be sure to grieve with hope in the coming of our Lord.

Jesus, thank You for this beautiful picture of how very much You love us and how You feel our pain. When I grieve, help me to do so with hope. Amen.

SELF-SACRIFICE, NOT SELF-HELP

*Then Jesus went to work on his disciples. . . . "Self-help is no help at all.
Self-sacrifice is the way, my way, to finding yourself, your true self."*
MATTHEW 16:24–25 MSG

Every so often, a self-help book captivates readers and soars onto bestseller lists. The text is usually a combination of common sense and New Age philosophy, with a few Bible verses thrown in for good measure. Its principles tout both good advice and bad, and its followers tend to become zealous about it. Sure, the book might have some merit, but it doesn't factor in God. And the scriptures say that anything not done with and for God is meaningless.

As Jesus told His disciples, anyone who intends to follow God must let Him lead. We can't make plans and ask God to bless them. Instead, we must accept Jesus' sacrifice, ask for His forgiveness and grace, and surrender ourselves to Him. In return, He will give us the Holy Spirit. The Spirit's presence gives us comfort, guidance, and the strength to follow Him. And He will empower us to embrace self-sacrifice.

Do you want to achieve big things? Ask God for His guidance, and follow the instructions He reveals. His dreams for us are perfect, because He created us. And the future He has for us will truly satisfy our souls, as we become all He created us to be.

Lord, help me to learn and follow Your way.

ANGER

"In your anger do not sin": Do not let the sun go down while you are still angry, and do not give the devil a foothold.
EPHESIANS 4:26–27 NIV

Anger is an emotion that can cause great harm if we leave it unchecked. Anger can result in sin that affects us personally and the people around us. How do we take charge of this emotion and handle it appropriately?

Anger may arise in our hearts because someone has hurt us. The pain ignites a tiny spark of fire deep within. We may fan the flame by allowing our minds to dwell on the hurt. As we dredge up past offenses, we add fuel to the fire. Soon the tiny spark has become a raging fire in our souls looking for an outlet. We seek retaliation, even wanting to inflict pain on the attacker. We lash out with our tongues to pay back the offense. As we sin in our anger, Satan enters the picture.

God has a better plan. Rather than allowing the fire in your heart to spew from your tongue, take your hurt to the Lord before you speak. Confess your anger and ask Him to help you to forgive. Forgiveness squelches anger like throwing cold water on a fire, and through forgiveness God is glorified in your life.

Dear Lord, help me deal with anger when it first arises in my heart. May I give You a foothold by choosing forgiveness. Amen.

JUMPING FOR JOY!

*I'm thanking You, God, from a full heart, I'm writing the book on Your
wonders. I'm whistling, laughing, and jumping for joy;
I'm singing Your song, High God.*
PSALM 9:1–2 MSG

A woman with a cancer scare was given a reprieve. What she
thought would be a life-threatening diagnosis turned out to be a
false alarm. When she got the news, she felt like jumping for joy.
She was ecstatic. The words to a favorite praise song found their
way to her lips, and she sang at the top of her lungs while driving
home in the car.

Have you ever experienced this kind of joy that couldn't
be contained? Such joy rises from a heart filled with hope. And
when it comes, you really could write a book on God's wonders.
You feel like telling everyone just what He's done for you.

This is the day the Lord has made. Go ahead, rejoice in it!
Celebrate the victories you've experienced, large or small. And
if you're in the midst of a battle right now, go ahead and jump
for joy anyway. It'll do you good, and it will prepare you for the
celebration that is yet to come when that battle has been won.

*Lord, my heart is overwhelmed with joy. You've done so much for me,
and I don't deserve it! I feel like laughing, singing, and whistling.
In fact, I might just do that right now!*

LIVING GOD'S WORD

*Do not merely listen to the word, and so deceive yourselves. Do what it
says. Anyone who listens to the word but does not do what it says is like a
man who looks at his face in a mirror and, after looking at himself,
goes away and immediately forgets what he looks like.*

JAMES 1:22–24 NIV

The Bible contains instructions, promises, and encouraging
words. It also contains warnings such as this one in James. The
Bible is just another book if we do not heed its teachings and
apply them to our lives. If we claim to be Christians, we must
take the Word of God seriously.

How does this play out in real life?

Throughout each day, we are faced with situations that give
us options. Some of our options are how to react when we are
treated unfairly at work or when we get cut off by another driver
in traffic. As you read God's Word, take time to consider how the
passages and insights apply to your daily life. Do not merely read
the words, but challenge yourself to *live* them. In doing so, your
life will be blessed and your God will be honored.

*Father, I admit that many times I simply read the Bible as if it were a
storybook. Remind me to apply its truths and commands to my life. Amen.*

LISTENING TO GOD

*Why do you spend money for what is not bread, and your wages for what
does not satisfy? Listen carefully to Me, and eat what is good, and let your
soul delight itself in abundance. Incline your ear, and come to Me. Hear,
and your soul shall live; and I will make an everlasting covenant with
you—the sure mercies of David.*
ISAIAH 55:2–3 NKJV

Who do you follow? Who do you listen to? Celebrities
and politicians? The mainstream media and pop culture? What
messages do they give? Are you satisfied with their advice and
their promises?

This world and its counsel have nothing lasting to offer us.
The culture's solutions are short-lived. The very thing we think we
must have or do brings only a temporary satisfaction.

The Lord calls us to listen to only Him. "Incline your ear.
Come. Hear," He says. Relationship with Him—the Bread of
Life—is what nourishes and sustains us, what fills the emptiness
inside us. He has the ability to delight our souls. Lasting joy and
peace come from knowing we are loved unconditionally by Him.

Whose voice are you listening to today? Hear the voice of
Jesus calling you to come to Him.

*Lord Jesus, forgive me for following the world's voice instead of Yours.
Cause me to listen and follow You.*

YOU'RE CHUBBY

*They can train the younger women to love their husbands and children,
to be self-controlled and pure.*
TITUS 2:4–5 NIV

As Dianne walked her niece to school, the six-year-old suddenly burst out with, "You're chubby," punctuated with a throaty giggle.

Dianne gulped and laughed back with, "Don't you want to grow up and have nice curves like me?"

"Nope," came the reply. "I don't want to get old. I want to stay young and skinny."

Dianne was speechless as they reached the elementary school steps and her niece skipped inside. She realized she had just missed a teachable moment, but—really—what should she have said?

Dianne knew her sister-in-law was trying to lose some baby fat to get into a new dress for a high school reunion. It wasn't a big deal—or was it? Was a six-year-old already forming a warped body image by watching her mother preen before a mirror like any other woman in her midthirties might do?

All women have a hand in shaping how these girls develop their body images. We are charged by God to protect their innocence and lead them to desire healthy bodies, minds, and souls.

*Dear Lord, help me to reach out to a girl in my circle of influence
and teach her to see herself as a beautiful creation of Yours, no matter how
the package has come wrapped.*

One Way

Jesus told him, "I am the way, the truth, and the life. No one can come to the Father except through me."
JOHN 14:6 NLT

Jenny had just finished reading the newest self-help bestseller—the one that all of Hollywood was raving about—and she couldn't help but be a little confused. The book focused on inner peace and happiness, and when it talked about God, the almighty Creator and heavenly Father that she knew seemed more like a mystical force that a person could experience through self-reflection and. . .well. . .just about anything else that someone wanted to try.

The truth is that there's only *one* way to the Father—through Jesus Christ. Since the dawn of time, humans have sought eagerly after other paths to God, but His Word spells it out plainly: Jesus is the way, the truth, and the life. Take comfort in knowing that an understanding Savior is the solitary way to the Creator. He's been here and opened the way to God, and He lives today at the right hand of the Father in heaven.

Father, forgive me for seeking You in ways other than through Jesus. I know in my heart that He is the way, the truth, and the life. Give me the strength to share this fact with people around me who are looking for answers in the wrong places. Amen.

A HARD DAY'S NIGHT

I am worn out from sobbing. All night I flood my bed with weeping,
drenching it with my tears.
PSALM 6:6 NLT

Do you ever get sick and tired of being sick and tired? Fed up with being fed up? If so, then today's scripture verse surely rings true for you. Maybe you're going through a tough season. Unexpected challenges. Hard stuff. And maybe you think the night will never end.

Consider that only a God-focused heart recognizes when enough is enough. You've already made progress! Recognizing that you're ready to jump the hurdle is a good thing. But before you do, remember that tears can have a positive effect. They're cleansing, after all. And being honest with yourself about your emotions is also a good thing, as long as you can still affirm that God is good in the midst of your pain.

So cry for a season. Get it all out. Let the cleansing take place. Then when you reach that place where you know it's time to move on, get to it! Acknowledge your need for God, then get up off that bed and back to work.

Father, I recognize that sometimes I need to cry. I just have to get things out.
Thank You for giving me tears. They're a great release. Today, I give my tears
and my fears to You. May I rise up off my bed, ready to face a new day!

RIGHTEOUS ANGER

"When Jesus saw this, he was indignant. He said to them, 'Let the little children come to me, and do not hinder them, for the kingdom of God belongs to such as these.'"
MARK 10:14 NIV

At first the disciples must have enjoyed the attention. After all, they were Jesus' closest friends. And Jesus was popular. Everywhere He went, a crowd seemed to gather.

However, this probably got old after a while. Especially because most of the people Jesus attracted were limping or blind or desperately poor. If that wasn't enough, there were always children running and screaming and hiding behind Jesus when they played tag—it was exasperating! Surely Jesus would be grateful not to have these pesky kids climbing all over Him. His response likely surprised them all. Scripture says Jesus became indignant when the disciples rebuked the children.

Can you relate to the disciples? We often get angry when we are annoyed, irritated, or our rights are violated in some way. Contrast this type of anger with Jesus' anger. He saved His anger for things like oppression. Injustice. Unfairness. Not for when *His* rights were violated, but when others' rights were violated— for when the powerful took advantage of the powerless.

Anger is a potent emotion. Save it for the issues that really matter.

Jesus, help me to be more like You, to be angry about the right things and to use my anger in a way that honors You. Amen.

SERVING OTHERS

*Love must be sincere. Hate what is evil; cling to what is good. Be devoted
to one another in brotherly love. Honor one another above yourselves.*
ROMANS 12:9–10 NIV

As the pastor read the weekly announcements, Alex noticed
a young mother come into the sanctuary for the first time. The
mother was trying to hold her fussy toddler, a diaper bag, purse,
and her Bible as she looked around for a place to sit.

Alex wasn't the scheduled greeter, but it was obvious that the
mother was getting embarrassed. Quietly, she stood and walked
to the mother and toddler and offered to carry her belongings
and help her find a seat. She let them know where the nursery
was in case she'd like to take her toddler there. After church,
she invited them to lunch and introduced the mother to other
women in the church.

God calls us daily to react in everyday situations in such a
way that we show Christ's love to others. When we put others'
needs before our own, we please God.

*Dear God, thank You that You have called me to love others with Your love.
Show me how I may demonstrate Your love in practical ways to those people
I am near today. Amen.*

HEAVENLY GOALS

Brethren, I count not myself to have apprehended: but this one thing I do, forgetting those things which are behind, and reaching forth unto those things which are before, I press toward the mark for the prize of the high calling of God in Christ Jesus.

PHILIPPIANS 3:13–14 KJV

Many women set personal goals and priorities. Your long-term goals may include career advancement, fitness or weight-loss, or some personal dream you hope to achieve. You might also have a list of short-term priorities like spending more time in God's Word, getting involved in a church ministry, or even volunteering at a local women's shelter.

New goals and priorities are always made with good intentions. At times, you may fall short of some of your goals or even neglect some of your priorities. You can, however, achieve those goals, no matter what you've done in the past. It's never too late to start over; you can accomplish anything with God's help.

As a child of God, your goals should always be those that glorify the Father. Continually strive toward the completion of your godly goals with faith and perseverance, and one day you'll reach your goals, and your eternal prize will be one of heaven's greatest rewards.

Dear God, help me to continuously aim for the dreams and goals that You've placed in my heart. Amen.

PONDERING

But Mary treasured all these things, pondering them in her heart.
LUKE 2:19 NASB

Mary was a young woman when she was chosen by God to bear His Son, Jesus. She had a lot to think about in the following days and months—a visitation from an angel that told her she would conceive a child even though she was a virgin, what Joseph would think, and then giving birth in a stable with shepherds showing up in the middle of the night to see her newborn son. Yes, Mary was young. But she possessed a great deal of depth. The Bible tells us that she pondered all of these things in her heart.

Do all women ponder? It seems that we do. We think about the good and the bad in our lives. We get lost in daydreams. We lie awake at night wondering. We question our decisions at times and second-guess them occasionally. We imagine. We wonder. We think.

Take a few moments today to ponder the blessings God has given you. You may be in the midst of a mountaintop experience in your life, or you may find yourself in a deep valley of turmoil. Wherever you are, remember this and treasure it in your heart: God sent His one and only Son to die for you. Ponder that kind of love.

Father, today when I am tempted to dwell on the troubles in my heart, help me instead to focus on the treasures. Amen.

Whom Shall I Fear?

*The LORD is my light and my salvation; whom shall I fear? The LORD is
the strength of my life; of whom shall I be afraid?*
PSALM 27:1 NKJV

If the tentacles of fear grip your heart today, rest assured the
Lord is not causing it. He's the author of peace. Even knowing
that, we often struggle with situations and circumstances that
make us afraid. So, what's a Christian woman to do?

First of all, we need to call on the Lord to protect us with His
mighty hand. After all, we're God's kids, and our Daddy watches
over us. And if anyone messes with us, they'd better watch out!

Next we have to recognize there's a huge difference between
being cautious and being fearful. We're wise to be the first, of
course. But anything—or anyone—that causes us to fear needs to
be examined.

So, what are you afraid of today? Being alone? Money
problems? Issues with children? Health-related concerns? Career
moves? Things that go bump in the night? Most of the things we
worry about never come to pass. They're mostly shadowy "what
ifs." But when God sweeps in with that heavenly flashlight of
His, He brings everything to light. And seeing our problems in
the light certainly makes them less scary.

*God, I'm ready to hand my fear over to You. I want to be cautious, Lord,
but not fearful. You are the strength of my life. I've got nothing—or no
one—to be afraid of.*

COVER CHARGE

"Come!" say the Spirit and the Bride. Whoever hears, echo, "Come!"
Is anyone thirsty? Come! All who will, come and drink,
drink freely of the Water of Life!
REVELATION 22:17 MSG

Sarah was preparing for church one Saturday evening when Mark called and asked what she was doing. She said, "Getting ready for church." On an impulse, she added, "Want to go?" To Sarah's surprise Mark said yes. Then he asked, "How much does it cost?" The woman was stymied and asked for clarification. "What's the cover charge?" He'd never attended church and assumed there was a monetary cost involved.

What an opportunity to minister in someone's life. Just a simple invitation could be life-changing. We often feel intimidated and do not want to impose our beliefs on others. But all throughout scripture, we are directed to encourage people. When we've accepted Jesus as our Savior, it should be contagious.

Those who do not know the Father will not know Christ has paid the price for sin: He died on the cross for us and the gift of eternal life is free! Pass it on. Tell another person. Spread the news: Jesus is our cover charge.

Heavenly Father, show me someone You'd have me invite to church. Give me the courage to speak about what You've done in my life. Amen.

Lasting Treasure

*"Do not store up for yourselves treasures on earth, where moth and rust
destroy, and where thieves break in and steal. But store up for yourselves
treasures in heaven, where moth and rust do not destroy,
and where thieves do not break in and steal. For where your treasure is,
there your heart will be also."*
MATTHEW 6:19–21 NIV

Thankfully, Tessa was home and awake when the smoke
detector sounded. Her heart raced as she screamed for her brother
who, only moments before, had been in the shower. She never
thought to grab anything as they raced for the door—her single
thought was for her brother's safety. As they stood across the
street arm in arm watching the firefighters battle the flames, Tessa
sobbed. It wasn't about the stuff—she knew it could be replaced.
She simply was overwhelmed with thanks that both of them
made it out alive.

There's nothing like a close call with disaster to reveal to us
what is really important. Many of us invest time, money, and
energy in acquiring things, and yet if we're faced with having to
choose between people and possessions, we would choose people
every time. We find that our hearts aren't really in material things
after all. Often we're tempted to invest our resources in acquiring
material goods—sometimes at the expense of relationships. Jesus
turns this principle upside down when He challenges us to invest
our lives in things that no disaster can destroy.

*Father, give me a heart like Yours. Teach me to invest my resources in
matters of eternal significance. Amen.*

CONFIDENCE

But You, O Lord, are a God full of compassion, and gracious,
longsuffering and abundant in mercy and truth.
PSALM 86:15 NKJV

Most of us base our confidence in our own knowledge,
skills, good looks, or natural abilities. The truth is, our confidence
should be in our Father God, not in our own efforts and talents.

Self-confidence is typically tied to our feelings. We feel good
when we think we have done well and bad when we think we
have not measured up. We may think of God as being like a
schoolteacher who grades us on our performance. But God does
not reward us based on what we do or do not do. That is the
world's way. God is our Redeemer, our Savior, and the One who
sees us through the righteousness and person of Jesus Christ.

Compassion, grace, longsuffering, mercy, and truth—these
are attributes of our God. Compassion is undeserved sympathy.
Grace is an unmerited gift. Longsuffering is patience beyond
reasonable standards. None of these gifts have to do with our
performance—but all come out of His extravagant love. We give
God our need, sin, dependence, and weakness. He gives us help,
forgiveness, power, and strength.

Heavenly Father, thank You that I may exchange all my sin and weakness
for Your forgiveness and strength. Help me to be confident in Your character,
not my performance.

Fountain of God

For with you is the fountain of life.
Psalm 36:9 esv

Fountains are objects of beauty. The dance of water is constant, but our eyes never see quite the same scene for more than a second. The sound of splashing water is soothing and relaxing. Fountains evoke thoughts of constancy and renewal, cleansing and refreshment. Fountains are also a needed source of water, the most essential element of life.

God is the source of life for all creation. All things begin and end in Him. His love is beyond the bounds of the heavens. His beauty is constant as we see Him through circumstances that come into our lives. Even if we're unfaithful, God's faithfulness remains. It does not run dry. Over and over, He comforts His people. Daily His mercy is new to us, like clean water bubbling up from a fountain.

When we see ourselves in Him—our very lives held in His—all of creation together belonging to, controlled, and preserved by Him, we gain perspective on who we are and how much we are loved. As the psalmist says, "With you is the fountain of life."

Heavenly Father, how little I know of Your majesty and beauty.
Your creation speaks more love to me than I can possibly comprehend.
Show me more and more of how my life is hidden in Yours.

AT ALL TIMES

I bless GOD every chance I get; my lungs expand with his praise.
PSALM 34:1 MSG

It's hard to imagine blessing God in the midst of a battle or when we're in pain. Yet He wants us to bless Him at all times: when the sink is clogged, when the bill collectors are calling, when things aren't going as planned in the workplace, when we battle discouragement or health problems. The solution to any struggle? Bless God!

There are so many ways we can bless the Lord. First, we can avoid feelings of bitterness when we're wronged. And we really bless His heart when we spend time in His Word and do what it says. When we look for the good in every person or situation we bless God. And nature's glorious display can be a catalyst for blessing as well. A misty morning, a bird bathing, a child laughing. These are all things that evoke blessings from a thankful heart.

Make a list of all the reasons you have to bless God. Then go over that list, speaking words of thanksgiving and praise for what He's done in your life!

Lord, I have so much to be grateful for. May I never miss the little things all around me. And may I bless You—not just when things are going well but at all times! May Your praise continually be on my lips!

PEOPLE NEED THE LORD

*When he saw the crowds, he had compassion on them because they were
confused and helpless, like sheep without a shepherd.*
MATTHEW 9:36 NLT

Look closely at the people around you. External appearances
are deceptive. Beneath the forced smiles lie hearts that reveal a
different story. Aimless. Wandering. Lost. Many people have no
idea why they are here, what they are doing, and where they are
going. Pain, fear, and anxiety are their constant companions.
They are like sheep without a shepherd.

We need the Lord's eyes to see people's hearts. Then
compassion will compel us to reach out. People need to know
that they are loved unconditionally. They need to understand that
God has a purpose for their lives. They need to realize that God
can guide them along life's journey. They need the hope of eternal
life and the assurance of a heavenly home. Putting it simply,
people need the Lord.

We are all sheep in need of the Good Shepherd. Live your
life before others with authenticity and humility. Allow them to
see God's peace in times of trials, the Father's comfort in times of
grief, the Savior's hope in times of uncertainty. Be real so you can
point others to Christ. Reach out and introduce someone to the
Good Shepherd.

*Dear Lord, open my eyes to see the lost sheep around me. May I be used to
introduce them to You, the Good Shepherd. Amen.*

KNOW YOURSELF

Bow down Your ear, O LORD, hear me; for I am poor and needy.
PSALM 86:1 NKJV

"Poor and needy" is not a phrase we use to describe ourselves. In fact, it is the last thing we would want said about us. We'd never find it on the pages of a self-help book or hear it from talk-show gurus. Daily we try to watch what we eat, get our exercise, and count on our talents, skills, and experience to secure our future. Though Philippians 3:3 tells us to put no confidence in our own human effort, we rely on ourselves every day.

Proverbs 29:23 (NKJV) says, "A man's pride will bring him low, but the humble in spirit will retain honor." How do we retain a humble spirit when the world is constantly telling us how great it is to be self-reliant?

One way is to acknowledge our poverty and neediness before our heavenly Father. We need Him, and we need Him to hear us. Regardless of what we accomplish in the world through our own efforts, ultimately all we have and each breath we draw is a gift from God. Take comfort in knowing that His sustaining power in our lives is all we need.

Heavenly Father, help me to remember who I am before You.
Enable me to see myself as You see me, and keep me
mindful of my constant dependence on You.

HAVING IT ALL

When the woman saw that the fruit of the tree was good
for food and pleasing to the eye, and also desirable for gaining
wisdom, she took some and ate it.

GENESIS 3:6 NIV

It wasn't called Paradise for nothing. Eve had it all. A secure home. Beautiful surroundings. Peace. An attentive man who longed for her companionship. Freedom to roam the garden and eat anything her heart desired. However, in spite of having the resources to fulfill all of her wants and needs, there was a nagging place of longing in Eve's soul. Satan saw this vulnerability and took advantage of the opportunity.

Of all the things Satan could have tempted Eve with, he chose food. While the fruit can be a metaphor for many things that might cause us to sin, it's interesting that he chose food. Eve was not physically hungry. She had plenty to eat. She was drawn to the fruit because it looked beautiful. She was drawn to it because she thought it might make her like God.

We sin for the same reasons. Like Eve, every time we exchange long-term fellowship with God for the short-term reward of a pleasurable (but sinful) experience, we are saying that something is better suited to meet our needs than God Himself. That's a lot of pressure to put on a person, place, or thing.

Don't be afraid of that longing in your soul. Identify and acknowledge it. Then realize that nothing on earth can satisfy it except God.

Father, You are enough. Help me to be satisfied with You alone. Amen.

WHAT DO YOU LONG FOR?

*"What good would it do to get everything you want and lose you,
the real you? What could you ever trade your soul for?"*
MARK 8:36–37 MSG

What do you long for? Is it financial freedom or more vacation time? Do you long to be married? Maybe you want to own your own home or to start a business.

More importantly, what are you willing to do to get what you long for? Some people will go to extremes to achieve their dreams. Sometime people lose their common sense as they chase after their desires: Anorexics give up their health in order to be thin. Sex addicts sacrifice their dignity—and much more—as they go after what they believe will fulfill them. Some women change their personalities to please men.

But as children of God, we are to trust in God's timing and His plan. We might plan and take steps to achieve our goals, but we shouldn't run ahead of God's leadership. And we should always filter our longings through the Word of God and the counsel of mature Christians.

If the thing you long for isn't happening, ask God what He wants to teach you through the waiting. Ask Him to show you how to grow and mature in your faith during this time.

*Lord, help me to want You more than I want anything else. And teach me
never to trade my soul for something temporary.*

Honest Work

Hard and honest work earns a good night's sleep, whether supper is beans or steak. But a rich man's belly gives him insomnia.
ECCLESIASTES 5:12 MSG

There's nothing like dropping into bed at the end of a long day. Sleep is precious when you've earned it. And we women certainly earn it!

We're called to give an honest day's work. Oh, it would be great to think we could work shorter hours and make more money. And maybe for some that will happen. But what would be the point of lollygagging all day and having all of your needs met without any work involved? Sure, we all need a day off every now and again, and God is pretty clear about taking a Sabbath rest. Concerning our workdays, though, He's got a different plan. We're called to give our very best.

Maybe you won't be having steak for dinner tonight. Maybe it'll be beans, instead. So what? If you've given your best, worked your hardest, and can settle into bed at night with a contented heart, what difference does it make? A hard day's work will earn you a great night's sleep. So, work hard and catch some great *Z*s after!

Lord, thank You for making me a hard worker. I give my days and nights to You. Thank You for the reminder that I'm already rich, regardless of my financial situation.

It's All Him

"For in him we live and move and have our being."
ACTS 17:28 NIV

It's our human nature to want to be self-reliant. After all, even as toddlers we're praised as being a "big girl" for feeding ourselves, picking up toys, and selecting our own outfits.

Just like so many other things in God's kingdom, His view of self-sufficiency is the exact opposite of the world's take on it. *"Rely on me,"* He tells us. *"You can't make it through this life alone, and I don't want you to do it on your own. Let me take care of you."*

The Bible tells us that when we become a part of God's family, our lives are no longer our own—we are bought with the blood of Jesus (1 Corinthians 6:20). Our independent nature may resist this notion, but in reality, letting God take control gives us the freedom we're looking for that we don't get when we try to rely on ourselves.

Problems? Give them to the One who bought you. Persecuted? Let Him deal with it. Lonely? Run to Him for the comfort you need. Living life inside the love of God has amazing benefits! Give up your need for independence and control and let Him do great things in the life you share with Him.

Father, teach me new ways to depend on You. My heart knows that You are waiting to bless me in immeasurable ways if only I trust in You. Take my life—all of it—and use it for Your great and perfect plan.

MARY'S STORY

When Jesus rose early on the first day of the week, he appeared first to Mary Magdalene, out of whom he had driven seven demons.
MARK 16:9 NIV

Mary Magdalene was once was filled with demons—seven, to be exact. This woman knew great affliction, confusion, and grief. To go to bed each night and to rise again each morning with strong demonic forces at work within her spirit must have been a miserable existence.

Then Mary of Magdala met Jesus of Nazareth, the One called the Messiah. He drove out the demons that had ruled her life, and she was never the same again. She became a part of Christ's inner circle of supporters. Mary Magdalene was a witness at His crucifixion and His burial. She saw the empty tomb, and she was the first person the risen Lord appeared to after His resurrection.

Perhaps you think your salvation story is not as exciting as Mary's. You walked an aisle at church in second grade and accepted Christ. You met Jesus at a Christian camp or through a relative. But truly, *every* story of salvation is exciting! However and whenever Jesus saved you, your story is powerful. Never think it less meaningful than another's. Our testimonies are meant to be told!

Do you know Jesus? If so, will you be a modern-day Mary? The world needs sold-out believers in Jesus. The world needs to know about the Messiah. Don't keep Him a secret.

Father, give me courage to share my testimony with someone who needs to know You. Amen.

BLOOM WHERE
YOU'RE PLANTED

Then Joseph said to them, "Do not interpretations belong to God?
Tell me your dreams."
GENESIS 40:8 NIV

From the time she was a little girl, Rochelle knew she wanted to be a teacher. She dreamed about interacting with students, investing in their lives, and making a big difference in the world. Yet receiving her teaching certificate didn't automatically lead to a teaching position. Weeks turned into months but still no job materialized.

Just when Rochelle thought things couldn't get any worse, circumstances forced her to move back into her childhood home to take care of her seriously ill mother. Although she was glad to help, Rochelle found herself becoming increasingly resentful.

Everything changed one afternoon when a neighbor called on Rochelle to tutor her son, who struggled in math. Years later, Rochelle was living out her dream in her hometown, providing tutoring and mentoring services for children from low-income families.

What is your dream? Don't wait for circumstances to change. Make a choice today to bloom right where you're planted.

Father, help me to bloom where I am planted, in spite of my circumstances.
Help me to accomplish Your dreams for me. Amen.

STRENGTH IN WEAKNESS

*For thus said the Lord G*OD*, the Holy One of Israel, "In returning and rest*
you shall be saved; in quietness and in trust shall be your strength."
ISAIAH 30:15 ESV

Assert yourself, work hard, make progress, speak up, and believe in yourself. These are ways the world defines personal strength. But God's Word gives a paradoxical view of strength. Rest, quietness, and trust—these words all reflect a state of dependence.

Strength, at its core, is depending on God. Strength comes when we acknowledge our weakness and our need for God. When our sin overwhelms us, we repent and turn to Him for forgiveness. When we are weary of trying to earn His favor, we stop and remember that we only have to receive His grace. In solitude, we hear Him speak and we learn to pray. In getting to the end of our self-reliance, we trust Him for our needs. When we are willing to be emptied of self, then He can fill us with His life. 2 Corinthians 12:9 (NKJV) says, "And He said to me, 'My grace is sufficient for you, for My strength is made perfect in weakness.' Therefore most gladly I will rather boast in my infirmities, that the power of Christ may rest upon me."

What are the areas of your life where you need to depend more on God?

Father, remind me today that You are not asking me to be strong,
but to depend on You. In my weakness, You will be strong.
Help me to return, rest, listen, and trust.

LEAVE NO TRACE

Whoever sows sparingly will also reap sparingly, and whoever sows generously will also reap generously.
2 CORINTHIANS 9:6 NIV

When you enter any state or national park, you will notice a recurring sign posted with a plea to hikers, climbers, campers, bicyclers, and horseback riders to leave no trace of their passing— no trash, no damaged vegetation, no fire rings, and so on. Where park visitors pass is to remain just as it was before—as if humans had never been there.

In our Christian lives, the "leave no trace" rule goes against all that Christ taught His disciples to do. The Christian's calling is to leave an imprint on all the lives we touch, sharing our relationship with Jesus through our words and actions.

There are unbelievers who have tried—and continue to try— to enforce a "no trace" rule upon Christians, because they know the power of the gospel to change lives—even turn the political will of a whole country. But truth cannot be stopped.

The nature of Christianity is to bring others to a saving knowledge of Christ, sowing seeds of truth wherever we can. If a Christian passed through life without leaving a trace of their presence, then their life would be a tragic waste indeed.

Dear Lord, I want to mark trails that will lead others to the wonder of knowing You as Savior and friend. Help me not to waste my life in fear of telling others about You.

THE MORNING SUN

The sun comes out like a bridegroom from his bedroom.
It rejoices like an athlete eager to run a race.
PSALM 19:5 NCV

Are you a morning person? Do you spring out of bed with a smile on your face, ready to face the day ahead? Are you ready to run the race? To rejoice in unseen victories? To head to your workplace with a spring in your step and an enthusiastic heart?

If you don't "do mornings," you might want to memorize today's verse. It's a great reminder that each rising sun is a blessing from God. It's a new opportunity to accomplish great things for the Lord and to watch Him work. And the heavenly Father paints a beautiful picture—likening the sun to a bridegroom emerging from the inner sanctum. His personal time with his bride gives him the ability to face each new day. In fact, he rejoices like an athlete!

Today, spend some time in the inner sanctum with your Lord, and watch Him energize you for the day ahead. You'll be amazed at the joy and strength that rise up as you head off to your workplace. And surely that joy will spill over onto all you meet.

Lord, I thank You that each new morning is a new opportunity to do great things for You. I'm excited and blessed for every sunrise and grateful that You've given me this race to run.

Only God

"You intended to harm me, but God intended it for good."
Genesis 50:20 NIV

It was a dark part of her past, but Dana considered it to be essential to her testimony. When she was twelve she was abused by her soccer coach, a man that her overworked single mother depended on to give Dana rides to and from practice several times each week. Dana made the courageous decision to tell her mother, and together they saw to it that her abuser was brought to justice.

With the love and support of her mother and lots of counseling, Dana eventually was able to work through her feelings of betrayal and brokenness. Today she is a successful and confident young woman who ministers to girls in vulnerable situations with the hope that she can help protect them from similar types of abuse. When Dana shares her testimony, she always ends with this verse spoken by Joseph to his brothers, "You intended to harm me, but God intended it for good."

Many women can identify with Dana's story. Abuse has far-reaching consequences, but healing and redemption are available for those who seek it. Only God can take the most hurtful circumstances of our lives and weave them into His plan for us. There is no question that Satan's only goal is to harm. However, when we yield ourselves to God's purposes, even Satan's most blatant attacks can turn into joyous victories.

Father, take my pain and redeem it. Use it for Your glory. Amen.

PEACEFUL SLEEP

In peace I will both lie down and sleep, for You alone,
O LORD, make me to dwell in safety.
PSALM 4:8 NASB

Do you have trouble sleeping? Do you lie awake thinking, worrying about your future, or doubting your decisions? If this sounds familiar, you are normal. Welcome to the club! At some points in our lives, most women struggle with not being able to get to sleep at night.

The days are so hectic that often by the time you collapse into bed, your mind probably has not had time to settle down. It is still going a hundred miles an hour. Try reading the Psalms when you get into bed. Fill your mind and heart with God's Word. His Word will calm those worries that loop through your mind like a hamster on its wheel.

The Lord will bring you peaceful sleep. Say aloud to Him, "God, I know that I am safe with You. Give me a good night's sleep." He wants His precious daughter to rest in His care.

Lord, remind me to read the Bible before I go to bed at night so that the last thoughts of the day are Your promises. Amen.

THE GREATEST IS LOVE

And now these three remain: faith, hope and love.
But the greatest of these is love.
1 CORINTHIANS 13:13 NIV

Faith. . .hope. . .love. Without faith, it's impossible to please God. The truth is, it's often hard to look beyond our current circumstances and believe that all will turn out well. There are times our faith will be tested and tried. During these times, it's important to know what God's Word says about faith: "Now faith is the substance of things hoped for, the evidence of things not seen" (Hebrews 11:1 KJV).

Then there's hope. Are you hoping for something you're still waiting for? Remember, your hope is found in Jesus. He's your hope for a life full of happiness and love. He's your hope for a victorious life and, most important, your hope for an eternal future.

You may encounter times in life when your faith runs low. You may even feel you have no hope. But always know that nothing can ever separate you from the almighty love of God. His Word says that faith, hope, and love all remain, but the greatest of these is definitely God's love.

Dear God, help me to always share that same unconditional
love that You give me with others. Amen.

FINDING TIME TO COMMUNE WITH GOD

[Your words] will always be my most prized possession
and my source of joy.
PSALM 119:111 CEV

Do you want to spend time with God but wonder how to fit it into your day? Ask God to give you creative ideas on ways to cultivate an intimate relationship with Him.

Linda lights a candle that reminds her to pray whenever she sees the flame. Elizabeth sets her PDA to beep when she needs to pray about a friend's doctor's appointment or other time-related prayer request. Brenda listens to Bible verses set to music.

Other ideas: Sign up for e-mail prayer newsletters for your favorite ministries and pray over them before you check your personal e-mail. Keep a Bible and devotional book in your purse so you can pray and study while waiting on appointments. Or write requests and Bible verses on index cards and tape them on your mirror and review them while you primp for the day. Why not pray while exercising, walking the dog, or performing other mundane tasks? And you could listen to audio devotionals and the Bible on CD while driving.

Above all, know that God desires for you to desire Him. If you ask Him to, He will help you create time for the things that will bring you closer to His heart.

Father God, I love Your Word. Help me to make it a priority,
so we can get to know one another better.

WORK FOR THE LORD

Whatever you do, work at it with all your heart, as working for the Lord,
not for men, since you know that you will receive an inheritance from the
Lord as a reward. It is the Lord Christ you are serving.
COLOSSIANS 3:23–24 NIV

An elementary school teacher gave her class the following assignment: Draw a picture of what you want to be when you grow up. Emily drew a picture of herself sitting in a lounge chair on the beach. When asked to explain, she responded, "When I grow up, I want to be *retired*!"

Retirement is a coveted goal in our society. A career of hard work is rewarded by a life of ease. But is that really what we learn from heroes of the faith? Moses didn't ride off into the sunset after he'd led the Israelites out of Egypt, and the apostle Paul didn't stop preaching after a certain number of people became Christians. Why not? Moses and Paul knew whom they were working for. The Boss kept giving them new assignments, and they continued to be obedient. Their real employer was the Lord.

Whether we're employed or retired, we never stop working for the Lord. Since He is our ultimate boss, we serve Him in our jobs, homes, and communities. Work with all your heart, giving the Lord 100 percent. The Lord promises to reward you. Someday He'll say to you, *"Well done, my good and faithful servant!"*

Dear Lord, my life is Yours. Use my time, talents, and efforts as You desire.
May I serve You with all my heart. Amen.

RED AS CRIMSON

"Come now, let us reason together," says the LORD. "Though your sins are like scarlet, they shall be as white as snow; though they are red as crimson, they shall be like wool."
ISAIAH 1:18 NIV

A woman entered a relationship with a Christian man with the best of intentions. She never dreamed she would ever compromise herself in any way, but by the time the relationship ended, she'd stumbled in a major way. She couldn't forgive herself. Though she never admitted it to anyone other than herself, she secretly struggled with shame.

Have you ever walked in this woman's shoes? Found yourself falling. . .not just away from God, but away from the standards you felt certain were unshakable in your life? Did you struggle to forgive yourself after the fact?

It's often easier to forgive others for the things they've done to us than to forgive ourselves when we mess up. Thankfully, God stands ready to forgive. Today, if you have unconfessed sin in your life, take it to the One who longs to reason it out with you. Confess. . .and watch as those sins are washed whiter than snow. Then observe how your loving heavenly Father teaches you to forgive yourself.

Lord, I come to You today, desperate for a clean slate. My sins are red as crimson, but today I ask that You wash me clean. Forgive me, Father, then teach me to forgive myself.

CHOSEN FIRST

"I have chosen you," declares the LORD Almighty.
HAGGAI 2:23 NIV

Lydia felt like she was back in grade school, waiting for one of the team captains to choose her for their kickball team. Who knew that job hunting was going to be such a blow to her self-esteem? Silence from some potential employers coupled with immediate rejections from others left her discouraged and deflated.

Have you ever felt this way about a situation in your life? Whether it's a job hunt, a potential job promotion, a relationship, or something else, it's hard to deal with feeling like we're being overlooked or picked last.

God, in His loving plan, guaranteed your place in His family by picking you—first! Before you accepted His gift of grace, before you knew who God is, even before you were conceived, He chose you. He chose you, not as a nameless individual in a sea of faces, but as the person you uniquely are to Him. He loves you that much.

No position or promotion or relationship is as important as being handpicked by God for His team. Today, thank Him that He doesn't make us stand on the baseline kicking dust until He decides we're worthy enough to be on His team. And then get out there and play like you are the first pick that you are!

God, You know what it feels like to be rejected—to be overlooked.
Thank You for choosing me, even though I am unworthy of such an honor.
Help me to show Your love to others.

MEET THE MAN

"Come, see a Man who told me all things that I ever did."
JOHN 4:29 NKJV

After a long relationship, the couple broke up. Months passed and the young woman met another man. They began to date, but it soon became apparent they weren't a good match. Devastated at another loss, the young woman dropped to her pillow in tears. She was wounded and weary—and longed to know His plan.

Because we're human, we often make decisions that aren't necessarily what God intends for us. We get into situations that leave us wounded. And those wounds can't be healed by another person. They can only be healed by God.

The woman at the well learned her life choices had not benefited her. She called to her friends to come and meet the Man who knew her inside out, and she made a decision to ask Him to fill the void in her heart.

When life leaves us scarred, God gives us the strength to continue. He longs for us to lift our arms in surrender and listen for Him to speak. It takes patience and resolve, but when we give up, He gives. We should take a moment and listen. Meet the Man who will bind up our broken hearts.

Dear Jesus, how I need You. Be with me now. I choose this day to surrender to Your will. Amen.

PROFESSING THE
POWER OF PRAYER

I will meditate on all your works and consider all your mighty deeds.
PSALM 77:12 NIV

Often when we are faced with difficult situations, we ask close friends to pray for us. If we face a challenging situation at work, we ask people in our Bible study to pray about it. If we are confronting an illness, we ask church leaders to pray for our healing. If we are struggling with a personal or spiritual issue, we ask a trusted prayer partner to pray and hold us accountable for our actions. Asking others to join us in praying about tough situations demonstrates that we believe that God is faithful in answering prayers.

We also encourage people to believe in God's faithfulness when we report back on how He has met our needs. It encourages those who are facing a challenging work situation when we tell them how God set things right at work for us. When a friend is sick, we can encourage her by testifying to an instance when God healed us. If we know someone who is weighed down with a personal or spiritual issue, we can tell them how God delivered us in a time of need.

Asking for prayer and proclaiming God's faithful responses are essential ways in which we glorify Him and encourage each other.

Dear Lord, I praise You for the amazing works that You do. Bring to my mind specific great works so I can focus on glorifying You for them. Amen.

PLANNING
FOR THE FUTURE

Why, you do not even know what will happen tomorrow.
What is your life? You are a mist that appears for a little while
and then vanishes. Instead, you ought to say, "If it is the Lord's
will, we will live and do this or that."

JAMES 4:14–15 NIV

It's hard not to look into the future and try to map out where
life will take you. Someone once said to go ahead and break out
the fine china instead of living with a paper-plate mentality! In
other words, don't wait for a special occasion or for your knight
in shining armor to appear. Experience life to the fullest each day
you are given.

It's natural to plan for the future, to imagine that special
relationship with a man that you hope will come along. God
knows the desires of your heart, and He is always interested in
blessing you with the very best. It can be dangerous to our hearts,
however, to plot out our future without giving heed to God's
Word.

James 4 warns us that we don't know how long this life will
last. When we make our plans, we should remember that our
sovereign God holds each day in His hands. Plan and pray within
His will.

Father, remind me that You are sovereign. Teach me to remember You as I
make plans. I want Your will above all else. Amen.

YOUR SONG OF PRAISE

"I will sing to the LORD, for he is highly exalted."
EXODUS 15:1 NIV

Throughout scripture, God's people composed songs of praise. In Exodus 15, Moses and his sister Miriam sang an anthem of praise when God delivered the Israelites from slavery. David composed many joyful psalms of triumph when God spared his life and gave him victory over his enemies. In 1 Samuel 2 Hannah responded in praise when God answered her earnest pleas for a son. And as she waited for the Messiah to be born, Mary's song was one of simple and poetic beauty (Luke 1:46–55).

What has God done for you today? In the past week? Month? Year? Take a moment and list some of the miracles He has worked in your life. Choose one of the songs of praise in scripture, write it out, and tailor it to your own life. Or if you are feeling creative, try composing your own song of praise and add it to the songs of believers from every generation.

My heart is steadfast, O God; I will sing and make music with all my soul. Awake, harp and lyre! I will awaken the dawn. I will praise You, O LORD, among the nations; I will sing of you among the peoples. For great is your love, higher than the heavens; your faithfulness reaches to the skies. Be exalted, O God, above the heavens, and let your glory be over all the earth (PSALM 108:1–5 NIV).

A Song in the Night

By day the LORD directs his love, at night his song is with me—
a prayer to the God of my life.
PSALM 42:8 NIV

Have you ever thought of your life as being like a symphony? There are some high highs and some low lows. There are crescendo moments—where everything seems to fall into place, and there are some pianissimo moments, where things draw to a quiet stillness. And in the midst of it all, there is the Conductor, standing with baton in hand, directing. He calls the shots. He tells the musicians when to play furiously and when to slow to a halt.

God is the director of your life. During the daytime—when most of the major decisions of life are made—He's there, leading you, guiding you. And at night, when His direction might not be as clear, His song plays over you.

Today, begin to see your life as a symphony with many movements. Allow the Lord—your Conductor—to lead you through the highs and lows, the crescendo moments and the pianissimo ones, as well. Then when night shadows fall, listen closely for the song He's playing over you.

Oh, Father! I can almost hear the music now. Thank You for the reminder that my life is a symphony and You are the Conductor. I don't want to carry the baton, Lord. I willingly remove it from my hands. Direct me in the daytime and sing Your song over me at night.

According to His Will

*This is the confidence which we have before Him, that, if we ask
anything according to His will, He hears us. And if we know that
He hears us in whatever we ask, we know that we have the
requests which we have asked from Him.*

1 John 5:14–15 nasb

The setting: a grocery store. The actors: one child and one
wise (but flustered) parent. The audience: customers at the
checkout lane, along with the cashier.

"Mommy, can I get some candy?"

"No, honey, you have some candy at home."

"But I want that kind of candy."

"We are not buying candy right now."

"Why? Pleeeeeease!"

"You don't need that much candy. It's not good for you."

We applaud the rare parents that stand their ground,
dooming their child to a healthy dinner and an appropriate
amount of sugar.

We come before God in much the same way. We pray for
blessings that we desire. God will always provide for us, but like
the parent that withholds candy from a child, God knows best.

Pray believing that God will provide for your requests.
Always remember, however, to pray in His will. He will not give
you what is not best for you.

*Help me, O Lord, to pray in Your will. I know that
You know what is best for me. Amen.*

STRONG TOWER

The name of the LORD is a strong tower; the righteous runs
into it and is safe.
PROVERBS 18:10 NASB

I want to go home," the little girl said, tugging at her mother's skirt in the department store. She knew that this big store, even with all its glamour, was not her *home*. Home is safe. Home is where we want to go when the world seems too big and frightening to face.

We read in Proverbs that the name of the Lord is safe. His name is like a home for His children. It is a haven, a strong tower into which we can run. But how do we do this? We claim His promises, read His Word, and pray. Sometimes, when we are too weak even to do these things, we simply speak His name. The Bible says there is power in the name of the Lord. Just speaking His name and giving Him praise in the midst of our circumstances will bring strength.

Call upon the name of the Lord. Run into the strong tower. There is safety there. He wants to be your protector from the pressures of this big world.

Lord, show Yourself to me. Give me wisdom to call upon
Your name when I am weak. Amen.

A PICTURE OF GOD

*For we do not have a high priest who is unable to sympathize with our
weaknesses, but we have one who has been tempted in every way,
just as we are—yet was without sin.*
HEBREWS 4:15 NIV

Beth was raised in a strict home. There were many rules to
follow and harsh consequences for breaking those rules. As a
result, Beth grew as an adult to have a distant relationship with
her parents.

Our parents provide an early template for our understanding of
God. For those raised in loving and affectionate homes, the picture
of God is one of love and security. But those who were raised in
less-than-ideal environments have a more difficult time conceiving
of a God who loves unconditionally. Thankfully, scripture paints a
far more accurate picture of God than we can produce on our own.
The Bible is filled with stories that illustrate God's character and His
unconditional, boundless love for His children.

What does your picture of God look like? Is your template
in line with what scripture says about Him? If you aren't sure,
examine what God's Word says about His character. Take notice
of how He interacts and communicates with biblical characters.
Ask Him to open your heart and your eyes so that you can see
Him for who He really is.

*Father, I confess that at times my picture of You is distorted.
I pray that You would reveal Yourself to me in a fresh way
so that I see You for who You are. Amen.*

GOD LONGS FOR YOU

Return to the LORD your God, for he is gracious and compassionate, slow to anger and abounding in love, and he relents from sending calamity.
JOEL 2:13 NIV

Felicia had spent a lifetime running from God. When she was twelve, she accepted Christ at a church camp, and she had spent two years involved in a youth group. But then she started dating a guy who despised religion, and she promptly stopped attending church and reading her Bible.

Decades—and many heartaches—later, she longed to return to God, but felt unsure. *How in the world could I approach Him?* she wondered.

Then she visited a church close to her house, and the pastor preached on the prodigal son. "God misses you and longs for you to come back to Him," he said.

Hearing that, Felicia cried, and at the end of the service, she went forward to the altar to pray for forgiveness.

Have you wandered from the Father? If you've spent time away from prayer and Bible study, or if you've wandered into sin, you may feel God is angry with you. And yes, God despises sin, but He *always* loves you. Don't believe the lie that He doesn't want you back.

Ask God to forgive you for wandering, and run to Him. He will be waiting with open arms.

Lord, I praise You for Your compassion and grace.
Thank You for being slow to anger and abounding in love.

PRAISE ANOTHER,
NOT YOURSELF

Let another praise you, and not your own mouth;
a stranger, and not your own lips.
PROVERBS 27:2 NASB

Sometimes when we women feel insecure, we try to make ourselves look good in a group. We may do this by spending too much money on name-brand clothing either to fit in or stand out as something special. We may attempt to lift ourselves up by boasting. We may drop names of important people into the conversation as if our association with them makes us better than others. We may tell of our accomplishments at work or even make mention of our good deeds in the community.

The Bible instructs us to find our worth in the knowledge that we are daughters of the King. We do not need to lift ourselves up by speaking highly of our works. In fact, in Proverbs, we are told not to praise ourselves with our own mouths.

Instead, find an opportunity to praise another person today. If there is a particular character trait that stands out to you in his or her life, acknowledge it verbally. You will find that in lifting others up, your heart is much more at peace than when you seek to elevate yourself.

God, show me someone today that I may honor. Remind me that I should not seek to bring attention to myself for my good deeds but should do them for Your glory alone. Amen.

A Saving Faith

And he said to the woman, Thy faith hath saved thee; go in peace.
Luke 7:50 kjv

Today's verse comes at the tail end of a remarkable story about a woman—a sinner—who washed Jesus' feet with her tears. In fact, she was so overcome with joy that she couldn't stop the unplanned praise service that took place at His feet. Instead of pronouncing her a sinner, Jesus said, "Thy faith hath saved thee; go in peace."

Have you ever been afraid to approach God because of your sinful condition? Ever feel like your faith just floated out the window? He longs for you to come to Him, even at your very lowest point, and pour yourself out at His feet. Let every problem, every sin, tumble forth. Then watch as your faith is restored. . .not faith in yourself or your deeds, not even faith in your ability to worship your way through life's problems, but faith in Him.

Today, run to Jesus with whatever problems you're carrying. Lay them at His feet. Then, while you're down there, spend some time pouring yourself out to Him in worship. Let your joy spur you on. In that place—on your knees—your faith will grow like a wildflower.

Dear Lord, my faith often seems so small. But today I'm running to You. I'm washing Your feet with my tears. And in that precious place, I ask You to restore and renew my faith.

CRAVINGS

*I decide to do good, but I don't really do it; I decide not to do bad,
but then I do it anyway. My decisions, such as they are, don't
result in actions. Something has gone wrong deep within me
and gets the better of me every time.*

ROMANS 7:18–20 MSG

We women love our chocolate. Maybe if we consumed it
only in pure cocoa form it would be good for us, but most of
us love it with sugar and fat added and could eat it every day.
Of course, our taste buds also may like broccoli, but unlike
chocolate, we prefer it in small doses.

You might find yourself feasting daily on fears, worries,
jealousies, and stress—the fat-laden chocolate of life. And just as
we know we should eat good foods like broccoli, we know love,
forgiveness, patience, and self-control are good for us, but most
of us struggle to consume enough of them to keep our spiritual
life healthy.

What we need is discipline in our spiritual (and physical)
diet, but we can't do it on our own. We need God's power to help
us crave those things that are the healthiest. Through prayer and
biblical guidance, it is possible to change our taste buds to want
the things that are the best for our bodies and souls.

*Lord, help me to feed my body and soul the things that will keep me most
healthy and useful to You. Help me to crave the things that are best for me.*

Plotting or Praying

Why do the nations conspire and the peoples plot in vain?
PSALM 2:1 NIV

Think for a minute about the intricacies of the human body. Consider all the involuntary functions the brain tells our bodies to carry on while we are conscious of only a few they are doing, like holding this book or reading this page.

Consider the many patterns and colors of nature and the cycles in which they occur. What about the complexity and beauty of various kinds of music and the ear that can hear it? Recall the myriad number of creatures and plants that live in the ocean. The Creator who made it is beyond our imagination. He is also beyond our control.

Why do we try to make our path without the all-powerful Creator God who does all things magnificently? Jeremiah 29:11 reminds us that God knows the plans He has for us, to give us a future and a hope. Wouldn't it be wiser to pray instead of plot?

Why not ask God what His plans are for your life? He knows the future, and He will lovingly lead you there. Pray first before planning. Ask Him. He will show you the way. With bowed head and bended knee, worship this One who spoke the world into being. And ask Him what plans you should make.

Father, You made the world and all that is in it. You are the author of past, present, and future. Forgive me for wasting much time in vain plotting. Show me the plans You have for me.

Fight the Good Fight

I have fought the good fight, I have finished the race, I have kept the faith.
2 Timothy 4:7 niv

After his conversion on the road to Damascus, the apostle Paul was irrevocably committed to the Lord. His single purpose in life was to be a living testimony for Christ. He was intensely focused and passionately dedicated to sharing the gospel. Whatever it took, he was willing to give, even if it meant hardships and suffering.

Will we be able to say the same as we look back on our lives? The Christian life is a daily spiritual battle. Take captive every thought and make it obedient to God's truth. Run the race with perseverance in the strength that God can give. Don't give up when the road is difficult. Keep your eyes on Jesus.

Paul's reward was a crown of righteousness given to him by the Lord. We can hope for the same. Keep focused and determined. God doesn't promise smooth sailing through life, but He does promise to be with us every step of the way. Let's run past the finish line of life's race as we fall into the arms of Jesus.

Dear Lord, help me persevere in my Christian walk.
May I be used by You for eternal purposes. Amen.

CREATIVITY

Huram was highly skilled and experienced in all kinds of bronze work. He came to King Solomon and did all the work assigned to him.

1 KINGS 7:14 NIV

Imagine Huram working quietly in his metal shop late one afternoon. So intent is he on his latest project that he doesn't notice the king's messenger waiting to talk to him.

"Huram?" the man asks. "The king wants to see you."

Huram is confused. "Me? What on earth could he possibly want with me?" Huram must have wondered how an ordinary guy like him could be used in such an extraordinary way.

We see creativity throughout scripture. David wrote songs, Abraham built altars. The Israelites used their gifts of metalworking, sewing, and woodworking to build the Ark of the Covenant and God's temple.

God delights in creating and in watching His children create with the gifts and abilities He has given them. What gifts, skills, and abilities has God given *you*? How can you use these things to honor Him?

Whether it's compiling and editing a newsletter for a local ministry, painting the walls of a Sunday school room, making meals for shut-ins, or sewing blankets for needy children, every gift and ability counts. Each time you find an opportunity to use your God-given talents and abilities, think about Huram and what an honor it is for ordinary people to serve God in extraordinary ways.

Father, help me to use my unique gifts and abilities to serve You. Amen.

REDEMPTION

*Praise the LORD, O my soul, and forget not all his benefits. . .who redeems
your life from the pit and crowns you with love and compassion.*
PSALM 103:2, 4 NIV

You were in a pit. Not just clinging to the side, climbing your
way out, almost to the top. You were deep down in the darkness
of a pit with no escape route, no way out.

Whether you came to know Jesus at age nine or eighty-nine,
you were not any closer to being able to save yourself. If your sins
were many or few, it made no difference before a holy God. You
were a sinner.

You needed a redeemer, a rescuer. You were desperate and
doomed. You may have appeared to be alive, but in reality you
were dead. Your soul was in darkness, longing for light. Your
spirit was empty, longing to be filled.

And then you saw Him. You may have heard His name
before, but it was nothing more than a name. You may have seen
the cross, but it was just a symbol. This time was different. You
realized you were lost without Him. You saw your situation for
what it was. You were in a pit. You were stuck. You called out His
name. "Jesus!"

Christ came down into the pit and lifted you up in His arms
out of the muck and mire of disbelief. You were helpless, unable
to save yourself. And then, simply by asking, by calling out for
help, You were saved. He redeemed your life.

*Jesus, You lowered Yourself unto death to redeem my soul.
May I never forget. Amen.*

A Vow of Friendship

And Jonathan made David reaffirm his vow of friendship again,
for Jonathan loved David as he loved himself.
1 Samuel 20:17 nlt

The friendship between Jonathan and David was pretty remarkable. From the moment Jonathan met David, he knew he had a friend who was a real keeper. Thanks to King Saul, Jonathan's evil father, the friendship was severely challenged. Still, in the very midst of the turmoil, Jonathan and David reaffirmed their vow to keep their relationship going, no matter what.

Do you have a Jonathan in your life—a friend who's a real keeper? One you know will stick with you, even under the worst of circumstances? Has the friendship been tried by fire and is still going strong? If so, then the two of you have a very special bond! Commit that person to the Lord daily in prayer. Let her know just how much she means to you. And make up your mind not to let any problems—big or small—destroy the relationship that God has blessed you with.

Friends are a gift from God. Today, thank the Lord for the "Jonathans" in your life.

Lord, today my good friend (insert name) is on my heart and mind. Father,
I thank You for this unique and special friendship. May it truly stand the
test of time. Bless my friend today, Lord.

REJOICE AND BE GLAD!

This is the day the LORD has made; let us rejoice and be glad in it.
PSALM 118:24 NIV

Today is a day that you can live for Christ. Today you can approach the throne of the Father in prayer. It's a day that you can study His Word and grow closer to Him. Today is a day to find contentment in the work God has given you to do, to find contentment in your current situation, to find joy in simple blessings. Today you are one step closer to heaven, to eternity in the love of the almighty Savior God.

Today is a day to reach out to others in love—to share the hope you have in Jesus. It's a day full of possibility, full of new discoveries hovering just below the surface. Look for these wonders, full of the expectation that God wants to bless you today.

God made a glorious today just for us. Now it's our responsibility to rejoice in it. What's holding you back from finding gladness in the dawn of each new morning? Ask God to show you what's so great about today, and tomorrow you may just wake up with a song of praise on your lips!

Father, today is the best day—because You made it just for me.
Help me always to put my problems in perspective with a
giant dose of rejoicing in You. Amen.

PERPETUAL COMMUNICATION

Listen to my prayer, O God, do not ignore my plea; hear me and answer me. My thoughts trouble me and I am distraught.
PSALM 55:1–2 NIV

For centuries, the handwritten letter was the main source of communication between friends who were separated by miles. Waiting for a reply could take several days or weeks.

With modern technology has come a revolution in how we communicate. We can exchange our thoughts with someone on the other side of the world in just a second or two. And we've become so enamored with communication that we now send notes, pictures, and our voice over a small device we carry with us everywhere.

So what does all this perpetual communication tell us about ourselves?

We want to be heard. We want to feel that others are listening to us and care about connecting with us. And we like to do it electronically.

But we have a significance that goes far beyond electronic wavelengths. God is tuning into our every little twitter of thought and activity, and He doesn't have to power up or log in to hear us.

Lord, thank You for hearing my cries for attention.
Help me to rest in knowing that my voice has significance to
You, and teach me to listen for Your replies.

CHILDLIKE FAITH

Jesus called the children to him and said, "Let the little children come to me, and do not hinder them, for the kingdom of God belongs to such as these."
LUKE 18:16 NIV

Jesus loved children. He even taught His disciples a lesson using them as an illustration: In order to enter the kingdom of God, one must receive Him like a little child.

What is childlike faith? It's an innocent, fearless faith a child places in his mom and dad. It's a kind of pure, unsoiled trust that leaves no room for distrust or sarcasm. Childlike faith doesn't have to be accompanied by a ton of Bible knowledge. A simple "I believe Jesus is the Christ, the Son of God" is all it requires.

This is the kind of faith Christ desires in those seeking Him. Once you become a follower of Christ, you will begin to grow in faith and learn to put your complete trust in God and His Word.

Jesus loves all His children. You can always depend on Him. His arms will always be there to hold and to keep you safe. Go to Him with childlike faith, with no fear and doubts.

Dear Jesus, I'm so glad that I'm Your child. Help me to always have that childlike faith that is pleasing to You. Amen.

DISCIPLINE

*"Behold, blessed is the one whom God reproves; therefore
despise not the discipline of the Almighty."*
JOB 5:17 ESV

Maria hung up the phone with disgust. She had just had her
weekly chat with her ex-husband in preparation for his having
the kids for the weekend. "What a jerk!" Maria said for the
umpteenth time. She let out a string of cusswords.

"Mom!" yelled her youngest son, and she jumped. She hadn't
realized he had entered the room.

Bobby's shock registered on his face. "You tell me not to use
words like that, or you'll wash out my mouth with soap."

Later, she prayed and confessed her sin to God. She realized
that she had begun to let her divorce cause bitterness and rage
in her heart. That night, God revealed to her that she needed
to forgive her husband for leaving her. God also reminded her
that the unwanted trial of divorce was an opportunity to grow in
Him.

Just as a parent disciplines his children, God disciplines us.
Sometimes He hones our character by allowing challenges that
will whittle away our selfishness, pride, and self-sufficiency. Even
hardships that are caused by other people are an opportunity for
growth. He disciplines not to punish us, but because He loves us.

*Lord, thank You for loving me enough to discipline me. Help me to accept
those things You ask of me, so I can grow up in You.*

TRANSFORM
YOUR ATTITUDE

*The thief's purpose is to steal and kill and destroy. My purpose is to give
them a rich and satisfying life.*
JOHN 10:10 NLT

Susan awoke with a migraine on the day she was scheduled
to meet with her boss for her yearly evaluation. She took her
medicine, ironed her gray suit, and went to take a cold shower—
her hot water heater was on the fritz again. When she came out
of the bathroom to get dressed, she was dismayed to find that her
dog had mistaken her new gray shoes for toys. What resulted was
a left shoe with no heel and a right shoe with the toe missing.

Before anything else could happen in her day, Susan had a
choice. She could let circumstances affect her attitude negatively,
or she could choose to have a good attitude, despite the
annoyances life threw her way.

When we choose to focus on only the upsetting things
that happen, we allow our hope and joy to be stolen from us.
God wants us to choose good attitudes even when it is difficult,
because He has called us to a life full of hope and joy resulting
from our focus on His abundant goodness.

*Dear God, I praise You for giving me a life meant to be complete in You.
Help my attitude be joyful as I consider this truth. Amen.*

CHASING THE WIND

*Enjoy what you have rather than desiring what you don't have. Just
dreaming about nice things is meaningless—like chasing the wind.*
ECCLESIASTES 6:9 NLT

Modern-day women are inundated with marketing
strategies. Every time we turn on the television, we're told what
type of toothpaste we should use, what shampoo is best for our
hair, and what jeans we should buy. And magazines are loaded
with photos of the latest and greatest handbags, shoes, clothes,
and makeup. Sometimes we get in the "To be my best, I have to
have the best" mentality. We dream about all the things we wish
we had, and even sacrifice to get them.

Chasing after the latest great "thing" is like chasing the wind.
By the time you actually purchase the things you're longing for,
trends will change. The winds will shift in a different direction.

What would it profit you to gain all of the goodies and still
lose your soul? Instead of dreaming about the things we don't
have, we should be praising God for the things we do!

Lay your dreams at the Lord's feet. Think of the many ways
He has blessed you, then begin to praise Him for the things you
already have.

*Father, I'll admit I've chased after the wind at times. I see pretty, trendy
things and want them. Today, I hand over my desires to You. Thank You for
the many ways You have already provided for me, Lord.*

WAKE-UP CALL

From inside the fish Jonah prayed to the LORD his God.
JONAH 2:1 NIV

Years later Betsy is able to joke about it being her wake-up call. But at the time, open heart surgery and the subsequent recovery were not a joking matter.

For most of her life, Betsy was sedentary, ate whatever she wanted, and basically neglected her body. Even so, when doctors discovered a potentially life-threatening blockage in her artery, Betsy was shocked. Thankfully, after she recovered from the surgery, Betsy determined to drastically change her lifestyle and alter her health for the better.

Wake-up calls come in various forms, but the underlying message is that something needs to change—*now*. For Jonah, it meant spending three days in the belly of a smelly fish. Saul had to be struck blind before he would stop persecuting Christians. Balaam refused to listen to God until his donkey opened his mouth and spoke.

Some wake-up calls are more dramatic than others, but all of them are designed to get our attention. God has shown over and over again that He is not opposed to taking drastic measures to get us to look to Him. Wake-up calls are often inconvenient, sometimes painful, and always memorable. Is God trying to get your attention today? Turn and look to Him.

Father, help me to listen to You, to adjust my life to You so that a major wake-up call does not become necessary. Amen.

Resisting Envy

A heart at peace gives life to the body, but envy rots the bones.
PROVERBS 14:30 NIV

Do you remember the story of the discontented little rabbit? He told his mother every day something different that he would become when he ran away from her—a sailboat, a cloud, other animals. . .and his list went on. That restless bunny was a bit discontented in the rabbit hole, even though it was the right place for him to be. He never ran away. He just thought about it. He envied those other creatures.

We are no different. We see another woman. We admire her style, her designer clothing, and what seems to be a better life than the humdrum everydayness of our own.

The longer our gaze is on others and what they have, the more we feel that we lack. You see that coworker's luxury automobile and remember that your compact car is leaking oil again. You wish for a nice house like your friend has, but finances limit you to an apartment. You live next door to Ken and Barbie, while you have not been so lucky in love.

You begin. . .slowly. . .over time. . .with each glance. . .with each little pity party. . .to envy. And you don't know it, but in doing so, your insides are affected. Especially your heart.

Let's be honest. It is not easy to be content. Ask God to plant in your heart a sense of peace in order that you might flourish.

God, keep my eyes fixed on You and not on the things I think I need from this world. Fill my heart with contentment. Amen.

THE BRIDEGROOM

For your Maker is your husband, the LORD of hosts is his name:
and the Holy One of Israel is your Redeemer, the God of the
whole earth he is called.
ISAIAH 54:5 ESV

From the time we are little girls, we women love weddings. Though we may not realize it, our personal relationship with God is beautifully portrayed to us in every wedding we attend. The bridegroom stands at the altar waiting, ready to commit himself to the bride. He brings his body, his provision, his name, and his future. He is choosing her. He loves her. He vows to cherish her. He promises to be with her through sickness and health, for better and for worse. He takes on her problems, assumes her debts, shares her joys, and suffers her pains.

Jesus committed Himself to us when He gave His own body for our redemption. He chose to love us and make us His own. He instructs us when we pray to ask in the authority of His name. The Bible says in 2 Peter 1:3 that He has given us everything we need for life and godliness. Our future is eternal life that He promised to those who believe in Him. He has given us the Holy Spirit to be with us always, through every joy and every trial.

Meditate on this image and all that you have as the bride of Christ.

Thank You, Lord Jesus, that You cherish me and have
committed Yourself fully to me forever.

SALVATION

*But he was pierced for our transgressions, he was crushed for our iniquities;
the punishment that brought us peace was upon him, and by his wounds
we are healed. We all, like sheep, have gone astray, each of us has turned to
his own way; and the LORD has laid on him the iniquity of us all.*

ISAIAH 53:5–6 NIV

Pierced. Crushed. Punished. Wounded.

As we read these verses in Isaiah, these words appear in black
and white on a page. Not so the reality of the cross. Nails driven
through hands and feet. A Roman soldier's sword through flesh.
Sweat. Blood. A brow gouged and scraped by a crown of thorns, a
crown of mockery.

It was not a neat and poetic paragraph, as it sometimes
appears to us as we read our leather-bound Bibles. Redeeming
love was a day when the sun did not shine, when God turned His
face from Jesus. It was excruciating suffering, torture, and death.

But that is only part of the story. It was a choice, a gift,
a chance for all mankind to enter into a holy God's presence.
Because of Christ's agonizing death, we may call God our *Father*,
speak personally with the King, and one day walk the streets of
heaven.

We must remember the price Jesus paid. God placed our
sins upon His only Son. And that Son, that precious lover of our
souls, accepted the mission.

By Christ's death, we have life.

*Jesus, I am humbled. Saying "thank You" does not seem enough. May my
"thank You" be a life well lived as a witness for You. Amen.*

SHARING THE
DEEP STUFF

Gideon arrived just as a man was telling a friend his dream.
JUDGES 7:13 NIV

Do you have a special friend you can share your dreams with?
Someone who knows the real you, the person deep down inside?
If so, then you've found a real treasure.

Finding a kindred spirit is so important, especially for
women. Knowing you have someone you can trust with your
hopes, your dreams, your ideas, and your failures makes you feel
safe. And when you receive the validation of a close friend, you
also receive the courage you need to step out and do what you've
been called to do. True friends not only give us their stamp of
approval, they invigorate us.

Consider something else from today's verse. Gideon arrived
"just as" a man was telling a friend his dream. Has the Lord ever
placed a godly friend in front of you "just as" you needed her?

There is a Friend you can trust above all others—the
One who gave you those dreams in the first place. Talk about
validation! He longs for you to confide in Him and to turn to
Him with your deepest longings, as well as any hurts and pains.
And He's always there. Talk about impeccable timing!

*Lord, thank You for planting dreams in my heart, and thank You for giving
me godly friends with whom to share those dreams. Today, I praise You for
the kindred spirits in my life.*

MAKE A JOYFUL NOISE

Speak to one another with psalms, hymns and spiritual songs. Sing and make music in your heart to the Lord.
EPHESIANS 5:19 NIV

A choir director asked a new parishioner to audition for the church choir. The woman answered, "The joyful noise I make is for the Lord's ears only. He has a special filter to turn my squawks into His praise." What a true statement. The Lord does sift our faltering songs into praise.

King David crawled in caves and crevasses hiding from his enemies, yet he found time to pen many praise songs to the King of Kings. Despite his circumstances, he knew God was in control.

Paul sang in the dank darkness of a dungeon cell, praising his Creator even though life looked bleak. God's grace was extended to him as he praised despite his suffering.

How much more should we make a melody to the Lord when we are free to move about, to worship, to sing? God wants to hear music from our hearts, not arias with perfect notes. So we lift up our voices and join in the praise to our Creator and Lord. Harmonious, harsh, or hoarse, He's filtering our melodies with His love.

Dear heavenly Father, I worship You. I adore You. Thank You for Your goodness and mercy. Amen.

LORD OF THE SABBATH

Then Jesus said to them, "I ask you, which is lawful on the Sabbath:
to do good or to do evil, to save life or to destroy it?"
LUKE 6:9 NIV

As if Jesus hadn't caused enough trouble, now He was
violating the rules of the Sabbath. The Pharisees' frustration turned
to anger as they confronted Jesus with His actions. Why did He
allow His disciples to pick grain on the Sabbath? As far as healing the
man with a withered hand—it was a blatant disregard of Sabbath
rules. The Pharisees were anxious and upset about Jesus breaking the
rules, and they were anxious and upset because *He* wasn't anxious
and upset about it. Didn't Jesus understand the Law?

Jesus did understand the Law. But more importantly, He
clearly understood the principle behind the Law. The Law was
about outward actions; Jesus was about the heart. As far as the
Pharisees were concerned, outward obedience meant the Law had
been kept. They paid no attention to and made no concessions
for the attitude with which obedience was done.

Jesus, on the other hand, was far more concerned about the
heart than with outward actions. In Jesus' mind, if you were
going to do the right thing with the wrong heart, you might as
well not even bother. In Jesus' book, a clean heart is far more
important than clean hands.

Father, help me not to get caught up in rules made by men. Instead,
help me to focus on the condition of my heart, just as You do. Amen.

THE MEMORY BOX

These things I remember as I pour out my soul.
PSALM 42:4 NIV

Katie loved her grandmother more than just about anyone else on earth. She was blessed to live right around the corner from her. Katie's grandma always had time for her and never seemed to be too busy to listen, offer advice, or work side by side with her in the kitchen or garden.

When Katie was twelve, her grandmother died suddenly. One afternoon, Katie was helping her mother go through her grandmother's things. Katie stumbled upon a box with her name on it. She could hardly contain her excitement as she gingerly lifted the lid. Within the box was a collection of recipes and clippings from seed catalogs. All of them were memories of projects that Katie and her grandmother had worked on side by side, along with little notes about their time together. At the bottom of the box was a list of scriptures about heaven and the hope that Katie would indeed be reunited with her grandmother again.

God's Word is like a treasured box of memories. In it we find stories of the past to remind us of His faithfulness and His unchanging character. In it we also can find hope for the future— that there is more to life, that this is not the final chapter.

When you find yourself grieving a loss, turn to God's Word for a treasure box of thankfulness for the past and hope for the future.

Father, remind me of Your great love and faithfulness, of my future and my hope. Amen.

SOARING

But those who hope in the LORD will renew their strength.
They will soar on wings like eagles; they will run and not grow weary,
they will walk and not be faint.

ISAIAH 40:31 NIV

A runner will tell you that a good run is exhilarating. Some may jog a mile or so each morning, while others tackle marathons. No matter one's skill level or degree of stamina, every runner eventually tires. The human body simply cannot run forever in its own strength.

Are you weary? Some days you may find yourself pulled in many directions—work, family, church, and perhaps with classes or raising children. You attempt to have some sort of a social life amid all the demands. You collapse at the end of each day.

Well, put on your sneakers because Isaiah 40:31 calls you a *runner*. In fact, this verse promises that you can soar! How is that possible, you may wonder? None of the responsibilities on your plate are going anywhere, and there remain merely twenty-four hours in a day.

In your own strength, there will be no running and certainly no soaring. That's why you need Jesus. Put your hope in Him. He promises to renew your strength. Marathon runners will never attain the ability to run and not grow weary, but you can. You are God's child, and He wants to see you soar.

God, I am weary from the demands of this life. Help me to place
just a tiny bit of hope, if that is all I have today, in You.
Renew my strength. I want to soar!

CHANGE YOUR MIND

"Study this Book of Instruction continually. Meditate on it day and night so you will be sure to obey everything written in it. Only then will you prosper and succeed in all you do."
JOSHUA 1:8 NLT

Cami had always been an optimistic and cheerful individual—until her car accident. When a teenager ran a red light and hit her car, Cami's confidence was greatly shaken. She became too anxious to drive, so she sought help from a qualified Christian counselor. It took several weeks, but her counselor helped her learned practical steps for managing her anxiety, and Cami found that scripture spoke to her heart now in a way it never had prior to the accident. Gradually, as her thoughts were transformed, Cami was able to drive again, and her cheerfulness and optimism returned.

Our thoughts influence our feelings and behaviors. In fact, our bodies physically respond to the things we think about. When we think negatively about ourselves or others, we are more likely to act on those thoughts. God designed our brains this way, which explains why scripture places such a high priority on maintaining our thought life. One of the most practical tools we have for improving it is to regularly meditate on scripture and commit it to memory. This discipline will literally transform our thoughts *and* our lives.

Father, help my thoughts to be pleasing to You. Amen.

WAITING
FOR THE UNSEEN

But if we hope for that we see not, then do we with patience wait for it.
ROMANS 8:25 KJV

Remember when you were a little girl and Christmas was coming? Maybe you hoped for a particular bicycle. You knew just what it looked like and could describe it perfectly. You waited with great anticipation for something you'd actually seen with your eyes. The image was crystal clear. And because you wanted it so badly, it was worth the wait.

It's one thing to wait on something you've seen, and it's another thing to wait on something you haven't seen. It's hard to get excited for something when you don't know what it looks like. And yet there are so many wonderful unseen things in our lives—blessings we haven't experienced yet. Jobs we haven't been given. Children who haven't been born. Relationships that haven't begun. Opportunities we haven't been offered. It's exciting to think of all the great things ahead.

Maybe you've been so stuck in the problems of the past that you can't see the future through hopeful eyes. Today, ask the Lord to renew your hope. The days ahead are filled with great adventure. . .and wonderful, unknown things. Oh, if only you could catch a glimpse! Then you would realize it's worth the wait.

Lord, sometimes I wish I could see what's coming. There are so many things I have yet to see, but I'm willing to wait, Lord. And while I'm waiting, please increase my hope and my patience.

RED SEA EXPERIENCES

"The LORD will fight for you; you need only to be still."
EXODUS 14:14 NIV

The Israelites found themselves in a terrifying predicament. The Red Sea was before them and the Egyptians were bearing down from behind. There was nowhere to go—no escape—no way out. They blamed Moses and questioned his judgment. In fear and desperation they cried out to the Lord for help. The Lord promised to fight for them as they demonstrated their trust by being still.

The Israelites' plight wasn't a surprise to the Lord. In fact, God brought them to that very place for His purposes. The Israelites would have to exercise their faith and trust Him to save them. The Egyptians would be destroyed when the parted waters engulfed them. The Lord would demonstrate His power and receive glory.

Have you ever encountered a Red Sea experience? Perhaps you felt hemmed in by life's circumstances. God is not taken by surprise. He allowed you to come to this place for certain reasons. Trust in the Lord with all your heart, and Satan will be destroyed as faith displaces fear. God will receive the glory. There is nothing we face that God cannot conquer. Be still. Know that the Lord will fight for you. If God is for us, there is no one and no circumstance that can be against us.

Dear Lord, give me confidence in You when I face Red Sea trials in life. As You made a way for the Israelites, do the same for me. Amen.

This Is Your Time

"Who knows? Maybe you were made queen for just such a time as this."
Esther 4:14 MSG

To live in the center of God's will—to walk, step by step, the path He's prepared before us—is no easy task. At some point in our lives, we each wonder, *Why am I here? What did God make me to do?*

Too often we look for the big Hollywood blockbuster answer: *I will find a cure for cancer. I will solve world hunger. I will save thirty-eight children from a burning school bus.* While these things are possible, they're unlikely to happen to most of us.

Instead, God wants us to be sensitive to the opportunities He places in our lives—sometimes on a daily basis—to make a difference for His kingdom. Do you see someone who needs a good meal or just someone to talk to? Could you help out a coworker who is burdened with a heavy workload? Big or small, the choices we make to help others are just one part of the puzzle that is the meaning of life.

Like Queen Esther in the Old Testament, we need to examine our daily lives and consider. . .maybe God brought us to this very place for such a time as this.

*Father, please show me the purpose for my day today. Open
my eyes to the opportunities that You put before me to make
a difference in other peoples' lives.*

ANYTHING IS POSSIBLE

Jesus replied, "What is impossible with men is possible with God."
LUKE 18:27 NIV

Have you ever lived through what appeared to be an impossible circumstance? Maybe it was starting over after a divorce or living through the loss of a loved one or surviving a devastating disease or facing a mortgage payment when you knew the money just wasn't there.

Webster defines the word *impossible* as "not capable of being, being done, or happening." As a Christian, you should know how Jesus defines the word. According to Luke 18:27, there are things that are impossible with men. But with God on your side, there is absolutely nothing that is impossible. No matter how difficult your problem may look, always remember that God can turn impossibilities into possibilities.

Are you facing a situation that seems totally impossible? Friend, don't dwell on your problem or circumstance. Instead look only to God, who makes all things possible. Put your complete trust in Him and His Word, and remove the word *impossible* from your vocabulary.

Dear God, I know there is nothing impossible with You. I choose to put my complete trust in You and Your Word. Amen.

LIGHT

Your word is a lamp to my feet and a light to my path.
PSALM 119:105 NKJV

One night in Guatemala, two American women who were on a mission trip slept in twin beds in their hotel room. There were no streetlights or hallway lights, and the room was black as pitch.

In the middle of the night, one of the women rose from her bed to go to the restroom. In the darkness, she held her hands out in front of her to avoid running into furniture or walls. At the very same time, the other woman got out of bed to head to the restroom. The incredible darkness, along with a loud air-conditioner unit, kept her from sensing that her friend was also walking through the room. The two ran into one another, and the shock caused both women to scream uncontrollably!

Psalm 119:105 says, "Your word is a lamp to my feet and a light to my path." This is a dark world. As we make choices regarding work, entertainment, purchases, marriage, and children, we need some light! We don't want to make those decisions stumbling through the dark like the two women in their hotel room.

God tells us plainly where to find light. The answers for life's tough choices lie within the Bible. It provides the light we need in order to walk with God daily.

*Lord, give me a hunger for Your Word like I have never had.
I want Your light to guide me. Amen.*

THE WEE LITTLE MAN

"For the Son of Man came to seek and to save what was lost."
LUKE 19:10 NIV

Annette was never in the popular crowd back in high school, but she did try to be friends with just about everyone—except the cheerleaders. There was just something about those girls that screamed insincere, and she had no desire to be a part of their fake little world. So several years later, when Kathryn, a former cheerleader, began working at the same company as Annette, Annette chose not to reconnect with her high school acquaintance. The problem was, Kathryn was in the midst of a painful divorce and really could have used Annette's friendship and encouragement.

Labels are often limiting, demeaning, and inaccurate. Zacchaeus understood the pain of a label. He was a tax collector. His peers had written him off as a thief and someone who definitely could not be trusted. As a result, there were probably very few people in Zacchaeus's world who were willing tell him about the love of Jesus. Thankfully, Jesus noticed Zacchaeus, because He never put people in a box. He loved them unconditionally.

What limiting labels might you be placing on people around you? If Jesus lived in your home or worked in your office, how would He see these people? Is there a label that prevents you from connecting with someone who needs His love?

*Father, enable me to see people through Your eyes, not
through the limiting eyes of a label. Amen.*

SAY IT. . .DO IT!

When you tell God you'll do something, do it—now. God takes no pleasure in foolish gabble. Vow it, then do it. Far better not to vow in the first place than to vow and not pay up.

ECCLESIASTES 5:4–5 MSG

Have you ever known people who made promises they didn't keep? Maybe they said they would call, but didn't. Perhaps they promised a lunch together or a movie, then simply got busy and forgot. It's frustrating, isn't it? A person like that is hard to trust. And when you have to work with someone who doesn't follow through, it can be even more frustrating.

How wonderful that God never forgets His promises. If He says it, He means it. And if He means it, He does it. Talk about keeping your word! God is the very epitome of trustworthiness.

Remember that you are created in God's image, and He's all about honesty. So, pray before making commitments; then do what you've said you would do. And when the Lord speaks into your life, giving you instruction—like ministering to someone in need or spending more time in the Word—better get to it! Be a woman of your word—both to people and to the Lord.

Lord, I want to be known as a woman of my word. I want to be trustworthy. Today, remind me of the commitments I've made, then set me back on the right track to get those things done.

GOD'S COMPASSION

As a father has compassion on his children, so the LORD has compassion on those who fear him.
PSALM 103:13 NIV

What does it mean that God has compassion on us? For some women, it means that God gives strength as they battle a chronic illness. For others, it means that He has forgotten their sins, because they came to Christ from a life of deep regrets.

How do you need God to show you His compassion today? Do you need guidance for a decision? Ask Him, and He will show you what to do. Perhaps you long for a companion to talk to. He is always available. Maybe you believe that God couldn't love you, because you've strayed from Him. Remember that He is the image of the loving father who ran to His prodigal son when he returned.

Another wonderful aspect of God's compassion is that once we've experienced it, we long to share it with others. So when you feel that God has met your needs, ask Him how you can be a blessing to the people around you. Does a coworker need some encouragement? Or maybe your best friend could use some girl time. If you ask Him, God will give you fresh ideas on ministering compassion to those in your circle of influence.

Lord, I am so thankful for—and in awe of—Your compassion.
Help me spread it to everyone I know.

STRENGTH FOR
THE WEARY

He gives strength to the weary and increases the power of the weak.
ISAIAH 40:29 NIV

Stress is part of every woman's life.

Stress is like a weight on one's shoulders. The load is heavy.

There are two "W" words in Isaiah 40:29—*weary* and *weak*.
Have you felt these culprits lately?

You start out Monday morning with things under control.
By Thursday, you have drawn arrows all across your calendar,
indicating that although the task wasn't accomplished today, it
will certainly take precedence tomorrow. Another task. Another
interruption. Another arrow in your calendar. Weary and weak?
Yes, you've been there.

Ask God for extra strength this week. While you are at it, ask
yourself which tasks should be removed in order to reduce your
stress. Give yourself permission to rest. Put it on your calendar!
God desires to give you strength when you need it. Your Father
also longs to see His daughter relax, enjoy a hobby, nurture
relationships, and draw close to Him through prayer and the
reading of His Word.

*Lord, please increase my strength and guide me as
I seek to decrease my stress level. Amen.*

His Waiting, Our Waiting

Therefore the LORD waits to be gracious to you, and therefore he exalts himself to show mercy to you. For the LORD is a God of justice; blessed are all those who wait for him.

ISAIAH 30:18 ESV

Expectation is a big part of waiting. Planting and tending a garden yields a harvest. Pregnancy results in a baby.

In the same way that we eagerly await happenings in our lives, God waits expectantly for us. He desires to be gracious to us; He longs to show us mercy. He uses time as His tool. He waits for opportunities to show kindness to us. Patiently He leads us along, a shepherd with His flock, one step at a time.

As God waits for us, we also wait for Him. He is a God of goodness and justice. He loves us and He hears our cries. He will do what is right. Though we may have problems to face, He promises to be with us through our trials. He says He will never forsake us. To wait for Him is to expect Him to act, so be watchful. He will make Himself known to you. He says if we seek Him, we will find Him.

Anticipate His voice and His leading. There is blessing for us in setting our focus on Him and waiting for His work in our lives.

*Almighty God, thank You for waiting to be gracious to me.
Show me how to watch and wait for Your goodness.*

LISTENING TO GOD

Let the wise listen.
PROVERBS 1:5 NIV

For years Shelia saw herself as an ugly duckling. In fact, her mom had even said as much when she was growing up.

Shelia carried this wound with her well into adulthood. Until one night she had a dream. In the dream a child was sitting on her father's lap. The father was speaking gently to the child, telling her over and over how beautiful and precious and unique she was. Shelia awoke from the dream in tears. She knew immediately that God was speaking to her heart, and from that moment on she never again doubted her worth in His sight.

Has God ever spoken to you in a dream? There are many biblical accounts of God speaking to His children through dreams, and there is no reason why He wouldn't use this method today. This does not mean that every dream is a message from God, nor that every dream contains deep spiritual meaning. Above all, meaning gleaned from dreams is never a substitute for biblical truth. But God can communicate with His children using any method He desires, and it is not surprising that He sometimes speaks to His children through dreams.

Whether you are awake or asleep, pray that God would open your eyes and your heart to whatever He wants to communicate to you.

Father, thank You for being the God of all of me, even my dreams.
Help me to listen whenever You speak to me. Amen.

DON'T SAY IT

Do not let any unwholesome talk come out of your mouths,
but only what is helpful for building others up according to their needs,
that it may benefit those who listen.
EPHESIANS 4:29 NIV

The sequence of events is very predictable: Random thoughts enter our minds; negative scenarios dominate our thinking; volatile emotions soon bubble up; and before we know it, hurtful words come out of our mouths. We may not be able to control every thought that enters our minds, but the good news is we *can* control what thoughts we dwell on and what words we utter.

Learning to tame the tongue is a difficult task. First we must acknowledge the destruction our tongues are capable of. James 3 addresses the consequences of an unbridled tongue. Although our tongues are a tiny part of the body, they can do great harm to us, and others, if left unchecked.

Edifying speech begins with a disciplined mind. Weigh your thoughts against God's truth found in His Word. Dismiss lies. Yield your thought life to God's control. When God is allowed to guard our minds, our speech will be pleasing to Him and will truly benefit others.

Dear Lord, help me win the battle of the tongue
by dwelling on Your truth. Amen.

IRON SHARPENS IRON

As iron sharpens iron, so a man sharpens the countenance of his friend.
PROVERBS 27:17 NKJV

Maybe you're familiar with the biblical expression "iron sharpens iron." But what does it mean? In order to keep things like knives sharp, they have to be rubbed against something equally as hard—something that can shape them into effective tools.

Godly friends will sharpen us. They won't let us grow dull in our relationship with God or with others. They will keep us on our toes and will work with the Lord to shape us into the most effective people we can be. Rubbing against them won't always be fun. In fact, we might feel the friction at times and wish we could run in the opposite direction. But don't run! Allow God to do the work He longs to do.

Take a good look at the friends God has placed in your life. Are there some who don't sharpen you? Perhaps you've been put in their lives to sharpen them. Are there a few who diligently participate in your life, growing you into a better, stronger person? Do they rub you the wrong way at times? Praise God! He's shaping and sharpening you into the person you are meant to be.

Father, thank You for my friends, especially the ones who keep me on my toes. Thank You for the sharpening work You are doing in my life—even when it hurts!

TEST YOUR THOUGHTS

Finally, brothers, whatever is true, whatever is noble, whatever is right,
whatever is pure, whatever is lovely, whatever is admirable—if anything
is excellent or praiseworthy—think about such things.
PHILIPPIANS 4:8 NIV

Have you been to a movie lately? Read a magazine? Glanced at a billboard? While there is still a lot of clean humor and purity in our world, there is so much that is not worthy of our attention.

In a chapter about peace with others, self, and circumstances, Philippians 4:8 gives us instructions about our thoughts. Put your thoughts to the test the verse provides:

Is this movie *pure*?

Is it *right* for me to share this bit of gossip?

Is the horoscope in the newspaper harmless? Is it *truth*?

Would slipping out of the restaurant without leaving a tip be *admirable*?

When you begin to assess your thoughts and actions in this way, you will see areas in which you could make better choices. Spend time in nature, admiring God's creation. That is pure. Read His Word. You will be dwelling on truth. Serve others who are less fortunate than you. Such service is praiseworthy.

The instructions for peace are there in the final chapter of the apostle Paul's letter to the Philippians. Will you overlook them, or will they lead you to a deeper peace and a cleaner conscience?

God, show me today things that are true, noble, right, pure, lovely,
admirable, excellent, and praiseworthy. Help me to fix my mind on such
things, I ask. Amen.

THANKSGIVING

*Offer to God a sacrifice of thanksgiving, and perform
your vows to the Most High.*
PSALM 50:14 ESV

It's not difficult to say thank you. So why does the psalmist
call thanksgiving a sacrifice? What are we giving up in order to
be thankful? When we list our blessings, we realize that we are
recipients of many gifts—things God has given us freely, through
no effort on our part.

Giving thanks is a means of letting go, of opening our
hands and acknowledging God's power, His control, and His
goodness. In the process, He frees us from ourselves. In the act of
thanksgiving we are letting go of the control we think we have.
We acknowledge once again that much of who we are and what
we have are gifts of a sovereign God who loves and blesses us. We
sacrifice our pride and self-sufficiency when we say thank You.

*Lord, give me a grateful heart. Cause me to turn daily to You in
thanksgiving and thus free myself from pride and self-importance.*

It's Okay

Forgive as quickly and completely as the Master forgave you.
COLOSSIANS 3:13 MSG

Each of us has been hurt by another—with words spoken in anger, disastrous relationships, wounded hearts. We know God wants us to forgive one another. But how in the world is this accomplished? As fallen creatures, we prefer to keep score and tally up the wrongs against us. And why should we forgive unfair treatment? Because God's Word tells us to.

Paul states in Colossians that we must clothe ourselves in mercy, kindness, and patience. These qualities will make it easier to get over the hurt and pardon the grievance. He reminds us that the Lord forgave us, so we must forgive others. That's easier said than done, certainly. We need to focus on a person's worth, not their weaknesses, and turn our hearts to what can be, not what was.

An anonymous author wrote, "There's so much good in the worst of us and so much bad in the best of us, that we'll spend much of our lives learning to forgive and forget. Until you make the decision to forgive, the process of healing cannot begin." Releasing the grip we have on our anger will, in turn, release God's blessings.

Dear heavenly Father, I know You command us to forgive, but genuine forgiveness is difficult. Help me to forgive those who have injured me. Amen.

AFRAID OF THE DARK

*You know everything I do. You know what I am going to say even before
I say it, LORD. You go before me and follow me. You place your hand of
blessing on my head.*

PSALM 139:3–5 NLT

Rhonda, widowed with three young children, hated the
darkness. Often, coming home after sunset, she would look at her
dark house and let her fears run wild. A criminal could be lurking
in the bushes or even inside. She would be almost paralyzed with
her fears of the "what if" scenarios, and she lashed out at God for
taking her husband and protector.

One evening after a particularly stressful homecoming, she
withdrew to pray and ask the Lord to remove her fears. She knew
God could choose to protect her and keep all dangers away, but she
also came to realize that even if a dangerous intruder did invade her
home, God would still be there and would help her through.

Rhonda went on to raise her three children alone, surrounded
by God's loving presence that is available to anyone who seeks
Him. She still had times when she feared the unknown, but with
God she could overcome her fears and press on.

*Heavenly Father, You know more about me and my needs than even I do.
Thank You for being always present, comforting and guiding me.*

MOVING TOWARD

*Not that I have already obtained all this, or have already
been made perfect, but I press on to take hold of that for which
Christ Jesus took hold of me.*
PHILIPPIANS 3:12 NIV

Amy was a perfectionist. Whether she was working to get
good grades, clean her apartment, or complete a work project,
she spent countless hours tweaking, changing, and rearranging
to be sure that she attended to every minute detail. The problem
was, no matter how hard Amy worked, she never felt successful.
She eventually realized that this mind set was keeping her from
accomplishing much of anything, since she was reluctant to start
a project if she felt she couldn't do it perfectly.

This type of thinking can be very debilitating. We conclude
that if we fail in one area, we are dismal failures. And that is a
very accurate picture of what life was like under Old Testament
law. Indeed, James 2:10 (NIV) says, "For whoever keeps the whole
law and yet stumbles at just one point is guilty of breaking all of
it." That's the bad news. The good news is that we no longer live
under the law. Romans 5:1–2 (NIV) says, "We have peace with
God through our Lord Jesus Christ, through whom we have
gained access by faith into this grace in which we now stand."

Now we live under grace. Grace frees us from the bondage of
perfection. Praise God for His gift of grace.

*Father, thank You that I can be done with being a perfectionist
since I am under grace. Amen.*

SET APART FOR HIM

You can be sure of this: The LORD set apart the godly for himself.
The LORD will answer when I call to him.
PSALM 4:3 NLT

Doesn't it make you feel special to know you are called, chosen, and set apart to do great things for God? And while the Lord doesn't play favorites, He does have a way of making you feel pretty special. You are dearly loved—one of His little darlings. And His ear is always tuned into your heart. That's pretty amazing, isn't it? Parents always know the voices of their children, and God is no different. He hears your every cry, even before you make it!

Today, ponder the realization that you've been set apart. What does that mean to you, and how does it affect your walk with God? Does it change the way you view Him? Does it put a spring in your step? Make you feel like curling up with Him for a long chat?

God desires an intimate relationship with you. That's why you've been set apart—to be with Him. Take full advantage of that! Head to your prayer closet and let the Lord share His heart with you. Then open up your heart and share it with Him, as well.

Lord, I feel so special knowing You've set me apart for Yourself. I long for an intimate relationship with You and I gladly come into Your throne room for some serious one-on-one time today.

THE SABBATH

Remember the Sabbath day by keeping it holy.
EXODUS 20:8 NIV

Remembering the Sabbath is not something God takes lightly. It is included in the Ten Commandments. Keeping the Sabbath holy goes back to Genesis. God made the world in six days. He worked. He created. He delighted in His masterpieces— the ocean, the land, the trees, flowers, and animals of all types. Best of all, He made man and woman in His own likeness. On the seventh day work ceased, and God rested.

Work is a good thing. After all, God created it. And there are many warnings in His Word against idleness. God takes work seriously. We are to work for six days and rest on the Sabbath. We are to keep the Sabbath day holy. It is meant for rest.

Many of us worship with other believers on Sunday but don't really rest throughout the remainder of the day. Take this challenge. For one month, strive to keep the fourth commandment. Keep the Sabbath holy. Don't clean your home, wash your car, or break out the laptop to complete that project you'd like to submit on Monday morning. Rest. Meditate upon the Lord. Relax. Take it easy. What a great commandment!

The book of Exodus tells us that the Lord blessed the Sabbath and made it holy. You will find great blessing as you set apart this one day each week for rest.

God, in this busy world, often Sunday becomes just another day.
Help me to keep it holy as You have commanded. Amen.

GREATEST LOVE

Set your affection on things above, not on things on the earth.
COLOSSIANS 3:2 KJV

A camp counselor gathered her sixth-grade campers together for a nighttime devotion. They crowded around her bed in their pajamas.

"What are some of the things you love?" the counselor asked. Immediately the preteens chirped out their answers: "My parents." "Sometimes my brother. . .when he's nice to me!" "Camp!" "My cool new cell phone." "My friends." "My dog." "Going to my grandparents' farm." "Boys!"

"All of these things are good," the counselor said, smiling. After reading Colossians 3:2, she asked them what the verse meant to them.

"God wasn't even on our list," said one girl, looking down at the floor, ashamed.

The counselor explained that as humans, naturally we get caught up in gadgets, people that are special to us, and pleasures of the world. She then encouraged the girls to think of things above. "As we go to bed tonight, let's think on things above. Let's thank God for who He is, for sending Jesus to die for our sins, for the promise of heaven. Let's practice reserving our deepest love for God, rather than anything in this world."

God, may my greatest love always be for You. Amen.

COMPLAINING
OR TRUSTING?

Do everything without complaining or arguing.
PHILIPPIANS 2:14 NIV

It is our nature to look out for number one. We want our opinion to count. We want our voice to be heard. We want things to go the way we plan, but life often does not measure up to our expectations. So we complain, bellyache, whine, and grumble. Resisting the urge to be the squeaky wheel is difficult, especially when we are in a situation where we feel we are treated unjustly.

Consider that maybe God tells us not to complain because He wants us to acknowledge that *He's* in control and is powerful enough to take care of everything. Psalm 10:17 tells us the Lord hears the desires of the humble. Romans 8:26 says that the Holy Spirit prays for us and helps us in our weakness. We have these assurances that our God is both hearing our prayers and helping us pray them. Why do we need to keep muttering our dissatisfaction to those around us?

*Father, help me to break the habit of complaining. Help
me to remember I can bring all my problems to You.
You will help me to pray and will hear my prayers.*

FATHERS MOCKERS

The apostles left the Sanhedrin, rejoicing because they had been counted worthy of suffering disgrace for the Name.
ACTS 5:41 NIV

A magazine recently ran an article with the headline: NOT SINCE JESUS. In the opening, the author wrote that not since Jesus' birth had a baby been so highly anticipated. He even wrote that the Christ child only had three wise men to greet Him in the manger while there are millions of people anxiously awaiting the Hollywood babe's arrival.

The Bible says we shouldn't be surprised when people mock our faith. But there's also a balance. Jesus didn't respond to His persecutors when He was crucified because He knew they were part of the fulfillment of God's plan. But He was livid when a bunch of first-century entrepreneurs tried to make the temple into a shopping mall. Like Jesus, we shouldn't react angrily every time we're misunderstood, misquoted, or mistreated. But we don't have to sit quietly when people take the name of the Lord in vain and mock the Savior we love.

We can be a shining light for God's name when we remain steadfast, faithful, and positive in the face of a world that belittles our faith. And we can pray for those who ridicule Christians, knowing that they'll ultimately answer to the One they are mocking.

Lord, help me to be strong when others ridicule my faith. And give me the courage to say something when I need to.

WHAT IS YOUR ISAAC?

Abraham built an altar there and arranged the wood on it. He bound his
son Isaac and laid him on the altar, on top of the wood. Then he reached out
his hand and took the knife to slay his son. But the angel of the LORD called
out to him from heaven, "Abraham! Abraham!" "Here I am," he replied.
"Do not lay a hand on the boy," he said. "Do not do anything to him. Now
I know that you fear God, because you have not withheld from me your
son, your only son."
GENESIS 22:9–12 NIV

God asked Abraham to sacrifice his only son. Isaac had
been born to Abraham and his wife, Sarah, in their old age
and was very special to his father. Yet Genesis tells us Abraham
did not hesitate when God asked him to make this enormous
sacrifice. He rose early the next morning and took Isaac to the
mountaintop.

Abraham would not withhold even his precious son from the
Lord. He didn't understand God's request, and certainly his hand
must have been shaking as he raised the knife. Nonetheless, he
was willing. His answer was yes.

What is your Isaac? What would be hard to lay upon the
altar if God called you to give it up? Is it your job or reputation, a
relationship, or a dream? Often the Lord just wants to know that
following Him is number one in your life—no matter the cost.

Lord, search my heart. Is there something I need to give up
so that I might follow You more closely?

PEACEFUL SLUMBER

I lie down and sleep; I wake again, because the LORD sustains me.
PSALM 3:5 NIV

There's nothing better than a good night's sleep, especially when you've worked hard all day. But sometimes the pressures of the daytime hours spill over into the night. You may find yourself unable to get the rest you need. Peaceful slumber seems to elude you. Instead of sleeping, you toss and turn, thinking, thinking, thinking about all sorts of things. Bills. Relationships. Work-related issues. Your mind won't rest.

If you're someone who struggles to sleep at night, it's likely you're trying to carry the load on your own. God never meant for you to bear that weight. He longs for you to give your problems, concerns, and issues to Him—not just so you can sleep well at night, but because He's big enough to carry them and you're not.

Today, acknowledge that you aren't big enough to handle the issues you're facing. Make a list. Write them down. Then give every item on the list to the Lord, each and every one. There! Doesn't that feel good? Now, see what a great night's sleep you'll have tonight!

Lord, I confess I'm not very good at handling my own problems and issues. Today, I release my hold on the things I've been gripping tightly. I give them to You. Thank You, Lord, for peaceful slumber in the nights ahead.

A Gracious Witness

Live wisely among those who are not believers, and make the most of every opportunity. Let your conversation be gracious and attractive so that you will have the right response for everyone.
Colossians 4:5–6 nlt

After moving to a new apartment, Maria met Kim and Steve, the couple across the hall. She made an effort to get to know them, and soon they became friends.

When Maria discovered that Kim and Steve weren't married, she began to pray that they would accept Christ and get married or stop living together. She became more outspoken and often challenged them with pertinent scriptures. Soon the friendship cooled, and Kim and Steve wanted nothing to do with Maria or her faith.

Many well-meaning believers have faced similar dilemmas. When we meet someone who doesn't know Christ, we want them to become a part of God's kingdom and give up sinful lifestyles. These desires aren't wrong; however, it isn't our job to make them follow through. Nowhere in scripture are we told cajole, connive, push, pull, or prod people into God's kingdom. Our responsibility is to love them, speak truth when asked, and let our Christ-light shine by modeling a godly lifestyle. It is God's responsibility to draw them to Himself, through the work of the Holy Spirit and the love of Christ. Cooperating with God is far more rewarding than trying to do His job.

Father, help me to see others through Your eyes and share my faith with love and authenticity in ways that attract others to You. Amen.

I'm Waiting, Lord

Be still before the LORD and wait patiently for him.
PSALM 37:7 NIV

If you want to see a picture of impatience, just talk to a small child in the weeks leading up to Christmas. To a kid with visions of sugarplums dancing in his head, waiting for the big day to arrive is torture, pure and simple.

We adults like to think we've grown past the impatient stage of our lives. But aren't we just as impatient as a child when we're waiting for an answer to prayer? God answers prayer in three ways: yes, no, and wait. An immediate yes or no we can deal with. Wait, on the other hand, is a little more difficult to accept.

What answer to prayer are you awaiting today? No matter what it is, God has it under control. Resist the temptation to fret and worry about the prayer request; instead, as Psalm 37:7 wisely recommends, be still before the Father and wait patiently for Him. The blessings He has in store for you far outweigh this time of waiting.

Father, calm my heart as I wait for You. I have confidence that You will act mightily in my life. Help me to be patient during this time and to trust completely in Your perfect plan.

SECURE YOUR OWN MASK FIRST

Keep a close watch on how you live and on your teaching.
Stay true to what is right for the sake of your own salvation
and the salvation of those who hear you.
1 TIMOTHY 4:16 NLT

Every woman needs to guard her time wisely—whether single or married. We are all in danger of getting exhausted running here and there to do all the things that are seemingly good and intended to bring glory to God.

So before agreeing to take on a volunteer position, recall how flight attendants remind airline passengers in the event of emergency to secure their own oxygen masks before helping others around them. In many ways God tries to tell us this also as He reminds us not to neglect our time in prayer, study, and fellowship with Him. If our spiritual oxygen isn't flowing from a full tank, our ability to assist others will run out and we'll become useless.

Securing our own mask first sometimes means saying "no" to groups that see us as "singularly" available and "yes" to God, who truly requires our time. Only then will we be alert and equipped to serve others in His strength.

Dear Lord, help me to prioritize my schedule so I can be
refreshed and energized by time with You and in turn be
inspired to do the tasks You place before me.

PRACTICING QUIET

*He who guards his mouth preserves his life, but he who
opens wide his lips shall have destruction.*
PROVERBS 13:3 NKJV

We all have times in our lives when we wish we had just kept
our mouths shut. Maybe you've let casual conversation slip into
gossip or accidentally revealed a secret. Scripture tells us our tongues
are powerful and dangerous and that no one can tame them. When
we sin with our mouths, it is because we lack self-control; but self-
control as we think of it seems impossible to attain.

The world's definition of self-control is personal discipline or
willpower, but the Bible says self-control is the fruit of the Spirit,
a result of God's work in our lives. His power can keep us from
sinning in our speech.

Invite Him into this part of your life. Pray Psalm 141:3
(NIV): "Set a guard over my mouth, O LORD; keep watch over the
door of my lips." Watch and see Him help you tame your tongue.

*Lord, so many of my words have been unhelpful
and even destructive. Forgive me. By Your Spirit,
watch the door of my lips and produce control in me.*

I Love You. . .Even in the Hard Times

A friend loves at all times.
Proverbs 17:17 NKJV

A woman walked her best friend through a difficult season. Health problems, a death in the family, and a serious bout with depression threatened to be her friend's undoing. Still, the woman stuck with it. Even when her friend insisted she didn't want anyone around. *Especially* when her friend insisted she didn't want anyone around.

Have you ever walked a friend though a tough season? Been there when she faced depression or pain? Held her hand as she mourned the loss of someone she loved? Walked with her through an illness or job-related challenge? Cried with her as her marriage came to a painful end? If so, then you truly know what it means to love at all times. Friendship—true friendship—runs deeper than the unexpected challenges of life.

Today, think of a friend who is going through a particularly difficult season. What can you do to lift her spirits? How can you encourage her to keep going? Should you send a card? Flowers? Make a phone call? Write an encouraging note? Take her to see a movie? Remember: God-breathed love pours itself out at all times.

Lord, I want to be a blessing to my friends who are hurting, to show my love at all times. Today I recommit myself to caring for my friends, especially during the difficult times. Give me Your heart and show me what I can do to lift my friend's spirits when she's down.

YES, LORD, AMEN

"The joy of the LORD is your strength."
NEHEMIAH 8:10 NIV

In our success-driven world, fun is an often-overlooked commodity. There's a corporate ladder to climb, a glass ceiling to break through, another committee meeting to attend. Serious, staid, and structured, our lives lack joy. We race a ticking clock with a sweep hand.

Paul exhorted the Christian community to be full of joy *now*. The Psalms encourage us to sing and dance and praise His name. How is that possible with a solemn face? A little lighthearted fun releases pent-up tension and balances life's scales. Laughter will lower our blood pressure. That cheerful heart is good medicine.

Surely it's time for a bit of spontaneity. 1 Thessalonians 5:16 (NIV) says to "be joyful always." In our cyberspace world, we can share jokes and hilarious videos. Pull one up on the screen, throw back your head, and laugh. Realize God intended for us to have joy in our lives. Say, "Yes, Lord," and chuckle.

Father, I live in a world loaded with danger, serious issues, and worry.
Help me to find joy in my life this day. Amen.

PRIDE

Pride goes before destruction, a haughty spirit before a fall.
PROVERBS 16:18 NIV

Pride, arrogance, conceit—all are sinful attitudes of the heart everyone struggles with. Pride is a Miss Know-It-All who has all the answers to everyone's questions. Arrogance always has to have the last word. She views herself as spiritually mature and looks down on others. Conceit is a control freak, masquerading as if she were God.

God does not take these attitudes lightly. He will put an end to our puffed-up behavior by allowing us to fall, bringing us to our knees.

Humility is the antithesis of pride. Jesus is the perfect example of humility—putting others above self. Although He was God, He humbled Himself and became obedient to His heavenly Father by dying on the cross.

Humility is self-sacrificing, not self-promoting. Humility realizes that God is God. Let's learn this important lesson before it's too late.

If your heart is prideful, confess it. Clothe yourself with humility by worshipping the Lord.

*Dear Lord, convict me of any prideful spirit within me
and teach me humility. Amen.*

CLUTTER

*When he heard this, he became very sad, because he
was a man of great wealth.*
LUKE 18:23 NIV

Donna's life was full to the brim. Known for her ability to
multitask, she often worked from her laptop with music playing
through the speakers. She simultaneously conversed with friends
via text and online messaging. While driving to work she'd also
talk on her cell phone, put on makeup, or jot down items on a
grocery list. She couldn't fall asleep at night without the television
on. Each morning she awoke to the sounds of talk radio.

Our lives quickly become cluttered. We think of constant
noise and activity as a contemporary issue, but it's a problem that
has been around for centuries.

The rich young ruler was a careful rule-follower, an expert at
keeping all of them since he'd been a boy. But his life had become
so cluttered that he couldn't find God. He came to Jesus looking
for something else to put on his to-do list; but instead, Jesus
challenged him to get rid of clutter that stood between him and
God. This saddened the ruler, because he wasn't willing to part
with it.

What clutters your life? It could be physical, mental, or
emotional. Set aside time to take an inventory. Ask God to
cleanse your heart and bring to mind things you need to get rid
of to draw closer to Him.

Father, search my heart and reveal anything that keeps me from You. Amen.

I Want My Mommy

For God is greater than our hearts, and he knows everything.
1 John 3:20 niv

Being sick isn't fun, but it can be made a lot better when you have someone to wait on you.

Mom always knows what food to suggest for an upset stomach. She knows just which blanket is your favorite or where to find that elusive thermometer. It's hard being a grown-up who has to take care of these things for yourself. It is much easier to rely on someone else to be there while you shut down and let your body heal.

Sometimes our sicknesses come in emotional forms. When we are not physically sick, it is hard for those around us to see how we can need a sick day to evaluate our mental health. In times like this, only God knows what we need and is the One we can turn to for a blanket of comfort to wrap around our wounded soul. He also knows just the type of food for our thoughts that will nourish and heal us.

So the next time you are feeling emotionally sick, take a little time to rest, and let Him comfort you until the pain and confusion are gone.

Thank You, Lord, for the comfort You bring to me when I'm feeling down and overwhelmed by life. Each day I'm learning to turn to You so that I can keep my emotional health in balance.

SAFETY IN SLAVERY

*"Didn't we say to you in Egypt, 'Leave us alone; let us
serve the Egyptians'? It would have been better for us to serve the
Egyptians than to die in the desert!"*

EXODUS 14:12 NIV

Millions of lives are affected by drug and alcohol abuse.
The consequences are far-reaching and can damage families for
generations. Statistics show that 50–90 percent of those with
addiction problems will eventually relapse. This is perhaps one
of the most tragic consequences of all. Why would someone who
experienced the devastation of addiction and the freedom of
sobriety want to become enslaved again?

The Israelites were faced with a similar choice. For years,
enslaved and abused by the Egyptians, they were forced to work
under miserable conditions. Pharaoh even ordered the deaths of
every Israelite baby boy.

Mere days after God miraculously freed them from their
oppressors they begged to go back. Why? Because the future was
unknown. They were terrified at what might lie ahead. At least in
slavery they knew what to expect and found security in knowing
where their next meal came from.

Satan uses the fear of freedom to keep us from experiencing
the freedom Christ offers us. But slavery is never better than
freedom. Hold tight to the promises of God. Freedom is yours
for the taking.

*Father, when slavery begins to look attractive, remind
me of the freedom-filled future I have with You. Amen.*

What to Wear

Therefore, as God's chosen people, holy and dearly loved, clothe yourselves
with compassion, kindness, humility, gentleness and patience.
Colossians 3:12 niv

We all spend time selecting what to wear each day.
Sometimes it is simply a matter of what is clean (or can at least be
resurrected from the dirty clothes hamper!).

Some women are trendy, which requires them to keep up
with the latest fashions. Others are more practical as they piece
together a week's worth of outfits with just a couple pairs of
neutral-colored pants and some solid-colored tops.

Clothing is important. It says something about a person.
Think about a black-tie affair, interview, tennis match, or a day
on the beach. Each calls for a different type of attire. To show up
on the beach in a tuxedo or at the tennis match in a business suit
would be ridiculous!

As believers, God tells us to clothe ourselves with
compassion, kindness, humility, gentleness, and patience. These
traits cannot be found in a department store or in the latest
fashion magazine. They can only come from the Holy Spirit
living in and through us.

Today as you choose the clothing you will wear, choose also
to clothe yourself with godly characteristics that will cause you to
shine as a daughter of the Lord.

God, it is not always easy to be kind or compassionate. Sometimes humility,
gentleness, and especially patience are also difficult. Help me to be certain
I am fully clothed with these attitudes before I leave home each morning.
Amen.

Rags to Riches

A lazy person will end up poor, but a hard worker will become rich.
PROVERBS 10:4 NCV

These days, most everyone wants to figure out how to get rich quick—how to have the "gain" without the "pain." Infomercials share investment tactics, TV shows explain how to flip a house, and competition shows give folks the opportunity to make the most of their talent in a rushed setting.

We all want to be successful. Sure, it's appealing to think we won't have to exert much effort to get what we want. But there's no "get rich quick" scheme that actually works. There's no miracle cure for financial obligations. You can't lie around in your PJs all day watching soap operas and expect to be successful. If you want to succeed, you have to work hard.

Take a good look at today's scripture. There's a promise buried in the second half: A hard worker will become rich. The Lord isn't promising a huge windfall—a miraculous financial miracle. No, He's referring to a deeper richness that even money can't buy. A hard worker is rich in satisfaction, rich in contentment, rich in the realization that she's actually done what she was called to do. So get to work!

Lord, it's tempting to want to succeed without much effort on my part. I give my desires to You and ask You to give me the energy and stamina I need to do the necessary work so that I can be the best at what I'm called to do.

A HOLY PERFUME

Everywhere we go, people breathe in the exquisite fragrance. Because of Christ, we give off a sweet scent rising to God, which is recognized by those on the way of salvation—an aroma redolent with life.
2 CORINTHIANS 2:15–16 MSG

Smells are all around us. The aroma of lavender relaxes us, the scent of coffee jump-starts us, and the odor of a skunk offends us.

Have you ever considered how a person's spirit has an aroma? When you meet someone who is godly, gentle, and sincerely kind, their spirit seems to exude an inviting aroma like home-baked cookies or mulled apple cider that draws others in. But there are also people you meet who almost immediately seem to give off a sharp odor like vinegar or ammonia. They have an unsettled spirit in which bitterness and discontent are cultivated.

What kind of scent do you want your spirit to emanate? Remember that it has the power to change a room and even a whole community.

So as you perform your daily hygiene, putting perfume on your skin, consider also your spiritual perfume. Keep the scent fresh, not overpowering, and welcoming by keeping your spirit in line with the Spirit of God through prayer, Bible study, and praise.

Holy Spirit, I welcome You into my life. Be a perfume that proves to others that You are sovereign in my life and that draws them to Jesus Christ.

GOD AS OUR GUIDE

Whenever the cloud was taken up from above the tabernacle, after that the children of Israel would journey; and in the place where the cloud settled, there the children of Israel would pitch their tents.

NUMBERS 9:17 NKJV

When they escaped from the Egyptians into the desert, God gifted the children of Israel with His presence. During the day, a cloud accompanied them; at night, they had a pillar of fire. When it stopped or started, they followed suit.

Do we follow God that closely? Or do we make our own decisions and ask God to bless them? We should make Him an integral part of our daily life—instead of just someone tacked on to the beginning or end of our day.

When faced with a big decision, some of us ask our friends and family members for advice, and others of us tend to be more independent. But if we're seeking to be like Christ, we need to ask God to lead us. He desires to be the first and last person we lean on. And He promises never to lead us astray. What comfort we can take in that fact!

Today, ask God to make His will for you clear. Then read scripture, pray, and be on the lookout for His guidance. He promises to give it and to go with you wherever you go, just as He did for the Israelites.

Lord, thank You for Your promise to lead me. I'm so thankful that You want to be intimately involved in my life.

A Witness
in the Workplace

*Make it your ambition to lead a quiet life, to mind your own
business and to work with your hands, just as we told you, so
that your daily life may win the respect of outsiders and so that
you will not be dependent on anybody.*

1 Thessalonians 4:11–12 NIV

Mr. Smith is a custodian at an elementary school. He empties
trashcans and sweeps floors. He greets the children as they arrive,
occasionally stooping to tie a shoe for a kindergartner. Mr. Smith
is paged over the loudspeaker when a mess needs to be cleaned up.
He scrubs foul words off the restroom walls. He is the person who
scrapes gum from the bottom of desks. It is not a glamorous job, but
Mr. Smith never complains.

When choosing heroes for a writing assignment, the fourth
grade teacher was surprised that so many students wrote about
Mr. Smith. They wrote about times when he had fixed a broken
toy for them and occasions when he had encouraged them with a
personal story from his childhood or a Bible verse.

Living a quiet life—not being a busybody—and having a
strong work ethic, Mr. Smith won the respect of many a child
who passed through the halls of that elementary school.

Are you a Mr. Smith? Our workplaces need examples of Jesus.

*Father, make me humble in my work. Keep my ears and my lips from gossip.
Make me diligent in all that I do, and give me a sweet spirit that others
might see Jesus in me. Amen.*

HEALING TAKES TIME

He heals the brokenhearted and binds up their wounds.
PSALM 147:3 NKJV

Do you remember the scraped knees and bumped heads of your childhood? You probably recall running to your mother and the painful process that followed. The wound had to be cleaned, often with a stinging antiseptic. You probably screamed, trying to avoid this part. Then there was the annoyance of having a wound to protect, a cut that needed to be kept clean. Even after most of the healing was complete, there was the pain of having the sticky bandage tape ripped from your skin.

The process of healing takes time and can be painful, whether it's a physical, emotional, or spiritual wound. When God comes to heal your broken heart, there will be painful moments of cleansing, washing out the grit of sin. Soreness and tenderness set in during the healing process. The wounded place may need protection for a while. You may have to alter your circumstances for a season.

Open yourself to His healing. Ask Him what part is yours to do.

Father, thank You for healing my hurts. Help me to trust
You and not resist Your process.

"Yes" in Christ

For no matter how many promises God has made, they are "Yes" in Christ.
And so through him the "Amen" is spoken by us to the glory of God.
2 Corinthians 1:20 niv

God is a keeper of His word. The Bible tells us that all of God's promises are "yes" in Jesus, His Son. His promises are yours to rely on each day of your life.

God promises to provide for your needs. That promise is "yes" in Christ. He promises you eternal life. Another "yes" through the blood of Christ. God promises never to flood the earth again, never to leave you, never to harm you, but only to bring you hope and a future. All of these are "yes" in Christ. A resounding "yes."

The apostle Paul also declared that through Jesus, the "amen" is spoken by believers to the glory of God. If you have ever been to a church where praise is spoken freely or to a good old-fashioned revival meeting, you have heard the "amens." To speak an "amen" is to agree with what has been presented.

God promises. His promises are "yes" in Jesus.

Believers say "amen" to this.

If you ever begin to doubt God, if you ever wonder if He is going to come through for you, or ever question one of the promises in His Word, remember that He has given you a "yes" in your Savior, and God's "yes" is a powerful thing.

God, people let me down. Broken promises hurt, sometimes for years to come. I thank You that all of Your promises are "yes" in Christ. Amen.

THE GREATEST
COMMANDMENT

*Jesus replied: "'Love the Lord your God with all your heart and with
all your soul and with all your mind.' This is the first and greatest
commandment. And the second is like it: 'Love your neighbor as yourself.'
All the Law and the Prophets hang on these two commandments."*
MATTHEW 22:37–40 NIV

Love God and love people. The whole of the gospel can be
summed up in these two statements. Jesus taught us how to love.
He demonstrated it by giving all of Himself for others. And His
love for the Father was evident in everything He did.

If you love God with your whole heart, it just comes
naturally to love people. And we're told to love them as we love
ourselves. Think about that for a moment. How much do you
love yourself? Enough to make sure all of your needs are met,
right? Imagine that kind of love expressed to a friend. It's a
pouring-yourself-out kind of love.

It's interesting to note that Jesus says, "All the Law and the
Prophets hang on these two commandments." He's really saying,
"What's the point of all of the other stuff if you don't have love?"
That's a question we need to consider today. What's the point
of going to church, giving financially, teaching Bible studies, or
directing the children's ministry if you don't truly love those you
come in contact with on a daily basis? So, go forth and love!

*Father, I want to acknowledge how much I love You with all my
heart, soul, mind, and strength. Help me to love others as I love myself.*

THE POWER OF THANKS

It is a good thing to give thanks unto the Lord.
PSALM 92:1 KJV

Rhonda's morning had started out badly. As she sat on the commuter train on the way to work, she caught her breath, irritated that she had to run to catch the train. When the train arrived at its destination, Rhonda watched as a man lifted a paralyzed woman out of her seat, carried her down the stairs, and gingerly placed her in a wheelchair. Suddenly Rhonda's frustrations seemed pretty minor. She found herself thankful for two legs that enabled her to walk off the train all by herself.

Being thankful doesn't minimize life's difficulties. But God's Word does tell us to give thanks—in *all* circumstances. Giving thanks gives us perspective on our situation. It keeps us from feeling sorry for ourselves and wallowing in self-pity. It teaches us to rely on God and reminds us that all we have comes from Him.

The Bible teaches that hardships help us to grow, so that even when we feel we have nothing else for which to be thankful, we can be grateful that God loves us enough to want to make us more like Him. Take a moment today to count your blessings— you'll be so busy, you won't have time to feel bad.

Father, thank You for the ways that You reveal Yourself to me. Thank You for the many blessings You have given me, and thank You that I can always think of something for which to be grateful.

HIS GRACE
IS SUFFICIENT

But he said to me, "My grace is sufficient for you, for my
power is made perfect in weakness."
2 CORINTHIANS 12:9 NIV

The apostle Paul had what the Bible calls "a thorn in his
flesh." Many have speculated as to what this thorn was. Some
believe it may have been a physical affliction or even depression.
We do not know what it was, but we know Paul pleaded three
times with the Lord to remove the thorn.

Why would God not remove the thorn from Paul's life? Why
would a loving God allow a devoted servant to suffer pain? Why
was God's answer "no" instead of "yes"? It seems cruel, heartless
even. But we know that our God is a loving God.

God told Paul that His grace was sufficient. The power of
God was perfected when Paul was at his weakest. God knew
something Paul did not. Something we, many centuries later,
still struggle to grasp. He knew the best thing for Paul was not
for the pain to be taken away, but for Paul to trust in the Lord's
provision for strength to endure it. God's grace had to be enough.

When you feel that this world has gotten the best of you, and
you have reached the end of your rope. . .perhaps you have. But
God still has plenty of strength. In His strength and by His grace,
you can go on.

Father, where You allow weakness to
remain in my life, please be my strength. Amen.

FREE FALLING

The eternal God is your refuge, and underneath are the everlasting arms.
DEUTERONOMY 33:27 NIV

Stressful issues face us each day. Whether it's work, school, or the neighbors next door, there's always some problem to deal with. And when these bumps in the road arise, our natural tendency is to worry, fret, and be anxious. Not only is that attitude counterproductive, God's Word says it's disobedient. Scripture directs us to turn our worries over to our heavenly Father and rest in Him. To fret is wrong.

Hannah Whitall Smith said, "There are two things which are more utterly incompatible even than oil and water, and these two are trust and worry." We must trust in a God who is able to do all things. We must trust in a God who cares. We must trust in a God with whom we may have a personal relationship. The Bible says so.

When life's storms are overwhelming, we should take our troubles to Him and seek protection from the One who cannot be moved. Climb into the Father's lap and feel His embrace. He is still in heaven and cares about His beloved children. He is our refuge. He's bigger than any storm we might face.

Dear Lord, I admit worry turns my attention from You.
Help me realize You are ever-present and will care for me. Amen.

DIRECTIONALLY
CHALLENGED

Whether you turn to the right or to the left, you will hear a voice saying,
"This is the road! Now follow it."
ISAIAH 30:21 CEV

It's the most wonderful invention for the directionally
challenged. It can ride in your pocket or on the dash of your car.
It can guide you across town or across the country. It is a global
positioning system, or GPS.

It is fascinating how a satellite positioned miles above earth can
find your GPS signal and help you navigate a network of streets,
back roads, and highways to where you want to go. No longer is it
necessary to stop at the nearest gas station for directions.

But did you know that God has the first and best GPS? The
Bible tells us how He knows where we sit, what we think, and all
our habits (Psalm 139:2–3). No one knows us better than He, and
He is just waiting to guide our steps to where we need to go in life.
His GPS goes beyond physical travel from point A to B, for He can
navigate us through the emotional minefields of life, the potholes
of depression and loss, and the byways of joy and celebration. All
we need to do to tap into His navigational system is seek Him
through prayer and a spirit quieted to listen for His voice.

Lord, help me to quiet my thoughts and tune in to Your voice,
so that You can guide me through the crazy roads of life,
and I will rest in Your direction.

SUCH AS THESE

People were bringing little children to Jesus to have him touch them, but the disciples rebuked them. When Jesus saw this, he was indignant. He said to them, "Let the little children come to me, and do not hinder them, for the kingdom of God belongs to such as these."

MARK 10:13–14 NIV

Have you ever watched children worship? They do it with abandon. They're not restricted by the "I wonder if people are watching me" problem. In fact, they never even think about it. When the music begins, they just begin to celebrate. And they do it with pure hearts and no hidden motivations or agendas.

Jesus longs for us to come to Him as children. To give up worrying about what others think and to simply come with a pure heart, ready to worship. You might have to shake off some worries and fears, and you might have to abandon your traditional way of approaching Him, but it will be worth it.

Take a look at today's scripture. When the disciples tried to send the children away—thinking they were annoying Jesus—He stopped them in their tracks. *"Do not hinder them. The kingdom of heaven belongs to such as these."* Makes you want to have a childlike faith, doesn't it? Come to Him—on every occasion— as a child.

Lord, please restore my childlike faith today. Help me overcome any insecurities and simply come to You with unbridled affection.

SEEK JOY

When they saw the star, they were filled with joy!
MATTHEW 2:10 NLT

How is your Christmas to-do list shaping up? Are you so strapped for time that you're spending lunch breaks on last-minute shopping or online, searching for the ideal appetizer recipe for an upcoming party?

At the heart of it, our frenzied holiday madness, lavish parties, and gift-giving traditions are distractions from the message attached to the Christ Child: God loves us.

Strip away the stress of family and social obligations, and what's left? If you asked the shepherds who worshiped at the manger, they'd say that Christmas is about joy. They were so filled with the excitement and hope of the newborn King that they couldn't keep their exuberance to themselves. They had to tell everyone, everywhere, what they saw and heard!

This Christmas, put aside some of the world's expectations of the holiday and seek out the all-encompassing joy of Jesus' birth. You may just find that, like the shepherds, you can't keep the joy of the Savior to yourself!

Father, I want to experience the true joy of Jesus this Christmas season. Show me how to block out the distractions of the world and focus on Him and the gift of His birth. Amen.

THE GREATEST GIFT

For unto you is born this day in the city of David a Saviour,
which is Christ the Lord.
LUKE 2:11 KJV

Every Christmas, people celebrate the greatest gift ever given—
Jesus Christ. That perfect gift born more than two thousand years
ago in a lowly manger was a divine gift of love. It would result
in fulfilling God's ultimate goal to give eternal life to His fallen
creation.

Jesus knew He had a purpose when He came to earth.
He knew it would require suffering and death on a cross. His
ultimate purpose would be to give His life to save all mankind.
He understood it would be an excruciatingly painful task, but He
prayed for God's will to be done. He could see beyond His death
to His resurrection on the third day. He now sits at the right
hand of His Father, waiting for the completion of God's plan.

As a Christian, you also have a God-given purpose to fulfill.
The greatest gift you were ever given—eternal life through
Jesus' sacrifice—is one that must be shared with others. The
gift of God's love is that ultimate gift that keeps on giving. It's
an eternal, priceless gift, one that should be celebrated every
Christmas and every day of the year.

Dear God, You accomplished Your purpose through Your Son, Jesus Christ.
Jesus fulfilled His purpose by giving us eternal salvation. Please help me
fulfill my purpose by sharing Your love daily with others. Amen.

BEING A GIRL

*The LORD God said, "It is not good for man to be alone.
I will make a helper suitable for him."*
GENESIS 2:18 NIV

Being a girl is amazing. We are a vital piece of God's creation,
made to complete what was started in men.

Often a woman can add a new perspective to a problem
by seeing a solution from a direction a man wouldn't have
considered. She brings a nurturing touch that most men lack.
Her flare for hospitality exceeds the average man's.

You don't have to be married to be a helper to the men in
your life. A male relative, like a father or brother, needs you to
show respect and love through the little things you do, including
seeking their advice or remembering their birthdays. A male pastor
needs women who can help him see the ministry needs of women
in his church. A male boss needs women who can help him see
the importance of a soft approach with some customers or to
understand the family/work balance essential for all employees.

A single woman doesn't need to wait for marriage to be a
significant influence on those in her life. The day will come when
you can focus your attention on being a wife and mother, but
for now, don't neglect others around you who can use your help,
your perspective, your advice, and your Christlike love.

*Lord, thank You for making me a girl who is unique and special. Help me
use the gifts You placed within me to complement the men in my life.*

Day
361

VALUING PEOPLE
OVER THINGS

*Then Mary took about a pint of pure nard, an expensive perfume;
she poured it on Jesus' feet and wiped his feet with her hair.*
JOHN 12:3 NIV

Mary and Martha must have felt especially grateful to have
Jesus over for dinner. Only recently had He raised their brother
Lazarus from the dead. They couldn't believe Lazarus was still
with them, or that their beloved Jesus was in their home for
another meal.

To her guests' surprise, Mary took a pint of luxurious
perfume and washed Jesus' feet with it. As if that weren't shocking
enough, she stooped to wipe His feet with her hair. As the scent
of perfume and the outrageousness of Mary's act wafted through
the air, Judas jumped up from the table in indignation.

"This should have been sold! We should have given the
money to the poor!"

As always, Jesus saw through Judas' actions right to his heart.
He acknowledged the truth of Judas' heart (Jesus knew Judas had
been stealing), while acknowledging the purity of Mary's actions
(she was symbolically preparing Him for burial).

Jesus valued people over things. He considered the person's
heart to be more important than their actions or outward
appearance. What do you value?

Father, help me to value the things that You do. Amen.

STANDING UP
FOR CHRIST

*"Look!" he answered, "I see four men loose, walking in the midst of the fire;
and they are not hurt, and the form of the fourth is like the Son of God."*
DANIEL 3:25 NKJV

Daniel and his three friends Shadrach, Meshach, and
Abednego were hostages in a country in which believers in the
one true God were often mocked and ridiculed or killed. Because
Daniel's friends would not bow to King Nebuchadnezzar's idol,
they were sentenced to death in a fiery furnace.

But instead of allowing them to die in the furnace, God
spared them and sent a heavenly messenger to comfort and
strengthen them. When the three men emerged unharmed from
their fiery test, everyone around them marveled, and the king
declared that everyone would worship *their* God.

Whatever challenges you face in proclaiming Christ,
remember that just like Daniel's three friends, believers all over
the world are facing persecution and even death for their faith.
Ask God for the strength to stand up for Him, and believe that
He will equip and encourage you as you do so. Who knows? You
might even see an angel standing by your side.

*God, give me the courage to stand up for You in a world that often mocks
Your name. Thank You for Your promise to always be with me.*

Soul Satisfaction

*Just as the living Father sent me and I live because of the
Father, so the one who feeds on me will live because of me.*
JOHN 6:57 NIV

Have you ever stood in front of the refrigerator eating
something that doesn't even taste that good? Have you found
yourself staring at a closet full of clothes you don't wear? You
make resolutions and muster up willpower, but time and again
you eat too much or buy too many things you don't need and
that don't satisfy your desire. Perhaps you are trying to satisfy soul
hunger with physical things.

What are you really hungry for? What are you seeking
through the things you overindulge in? Jesus said He is the living
water and the bread of life. Water and food satisfy basic appetites.
Jesus alone satisfies our deepest desires and needs.

Seek Him. Ask Him to satisfy your heart. Ask Him for a
desire to know Him and receive His love for you. He will give
you a hunger and thirst for His presence in your life. That is His
will for you, and you can be sure He will answer that prayer.

*Christ Jesus, give me a desire for You. Help me
examine my soul hunger and turn to You to fill it.*

FIT TOGETHER

*He makes the whole body fit together perfectly. As each part does
its own special work, it helps the other parts grow, so that
the whole body is healthy and growing and full of love.*
EPHESIANS 4:16 NLT

Have you ever put together a really large jigsaw puzzle?
Maybe you struggled to get all of the pieces to fit in place. Some
were obvious and others were a challenge.

The body of Christ is a lot like a giant puzzle. It's filled with
many, many pieces, and they all fit together seamlessly to form
the most beautiful picture on earth—more beautiful than any
seascape or mountain peak.

Each piece in a puzzle is critical to the whole. Sure, when you
look at them individually, you might wonder, "How in the world
can this piece fit? It doesn't look like any of the others. It's not
shaped like any of the others." Still, it fits! And when you see it in
its proper place, it makes perfect sense.

This is a great day to praise the Lord for the many puzzle
pieces—Christian brothers and sisters—you've been given. Think
about the ones in the farthest reaches of the earth. They're all a
part of this glorious picture that makes up the church.

*Oh, Lord, I'm so grateful that everyone in the body of Christ has a place.
Thank You for fitting us together so beautifully. And thank You that we've
each been given our own job to do. May I learn to do mine well, so that
others might grow in You.*

ADOPTED BY GOD

*For he chose us in him before the creation of the world to be holy and
blameless in his sight. In love he predestined us to be adopted as his sons
through Jesus Christ, in accordance with his pleasure and will.*
EPHESIANS 1:4–5 NIV

Michelle was having a wonderful experience on a mission
trip to Russia. Somehow, though, as the mission team boarded
the plane to head back to the USA, Michelle felt God calling her
to do more. He reminded her of the babies she had held in the
orphanage.

God called Michelle to adopt a baby girl. One year after her
mission trip experience, Michelle returned to that same Russian
orphanage and took home a seventeen-month-old little girl. The
adoption was official within a matter of months.

You also have been adopted. God chose before His creation
of the world that you would be His daughter. When you accepted
Jesus, your sins were forgiven and you became a daughter of the
King. You are, in a sense, a princess!

Adoption is a beautiful thing. God chose you, and He will
never let you go.

If you haven't accepted Jesus, receive Him today. God still has
room in His family!

*Father, thank You for adopting me as Your daughter through Jesus.
It feels good to belong to You. Amen.*

CONTRIBUTORS

Banks, Tracy: Day 8, 44, 53, 80, 101, 137, 170, 200, 233, 236, 251, 272, 296, 313, 359

Tracy "Bobo" Banks is a freelance writer, award-winning poet, licensed minister, business owner, and Web site administrator. Her greatest blessings: God's unconditional love, family, friends, and autistic niece, Hailie. www.tracybobobanks.com

Biggers, Emily: Day 6, 17, 20, 21, 26, 32, 43, 56, 67, 70, 74, 85, 91, 97, 99, 128, 138, 146, 148, 150, 156, 166, 173, 178, 197, 209, 214, 244, 252, 265, 271, 279, 282, 283, 286, 292, 301, 303, 308, 314, 318, 323, 329, 330, 333, 345, 349, 351, 354, 365

Emily Biggers is a gifted education specialist in a north Texas public school district. She enjoys travel, freelance writing, and serving in a local apartment ministry through her church.

Bloss, Joanna: Day 7, 12, 31, 48, 49, 54, 57, 66, 72, 90, 96, 102, 107, 114, 123, 136, 145, 151, 152, 162, 169, 171, 176, 188, 196, 205, 213, 235, 237, 240, 249, 255, 261, 266, 270, 280, 284, 291, 300, 306, 307, 309, 315, 320, 327, 335, 342, 344, 353, 361

Joanna Bloss is a personal trainer, writer, and student living in the Midwest. She is a coauthor of *Grit for the Oyster: 250 Pearls of Wisdom for Aspiring Authors.*

Dena Dyer is a writer who resides in the Texas Hill Country. She has contributed to more than a dozen anthologies and has authored or coauthored three humor books. www.denadyer.com

Rebecca Germany lives in the Ohio Valley where she enjoys her local church, gardening, and tending poultry. She works in Christian publishing and loves to see the Lord glorified through the written word.

Janice Hanna, who lives in the Houston area, writes novels, nonfiction, magazine articles, and musical comedies for the stage. The mother of four married daughters, she is quickly adding grandchildren to the family mix.

277, 305, 325, 340, 355

Eileen Key resides in Texas near her three grown children and two wonderful grandchildren.

Ratliff, Sarah Mae: Day 16, 40, 60, 89, 111, 116, 129, 147, 175, 207, 220, 232, 250, 278, 298

Sarah Mae Ratliff enjoys worshipping God, writing, working with children, and spending time with her family. Sarah and her husband, Ryan, are high school sweethearts who are expecting a son in April.

Rayburn, Julie: Day 4, 18, 23, 35, 42, 58, 71, 88, 105, 119, 133, 142, 157, 159, 183, 211, 222, 231, 242, 259, 274, 290, 311, 321, 341

Julie Rayburn is a surgical nurse and Christian public speaker. Julie and her husband, Scott, live in Atlanta. They have two children and two grandchildren. www.julierayburn.com

Slawson, Leah: Day 2, 9, 25, 29, 34, 45, 61, 69, 77, 79, 94, 106, 115, 117, 124, 125, 127, 134, 140, 141, 155, 164, 165, 174, 181, 184, 187, 193, 194, 198, 203, 215, 216, 223, 224, 228, 229, 245, 256, 257, 260, 267, 289, 302, 319, 324, 331, 338, 350, 363

Leah Slawson has been married to her husband, Guice, for more than twenty years, and they have two teenagers, a son and daughter. She lives in Montgomery, Alabama.

Annie Tipton is an editor and writer living in small-town Ohio. A former newspaper reporter, she loves her family, friends, sushi, and beach vacations.

Scripture Index

Also available from Barbour Publishing

EVERYDAY *Comfort*

Comfort at home. Comfort at work.
Comfort—in every area of life. These are just
a few of the timely topics included in this
soul-soothing volume designed to lighten the
day and lift the spirit of today's woman.
ISBN 978-1-60260-211-3

EVERYDAY *Blessings*

These brief, but powerful, devotional
readings reveal the everyday—yet often
overlooked—gifts in life, encouraging
women to bask in the loving-kindness
of our awesome God.
ISBN 978-1-59789-660-3

EVERYDAY *Encouragement*

This portable book contains over
200 powerful messages accompanied
by a related scripture reading.
ISBN 978-1-59789-435-7

Available wherever books are sold.